Home Care Nursing
Delegation Skills
A Handbook for Practice

Ruth I. Hansten, MBA, RN
Principal
Hansten and Washburn
Bainbridge Island, Washington

Marilynn J. Washburn, MA, RN
Principal
Hansten and Washburn
Bainbridge Island, Washington

Virginia Kenyon, MN, RN
Vice President
Clinical Services
Health People, Inc.
Bellevue, Washington

AN ASPEN PUBLICATION®
Aspen Publishers, Inc.
Gaithersburg, Maryland
1999

The authors have made every effort to ensure the accuracy of the information herein. However, appropriate information sources should be consulted, especially for new or unfamiliar procedures. It is the responsibility of every practitioner to evaluate the appropriateness of a particular opinion in the context of actual clinical situations and with due considerations to new developments. Authors, editors, and the publisher cannot be held responsible for any typographical or other errors found in this book.

Library of Congress Cataloging-in-Publication Data

Hansten, Ruth I.
Home care nursing delegation skills: a handbook for practice
Ruth I. Hansten, Marilynn J. Washburn, Virginia Kenyon.
p. cm.
Includes bibliographical references and index
ISBN 0-8342-12331
1. Home nursing—Standards—Handboooks, manuals, etc. 2. Delegation of authority—
Handbooks, manuals, etc. 3. Clinical competence—Standards—Handbooks, manuals, etc.
4. Home care services—Administration—Handbooks, manuals, etc. I. Washburn, Marilynn.
II. Kenyon, Virginia. III. Title
[DNLM: 1. Home Care Services—organization & administration. 2. Nursing Care—organization
& administration. 3. Nursing Process. 4. Nursing, Supervisory. 5. Nursing, Team. WY 115
H251n 1999]
RT120.H65H36   1999
362.1'4—DC21
DNLM/DLC for Library of Congress
98-45705
CIP

Orders: (800) 638-8437
Customer Service: (800) 234-1660

About Aspen Publishers • For more than 35 years, Aspen has been a leading professional publisher in a variety of disciplines. Aspen's vast information resources are available in both print and electronic formats. We are committed to providing the highest quality information available in the most appropriate format for our customers. Visit Aspen's Internet site for more information resources, directories, articles, and a searchable version of Aspen's full catalog, including the most recent publications: **http://www.aspenpublishers.com**
Aspen Publishers, Inc. • The hallmark of quality in publishing
Member of the worldwide Wolters Kluwer group.

Editorial Services: Joan Sesma
Library of Congress Catalog Card Number: 98-45705
ISBN: 0-8342-1233-1

Printed in the United States of America

1 2 3 4 5

TABLE OF CONTENTS

ABOUT THE AUTHORS

Ruth I. Hansten, MBA, RN, and Marilynn J. Washburn, MA, RN, are accomplished national consultants, speakers, and seminar leaders with extensive experience in staff, middle management, education, and executive positions in hospitals and other health care settings. Together they are Principals at Hansten and Washburn on Bainbridge Island, Washington.

Hansten and Washburn both graduated from the BSN program at the University of Northern Colorado. Ms. Hansten completed her MBA in Health Care Administration in Seattle, while Ms. Washburn received her MA in Organizational Development and Management at the University of Phoenix. Ms. Hansten serves as adjunct faculty at the University of Washington and Ms. Washburn teaches in the graduate program for the University of Phoenix.

Hansten and Washburn are widely published in nursing literature. Their first book, *I Light the Lamp* (1990, Applied Therapeutics, Vancouver, WA), is an inspirational and motivational gift book and resource for nursing professionals. *The Nurse Manager's Answer Book* (Aspen, 1993) offers realistic, workable solutions to the challenging situations faced by health care managers daily. They have also completed a six-month project editing a monthly newsletter published by Aspen and launched in February of 1996, titled *Hansten and Washburn's Successful Restructuring,* and are now coeditors of *Reengineering the Hospital* (Aspen). These efforts have led to the publication of their fourth book, *Toolbook for Health Care Redesign*, released in August 1997.

Their third book, *Clinical Delegation Skills: A Handbook for Nurses* (Aspen, **AJN Book of the Year Award**, 1994), now in the second edition (1998), used dozens of real-life situations from all clinical settings and exercises to address the controversy of the use of assistive personnel in care delivery settings. Continuing to build on experiences gained in the seminars they conduct, as well as their consulting projects with nurses undergoing care delivery redesign, this new edition includes the decision-making models developed by hospitals and professional associations, and highlights the work of the National Council of State Boards of Nursing on the topic of delegation. In addition, the aspect of critical thinking is explored in depth as it relates to the process of decision making within team work.

Virginia L. Kenyon, MN, RN, has been in community health nursing for approximately 24 years. She has been a nurse for 34 years. She is presently the Vice President of Clinical Services for Health People Inc., a home health care agency that she helped establish in 1997. She has had extensive experience in community health nursing, including 10 years as a field nurse for the Visiting Nurses Services in Seattle and 14 years as an administrator in community health. As an administrator, she has managed both public health and home health agencies.

Ms. Kenyon received both her Bachelors and Masters degrees from the University of Washington. She serves as adjunct clinical faculty for the University of Washington. She has also served as advisor and guest lecturer at Pacific Lutheran University School of Nursing. She has had numerous articles published on the topics of community health nursing and clinical competencies for community health nurses.

She has been actively involved in her professional and community associations, serving as President and/or on the Board of Directors of the King County Nurses Association, SEARCHN (Service Education and Research in Community Health Nursing), Washington Case Manager Association, and SEED (Southeast Effective Development).

For more information regarding the work of Hansten and Washburn, their workshops and consulting options, please contact them at:

Hansten and Washburn
10042 NE Knight Road
Bainbridge Island, WA 98110
Telephone 206-842-1189/0912
Voice Mail 206-999-1640
Fax 206-842-4211/9921

CONTRIBUTORS

Karen Haase-Herrick, MN, RN
Executive Director
Northwest Organization of Nurse Executives
Seattle, Washington

Karen A. McGrath, RN
Associate Executive Director
Washington State Nurses Association
Seattle, Washington

Loretta O'Neill, MN, RN
Director of Nursing
Manorcare Health Services
Lebanon, Pennsylvania

FOREWORD

Changes in health care delivery, the rising costs of health care, and the surging growth of the aging population are applying pressure in many areas of health care delivery. Federal and state budgets are impacted, and care delivery resources are stretched thin. New and creative ways need to be found to provide the care and support needed to make resources cover more people over longer periods of time. Sites for the delivery of care change, jobs dissolve, organizations restructure, and new players appear in the system. States try new long-term care systems, methods of providing more care with the same dollars, to an increasing population of vulnerable and fragile recipients. They move clients from long-term care facilities into community-based care in order to make state budgets stretch further.

Nurses sometimes want to believe that all of these changes are someone else's problem. We see changes in our workplace that affect us directly. We naturally resist the change. We are even tired of changing. We know how we want nursing practiced and it doesn't include allowing others to do what we went to school to learn to do. But we forget what is really at the core of our nursing practice: our ability to assess the client's physical and mental status, the ability to determine what is needed and what is the best course of action to bring about the best outcome. We forget that others can put on a dressing, can give their own medications. We forget that what is important about nursing is our body of knowledge, our ability to know and understand, to make judgments, assessments and reassessments, and to produce positive outcomes for our clients. We lose focus on what is the most appropriate use of skills. Reluctantly we inch forward by letting go of some of our nursing tasks. We allow someone to do them for us. As nurses we know that our responsibility and accountability doesn't stop there. We continue to retain the responsibility to go back and check on the client, to reassess, to teach and re-teach, to change the plan of care, to work towards the best outcomes. In this lies the true essence of nursing practice, and nursing care delivered in the community. Nurses that come to community-based care settings may need to make adjustments in their thinking about their role. They bring with them their training and work experiences in other settings such as hospitals, nursing homes, and physician's offices. They are asked to learn a new set of policies and procedures, new regulations, new ways of practicing their nursing skills. These well-trained and very experienced nurses may not have thought a great deal about nursing delegation, indeed they may not have needed to within their previous work setting.

Nursing delegation is not a new concept in community health practice. Nurses in community-based settings have been teaching clients and families how to do nursing tasks, some very complex and highly technical, for a long time. But the concept of nurse delegation gets cloudy and murky as new and unlicensed players become part of the delivery system in community-based care. Legal issues arise. Nurses that work in community health have not questioned the practice of delegating nursing tasks to family members. However, they have to make new judgments about delegation to a new array of care providers, paid, or volunteer, that provide care in lieu of family members. As pressure to expand delegation to unlicensed caregivers builds, nurses will need to actively advocate for retaining their important role. Payer sources will attempt to set limits on the role of the nurse, paying for one return visit when two are needed. Nurses will struggle with models of care that are driven out of social service practice models, not out of medical delivery systems. Nurses will be important in establishing the framework and quality of the delivery of long-term care in community health practice.

This book *Home Care Nursing Delegation Skills* will encourage nurses in thinking through some of the systems changes that are occurring in health care delivery. Nurses reading this text will be challenged to look at the "big picture." They will be urged by the information in this book to focus on the important values in nursing practice and think through their changing role. Hopefully this book will also encourage nurses to be proactive in seeing that the provision of community-based health care services also delivers the highest quality of care possible and the very best outcomes for those who are recipients of that care.

Nancy James, RN, BSN
Professional Affairs Director
Home Care Association of Washington

ACKNOWLEDGMENTS

Those of you who have read *Clinical Delegation Skills: A Handbook for Nurses* (1994) or the second edition published in 1998 as *Clinical Delegation Skills: A Handbook for Professional Practice* will recognize that we have once again enjoyed the expert involvement and writing skills of colleagues who helped us before.

We express continued appreciation for the support and involvement of Karen Haase-Herrick, MN, RN, Executive Director of Northwest Organization of Nurse Executives, and Loretta O'Neill, MN, RN, in *Home Care Nursing Delegation Skills*. The first edition of *Clinical Delegation Skills* had its beginnings based on a workshop developed jointly by the efforts of these women, in conjunction with the authors, and the support of the membership of the Washington Organization of Nurse Executives (now Northwest Organization of Nurse Executives). Karen Herrick is a national leader in nursing administration and has a unique big picture view. Her discussion (in collaboration with Ginny Kenyon) of what's happening in health care and how this affects the home health arena, helps us place our often chaotic nursing world into some kind of sane perspective.

Loretta O'Neill is an expert in many health care areas, and now works in long-term care administration. Her ability to assist nurses in communicating assertively has not been equalled by other educators, so we have asked her to apply her knowledge to those situations that present themselves in community settings. We truly appreciate her continued collaboration in our work.

Numerous people have also generously shared their work, and it is highlighted throughout the book and in previous editions of *Clinical Delegation Skills*. We extend our thanks to the following:

Karen McGrath, RN, for her considerable expertise in the area of collective bargaining and her contribution to Chapter 4.

Dennis Burnside, for his creativity, patience, and impressive ability to transfer our visual images into reality. We relocated Dennis in his new home in the midwest as a result of publishing this edition, and we are thankful for the opportunity to work with him again!

Sandy Jeghers of Health People, for sharing vision and values from this innovative and growing home care organization.

Margaret Conger, RN, EdD, for her work in delegation decision making.

Pat Auracher, for the use of the decision-making model from Columbia Swedish Medical Center, Englewood, Colorado.

Cheryl Allen and the State of Washington Department of Social Health Services for their tool on delegation validation, including other folks who helped us locate the tools that Washington and Oregon have developed.

Nancy James of the Home Care Association of Washington, a leader and proponent of the best quality care for those in home environments.

Most of all, we extend our gratitude to the countless nurses throughout the country who have shared their thoughts, their fears, their frustrations, and their successes in the journey toward optimum professional performance.

CHAPTER 1

The Overall Process of Delegation

Ruth I. Hansten and Marilynn J. Washburn

"Why all this talk about delegation and working in a team right now? Community health nurses since Lillian Wald and the Henry Street Settlement more than one hundred years ago have used the strong hands of whoever was available to help them care for people in their homes, schools, and churches, anywhere outside of acute care. We already know how to supervise others!"

It's certainly true that nurses working in our communities and homes have historically developed excellent skills in assessment and treatment of families and populations, in working effectively with other professionals as well as unskilled but willing volunteers, and will continue to do so in the future. But because home health care is one of the most cost-effective methods of delivering care (a major concern for years to come), and has become one of the fastest growing employers for nurses and home care aides, it is apparent to us that we must prepare to better educate those who enter the community care workforce, to better understand how to work with other members of the health care team to provide the safest and most effective care to our clients. Because community care nurses have traditionally been leaders in nursing in assuming our rightful position as coordinators of care, systematically implementing the holistic approach that is the foundation of our profession, then we must be certain that our growing numbers of home health care providers are expert in the processes necessary for this coordination.

THE DEFINITION OF DELEGATION

Just as a surgeon establishes anatomical boundaries before he or she operates, we need to establish boundaries, in the form of a definition, when delegating to other personnel. We cite the operational definition adopted by the National

Council of State Boards of Nursing (1990, p. 1) in its *Concept Paper on Delegation* and will use this as the basis of our discussion throughout the book:

> Delegation: "Transferring to a competent individual the authority to perform a selected nursing task in a selected situation."

This definition has stood the test of time, being presented once again in the 1995 *Issues* publication by the National Council. It is important to note the generic approach of this definition, which makes it timeless while allowing the practicing nurse a great deal of freedom in selecting the task and the individual to perform that task. As we will note in some detail in future chapters, the primary ingredient of this concept is that the nurse ensures the competency of the individual to whom he or she is delegating. To some, this is an added dimension of responsibility—and one that is not always willingly adopted. The challenges for nurses in this area are apparent because many do not feel they are adequately prepared to teach individuals to perform tasks that have been a part of their own scope of practice. Further, many nurses do not welcome the added responsibility of assessing competency of teammates, although community-based registered nurses (RNs) have been teaching families and others to perform care for years. In the past few years, unlicensed assistive personnel who were routinely performing personal care and basic health assistance in the home setting have added tasks to their roles that have strained the boundaries of what some nurses believe belongs only within the RN role. Supervision of others has taken on new elements of risk. This has become a significant issue for our regulatory agencies and will be discussed in further detail in Chapter 3.

This book will assist in developing that skill by applying a process that is very familiar to all of us: the nursing process. By following the four major steps of the nursing process, we can systematically analyze what is necessary for any practicing professional nurse to know in order to develop a skill that will be a fundamental of practice.

Further, many nurses do not welcome the added responsibility of assessing competency of teammates, although community-based RNs have been teaching families and others to perform care for years.

THE MODEL: THE KEY TO DELEGATION

The activities of delegation, like those of the nursing process itself, are cyclical, beginning with a gathering of data, continuing with the use of those data as plans are made and carried out, and concluding with the analysis of the activity; the cycle then repeats itself. We have developed a key model that illustrates this process (Figure 1–1) and will refer to the sequence of events often to make our point that this is not a singular process. The ongoing cycle of events will be the result of your ability to connect one component with the other until you have an integrated skill that allows you to perform many of the fundamentals concurrently. For the purpose of our study, we will isolate each step and allow you to focus your attention on the areas of the process in which you determine you need the most skill building.

Assessment

- *Know Your World*
- *Know Your Organization*
- *Know Your Practice*
- *Know Yourself*
- *Know Your Delegate*

A foundation must be laid on which to build the decision making that is implied in the concept of delegation. Selecting the right task for the right individual sounds a little like the job of the personnel manager and is foreign to many of us. We must do a certain amount of assessment, as we would in any situation in which we were determining the best course of action for the patient.

Assessment implies knowledge: the interpretation of information to provide an overview of the total picture of factors that are affecting the current condition. Such a review will help us to understand how best to respond and to plan for the future of health care. "Knowing your world" in terms of demographics, economics, and social changes will be essential in understanding why we are pursuing a skill that some believe is not in the best interests of our profession. Analyzing these factors will help us to prepare for changes ahead and to position nursing as a profession to lead the way instead of following a path determined by others as a reaction to health care reform.

Knowledge of the nurse practice act, including the numerous regulatory changes that are being made as a result of the changes in care delivery systems, cannot be overemphasized. The re-

> Assessment implies knowledge: the interpretation of information to provide an overview of the total picture of factors that are affecting the current condition.

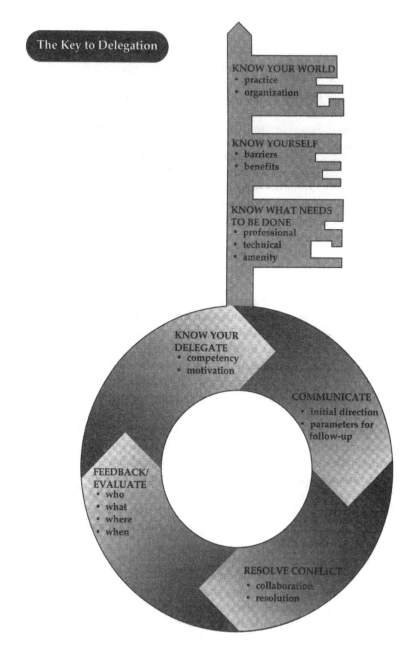

Figure 1–1 The Key to Delegation. *Source:* Reprinted from R. Hansten and M. Washburn, The Overall Process of Delegation, *Clinical Delegation Skills*, p. 3., © 1998, Aspen Publishers, Inc.

sponses of the individual boards of nursing, as they strive to protect the public by setting up ground rules for the changes in nursing personnel, have been significant. Many nurses feel at risk, voicing their concerns in the heartfelt statement, "I'm not putting my license on the line to work with those people!"

> Many nurses feel at risk, voicing their concerns in the heartfelt statement, "I'm not putting my license on the line to work with those people!"

Knowledge of the practice act, the statutes and rules that govern nursing practice and the policies of the employing institution will help the nurse to allay those fears and to practice professionally.

The knowledge of the organization in which we work, its mission and values, will help nurses to assess the attributes of their environment in terms of its support of nursing practice. What is the plan for quality? What are the policies for working with other personnel? Is nursing directly involved with the decision making regarding the changes in reimbursement and care settings, whether in schools, single family dwellings, or group home facilities? Answers to such questions will prepare the nurse for the decisions to be made regarding how he or she practices, delegates, and supervises clinically.

Knowledge of our own attitudes and beliefs is an area that each of us must explore if we are to develop fully the skill of delegation. Why did I choose home health nursing, and if I am transitioning from acute care to home health, what strategies will help me adjust? What personal barriers make it difficult for me to work with someone else? What do I do best that makes working with others the most reasonable choice? And what benefits can I get from this whole thing, anyway? How well do I understand my attitude toward leading and coordinating a health care team? Often we find that nurses know the fundamentals of delegation and appreciate the principles but that they just aren't buying it. There is no substitute for attitude, which will make all the difference in how successful you are in your practice with others.

Speaking of others, it is also necessary to assess the delegates. Who are these people you are being asked to share your practice with? Individuals with gifts and challenges like the rest of us, delegates have their own strengths, weaknesses, preferences, motivations, and cultural backgrounds. Because the basic tenet of safe delegation is to ensure the competency of the delegate, a careful assessment of this individual is an absolute necessity. We will ask you to refocus your thinking, however, by first emphasizing the strengths of your delegate and optimizing the resources you

> There is no substitute for attitude, which will make all the difference in how successful you are in your practice with others.

have available, rather than focusing on all of the tasks he or she cannot do. We will ask you to examine these areas of weakness as potential growth areas and to determine what can be done to overcome an apparent inability to perform a procedure—is more teaching necessary, or is this task truly beyond the scope of the individual?

Having completed an assessment of the external environment, the internal environment (that's you), and the delegates with whom you are asked to work, you are ready to proceed to the next step of the cycle. The foundation of knowledge you have developed in your assessment will allow you to plan the best use of resources and coordinate a high-performance team.

Plan

- *Know What Needs To Be Done*

The first step in planning involves gathering the knowledge of what needs to be done. You have some latitude here: as a practicing professional coordinating a plan of care, you are in the position to prioritize which outcomes are the most important to attain. Notice that we are talking about outcomes; we will continue to ask you to focus your attention in this direction. Before you can plan anything or determine who will carry out the plan, you must think in terms of outcomes and goals that you and, especially, your patient want to achieve from this experience. Often tasks are done for the sake of work, and very little thought is spent on the analysis of what the performance of these tasks contributes to the bottom line (and we don't mean budgets!).

> For many, thinking in terms of outcomes will be an unwelcome experience, when a "to do" or "task list" has been relied on to direct completion of work. Learning to focus on results rather than on tasks or processes can become a more meaningful means to a sense of accomplishment.

For many, thinking in terms of outcomes will be an unwelcome experience, when a "to do" or "task list" has been relied on to direct completion of work. Learning to focus on results rather than on tasks or processes can become a more meaningful means to a sense of accomplishment.

In Chapter 6, we will look at a model of nursing that divides our work into three areas of focus: the professional, the technical, and the amenities aspects of nursing care. From this "PTA model" we will be able to determine the emphasis of our care and those parts of our practice that may be performed by others.

Intervene

- *Prioritize, and Match the Job to the Delegate*
- *Know How To Communicate*
- *Know How To Resolve Conflict*

Continuing our cycle, we arrive at the point where the majority of delegation takes place. Procedures and tasks may be taught to unlicensed personnel, but the critical components of the remainder of the nursing process rely on the knowledge and experience of a professional licensed nurse. Herein lies one of our greatest challenges: we are faced with the need to determine which parts of our practice to "let go" of, and we often find that some of those direct care tasks may be what we have found the most personally satisfying. Once again, according to the operational definition of delegation, the RN is selecting the tasks and the appropriate situation in which to delegate. Matching the job to the delegate then becomes a decision we can control, and we must continue to make the choice wisely, based on sound judgment. Studies have demonstrated that nurses spend considerable time performing tasks that can be done more easily and efficiently by someone else. We owe it to ourselves and to our patients to free up this time so that we may do what we were educated to provide.

> Knowing when to take the lead and assuming a calm but assertive stance will assist you in clarifying the work to be done and by whom.

Working successfully with others requires communication. This skill is one we perform quite readily in interactions with our patients; we need to transfer this skill to directing and supervising our delegates. Clearly outlining the expectations we have, giving complete and concise directions for implementation, and providing parameters for following up with the nurse are essential ingredients for successful communication. Being able to be assertive without being aggressive when the response is not the eager and willing "yes" that we would like is also part of the skill of effective delegation.

Knowing when to take the lead and assuming a calm but assertive stance will assist you in clarifying the work to be done and by whom.

We have implied that the response given by the delegate may not be enthusiastic, and indeed it may be an absolute refusal. Knowing how to resolve conflict when the members of the health care team do not agree is fundamental to a successful working relationship. Passivity and a strong desire to avoid conflict will not lead to the desired outcome—a high-performing partnership with your delegates.

Evaluation

- *Know How To Give Feedback*
- *Evaluate and Problem Solve*

The final step of the process is one to which we are held accountable by law, yet it is the one area that we do not often find time for and that we willingly shift to management. However, the contract of delegation carries with it the legal expectation that you will supervise the delegate. Once again, an operational definition is provided by the National Council of State Boards of Nursing (1995, p. 2):

> Supervision: "Provision of guidance or direction, evaluation, and follow-up by the licensed nurse for accomplishment of a nursing task delegated to unlicensed assistive personnel."

Evaluation and follow-up of the activity means that you oversee the performance (again, you determine the frequency of this observation) and offer feedback to the delegate in terms of an appraisal of his or her performance. This is certainly part of your obligation of ensuring competency of the individual, as well as closing the loop by giving the delegate an evaluation of how things are going.

> Rules and statutes will tell us that the supervising nurse (that's you any time you delegate) will be held accountable for the correction of any error made by the delegate.

Whether you choose to pass that on to the manager for resolution or to take action yourself by discussing the situation directly with the delegate, corrective action must take place.

Feedback and follow-up may be as simple as a thank-you for a job well done or as formal as the documentation of an unusual occurrence form accompanied by a lengthy investigation. Whatever the situation calls for, you must be prepared to provide it. Just as you provide a thoughtful appraisal of the patient you have just taught to perform his or her own central line catheter care, you will need to evaluate the progress of the home health aide who is performing range of motion on an elderly patient with impaired mobility.

THE SKILL

Whether you are a nurse who has recently entered practice in a community setting or a seasoned home health expert, you have probably determined by now that the majority of the components of the delegation process are not new to you. In fact, you are performing many of them continually as you plan and implement your care for your patients. What will be required, then, is not the development of new knowledge but the transfer of skills that you have already developed. Assessment of the patient is a skill that you have developed and practiced all of your professional life and is no different in technique when you transfer that attention to the new delegate who arrives at your work setting ready and eager to do his or her job. The teaching that you do with each of your patients requires planning, clear communication, and evaluation to complete the process, and is similar to the planning, communication, and evaluation you will do with delegates.

Throughout this book we will focus on fundamentals, offering exercises for you to check your knowledge and to apply any new material. There will be repetition (we warn you) because this is a basic principle of learning. Using this book will help open the door to growth in professional nursing.

> Our goal, our planned outcome for you, is to develop your ability to implement the process of clinical delegation with confidence and completeness so that you have the time to do what you do best.

REFERENCES

National Council of State Boards of Nursing. 1990. *Concept paper on delegation.* Chicago: NCSBN.
National Council of State Boards of Nursing. 1995. Delegation: Concepts and decision-making process. *Issues* (December): 1–2.

CHAPTER 2

Know Your World: What in the World Is Going On?

WHY ALL THE CHANGE?

Virginia L. Kenyon

In the mid-1980s, home health began to experience dramatic changes. Prior to this time, the supply of clinically and educationally prepared registered nurses (RNs) for community health practice was fairly stable; supply and demand were within reasonable levels. By 1987, there was a major shift in the supply of RNs for home health practice. Several factors contributed to this change. First, the introduction of the diagnosis-related groups (DRGs) in the acute care arena resulted in efforts to reduce inpatient lengths of stay through the discharge of "quicker and sicker" patients (Murray, 1998), thus increasing the demand for home care services. Second, managed care continued to drive the "sicker and quicker" phenomenon further, but without the full authority to provide the kinds of services or the levels of care some nurses have felt are needed. Finally, the number of applicants to schools of nursing dropped, decreasing the general supply of nurses. By 1990, the shortage of nurses for community health practice was so acute that the long-held requirement of baccalaureate preparation for practice in community health nursing was no longer a reality (Kalnins, 1989).

Even with the hiring of nonbaccalaureate–prepared nurses, the shortage continued and worsened, but now there were additional problems. The primary source of nurses coming into home care

> By 1990, the shortage of nurses for community health practice was so acute that the long-held requirement of baccalaureate preparation for practice in community health nursing was no longer a reality (Kalnins, 1989).

> This act has placed even greater demands on the RN case managers in home care to delegate increasing portions of care to unlicensed personnel in order to maximize the services with the decreased funding limits.

was the acute care environment where for at least the past two decades "primary care" nursing had been the practice. This presented two problems: we were now hiring nurses who, one, had never been exposed to community health practice in their educational preparation, and, two, who had not practiced in a "team" environment where the delegation of selected nursing tasks was the norm. With the downsizing of the acute care facilities that began in 1993 and 1994, the movement of acute care nurses to home care accelerated. Now we must add to all of the above issues the effects of the Balanced Budget Act of 1997. This act has placed even greater demands on the RN case managers in home care to delegate increasing portions of care to unlicensed personnel in order to maximize the services with the decreased funding limits.

As if the noted changes in the regulatory and payor environment weren't enough, we are also experiencing a great surge in the use of alternative therapies by the public. Some states have recognized this surge and have placed certification requirements on certain alternative care providers. In addition, some states, including the state of Washington, have legalized the prescriptive authority of some of the alternative providers, thus allowing for nurses to take orders from them. The use of herbal therapy, aromatherapy, massage therapy, music therapy, and acupuncture are but a few examples. As a case manager in home care, you are required to manage the overall plan of care for the client. Because you are only one person, you cannot possibly provide all the services yourself. The knowledge base for home care with all the possible services offered is beyond any one person's ability to master; therefore, appropriate and effective delegation is a requirement if clients are to receive appropriate care. For tenured home care nurses, care plan oversight and delegation to other disciplines and unlicensed personnel are routine parts of their role.

THE NEW WORLD

Karen Haase-Herrick and Virginia L. Kenyon

For those of you new to home care or contemplating moving to home care from the acute care setting, the biggest area of change affecting each of you as an RN involves the giving of care through others—the delegation of some traditional nursing tasks to others (Blegen et al., 1992). You are switching from a model of nursing care delivery in which the RN provides all the care to a model in which you delegate to others some of the tasks involved in the care of patients. You are being asked to work on teams and/or in partnership with an-

> As a case manager in home care, you are required to manage the overall plan of care for the client.

other person. You are sometimes being asked to work with caregivers about whom you know nothing and in whom you have little or no trust. Later in this book, you'll be asked to explore fully your own personal barriers to the use of clinical delegation skills. To reach a point where you are ready to explore the why and how of clinical delegation skills for the management of patient care, however, you must first know the world in which you are working so that you will understand the driving forces behind this change. The purpose of this chapter is not to provide you with new information so much as to bring to the fore of your thinking those environmental factors that are influencing the world in which you work or are about to work. You know that all of these things are happening. What you may not have done until now is link them together in an assessment of why you are in such a period of change in your work life.

Consider your environment at large. Take a few minutes to think about things that are going on around you. What do you hear in the news? What articles in nursing journals have you read recently about changes in patient care delivery? What programs and systems has your facility initiated over the past five years? How many businesses in your area have laid off employees in the past five years

> For those of you new to home care or contemplating moving to home care from the acute care setting, the biggest area of change affecting each of you as an RN involves the giving of care through others—the delegation of some traditional nursing tasks to others (Blegen et al., 1992).

and may now be either rehiring or laying off even more? What is happening to your own health care costs? What are you seeing with respect to the length of time patients remain in an acute care facility? What types of patients are you now caring for in the home or in residential long-term care facilities whom you did not see five or ten years ago? What about the age of your patients? What about the knowledge level of your patients? In all honesty, what have you and your coworkers said about your workloads over the past five years? How many times have you been able to do all the necessary patient and family education prior to discharge?

List at least five things that you think are shaping these changes—things around you in your community, your state, and the country:

1. _____
2. _____
3. _____
4. _____
5. _____

Your list of five will most likely fit into one of the following six categories:

1. Influence and memories of the 1980s nursing shortage—the Bowen and Pew Commissions' reports
2. Evolution of health care system reform
3. Demographic trends
4. Health care delivery trends
5. Changing nature of work
6. Maturing of the nursing profession

INFLUENCE OF THE 1980s NURSE SHORTAGE

Vacancy rates for nursing personnel began to soar in the late 1980s. Hospitals, home health care agencies, nursing homes, and public health departments across the country reported persistent vacancies; nursing school enrollments dropped. A devastating nursing shortage had developed very quickly. Positions were going unfilled for more than a year in many rural facilities and agencies. And yet patients were in hospitals and needed care. Home care agencies had growing caseloads. Long-term care facilities were full and needed RNs. Public health agencies, schools, and prisons all had need of RNs. And schools of nursing had vacant faculty positions. States across the country set up commissions to study the nursing shortage and to identify ways in which to address and resolve the issue.

Otis R. Bowen, Secretary of the U.S. Department of Health and Human Services, established the Secretary's Commission on Nursing in December 1987. The commission, which became known as the Bowen Commission, delivered its final report with recommendations in 1988. The Bowen Commission held hearings across the country to hear firsthand from RNs what issues were contributing to the current shortage. The conclusion reached was that the nursing shortage was primarily the result of rapidly escalating demand for RNs. The Final Report of the Bowen Commission contained 16 specific recommendations that were grouped according to the following issues:

1. Use of nursing resources
2. Nurse compensation
3. Health care financing
4. Nurse decision making
5. Development of nursing resources
6. Maintenance of nursing resources

Recommendations in the "use of nursing resources" category called on employers of nurses to develop innovative models of care delivery that would use scarce RN resources efficiently and effectively (U.S. Dept. of Health and Human Services, 1988).

Meanwhile, back at the site of care delivery, nurse managers and staff nurses began talking about new ways to "get the job done." Out of this evolved the increased use of clinical delegation skills. However, the evolution of these innovative care delivery models was shaped by other environmental influences as well.

After months of study, the Pew Health Professions Commission released two reports in 1995 that set the health care industry abuzz: (1) *Reforming Health Care Workforce Regulation: Policy Considerations for the 21st Century* and (2) *Critical Challenges: Revitalizing the Health Professions for the Twenty-First Century*.

The first of these reports recommended broad changes in the regulatory environment for all health professions to increase consumer involvement as well as create a type of "shared governance," if you will, among the state licensing boards of all licensed health care professionals (Pew Health Professions Commission, 1995b). This report has certainly stimulated many state governments to look at their regulatory environments to better align the licensing processes across all health care professions. States are also seeking to increase consumer membership on licensing boards. In response to telemedicine and other interstate care modalities, the National Council of State Boards of Nursing issued the report of a task force on interstate licensure that lays the groundwork for a true "interstate license."

The second cited report focused more on the future look of the reformed health care system and what needed to be done for survival in this evolving system. Integrated training across all professions, where feasible, was viewed as a key recommendation—clearly an approach that will encourage an interdisciplinary team approach to care. Recommendations specific to nursing related to the need to decrease the numbers of nurses educated at the AD or diploma level and to increase the numbers of nurses trained at the master's level and above. Central to the concepts being discussed in this book was the recommendation for nursing that stated: "Recover the clinical management role of nursing and recognize it as an increasingly important strength of training and professional practice at all levels" (Pew Health Professions Commission, 1995a, p. vi).

The findings of the Pew Commission and their recommendations are support-ive of the practice in home health care where the use of the bachelor-prepared nurse has been the norm for many years. Though the nursing shortage of the 1980s forced some home health agencies to use diploma and associate degree nurses in the field, the focus and goal were always to hire the bachelor-prepared nurse. Major changes in future community health nursing are predicted. The projections are:

- Increased focus on at-risk, high acuity, and high needs populations
- Decreasing services to low-risk and well families
- Community development/community mobilization
- Closer links with institutions for discharge planning
- More acute care in the community
- More care of young disabled individuals at home
- Changes in nurses' working conditions (e.g., evening practice)
- Little case finding in the community
- Closer contact within the primary care team
- Greater specialization
- Increasing skills mix in the community
- Increasing first-contact primary care role/nurse-managed clinics (Chalmers et al., 1998)

If these predictions become a reality for community health practice, the recom-mendations of the Pew Commission will become even more important to imple-ment.

HEALTH CARE REFORM

Public debate over health care reform continues. Although national health care reform failed in the early 1990s, the passage of the Kennedy-Kassebaum bill in 1996 and the Children's Initiative in 1997 implemented steps to address fiscal access to care for defined, limited populations at the national level. Health care professionals in all disciplines have been talking about health care reform for decades. Starting in the late 1980s, American business leaders also began talking in the press about the costs of health care and their impact on the ability of American business to compete in a global economy. What brought the need for change in health care financing to the forum of public discussion?

Most Americans thought very little about the cost of health care for a long time. However, in the 1960s, when Medicare was passed, government became a major purchaser of health care services for one segment of the American people—the elderly. As this group grew in size, the amount of money paid out by the government increased. At the same time, federal and state governments were paying for additional health care services for the poor through the Medicaid program. The number of people served by Medicaid had also grown, adding to the percentage of federal dollars purchasing health care for certain groups of Americans. In efforts to hold down the amount of federal money spent for Medicare, prospective payment in the form of DRGs was introduced in the early 1980s. Medicaid budgets were also tightened. Con-

> Consequently, the amount the government reimbursed providers for Medicare and Medicaid patients ceased being equal to the actual cost of care. That reimbursement figure has run as low as 60 cents for every dollar of costs (ProPac, 1993).

sequently, the amount the government reimbursed providers for Medicare and Medicaid patients ceased being equal to the actual cost of care. That reimbursement figure has run as low as 60 cents for every dollar of costs (ProPac, 1993).

The costs of providing the care did not go down. Salary costs, overhead, new equipment, and expanding technology all contributed to skyrocketing health care costs. Providers had to secure additional revenue to continue to operate. Cost shifting to payers other than the government became the means by which to secure the additional revenue. The "payer other than the government" was most often a health care insurance plan. Insurance premiums had to rise to cover these increased costs. Premium increases of 15 percent for one year became common. Employers who provided health care insurance for their employees saw their costs of providing this benefit increasing annually and subsequently increased the costs of producing whatever widget or commodity they made. The options for businesses were to hold down the cost of the health care insurance benefit, discontinue the benefit, increase the price of the product, or allow for declining profits. The only real choice to businesses became holding down the cost of the health care insurance coverage they provided employees (Smith, 1988).

Insurance companies began developing innovative ways to curb the growth of premium increases. Managed care, securing discounts from providers, and narrowing the scope of coverage were methods employed. Preventive services were deleted. Experimental procedures were seldom covered. However, providers were still delivering these services. The costs to deliver the services continued to escalate due to the increased demand for services because of increasing life spans, increasing birth rate, the AIDS epidemic, new technology, supply cost increases, and personnel and structural expenses. The result of this cost spiral was an increase in health care expenditures that exceeded the rate of inflation by three times ("Rising Health Spending," 1994).

Since the mid-1990s, health care costs to individuals and corporations have leveled off. Increases for costs stayed at or below the level of inflation through 1996. In 1997, clear evidence showed that costs would once again rise to rates equal to or slightly above the rate of inflation. However, the number of uninsured individuals has increased from 37 million to almost 40 million. In 1994, 10 million U.S. children were uninsured, and each year the number of children with private insurance is decreasing (GAO, 1996). In addition, many over-50-year-olds find themselves caught in a gap. They lose their health care coverage when they are laid off or when their spouse dies. They cannot secure new coverage, they cannot afford coverage on their own, and they are too young for Medicare (Perkins, 1997). Employer-sponsored health insurance is on a downward trend.

> In 1990, 77.7 percent of American workers were covered by their employers. In 2002, the percentage is projected to be 70.4 (AHA, 1996). As of 1995, 17.3 percent of Americans under 65 were without insurance (Greene, 1997).

In August of 1997, Congress passed a major piece of legislation titled the "Balanced Budget Act of 1997." This legislation has had great impact on all community health care services, including long-term care and home care.

Elements of this bill reduced funding for home health services by placing a dollar cap on the amount that can be spent each year per beneficiary, as well as a limit of 100 visits per year under Medicare A. In addition, a surety bond of $50,000 or 15 percent of the gross Medicare revenues (whichever was greater) was required. The implementation of the collection of the Outcome Assessment Information System (OASIS) data was also mandated. And for the first time, Medicare would not reimburse the agencies for the additional costs of implementing the new requirements. These cuts and additional costs to home health agencies could be financially devastating. In fact, NurseHealth Home Care in Grapevine, Texas, reported that its new reimbursement rate would be $17.47 per nurse visit versus the $68 per nurse visit it had expected (*Star-Telegram News*, June 11, 1998). With this rate of reimbursement, it is clear that no home health agency will be able to stay in business. At the very least, to stay economically viable, high-use clients would not be admitted for care. Potentially, this could cause the sickest

> In August of 1997, Congress passed a major piece of legislation titled the "Balanced Budget Act of 1997." This legislation has had great impact on all community health care services, including long-term care and home care.

and most at-risk patients to be denied services (Pathfinders for Seniors Home Page, p. 11, 1998). Home care agencies will have to be much more conscious of the kind of patient they will admit for care. Very ill patients use increased amounts and more expensive types of services and increased health care dol-

> These cuts and additional costs to home health agencies could be financially devastating.

lars, thus making them less desirable as clients. The sickest and most frail among our elderly could become the latest victims of the attempt to save health care dollars. According to the National Association for Home Care, as of July 20, 1998, 1,015 home health agencies had either closed their doors or had stopped accepting Medicare clients. Reportedly, the association was receiving daily notices of agencies closing or getting out of the Medicare business. As agencies close or no longer accept Medicare or Medicaid clients, finding care for the elderly will become a challenge, and those remaining in the business will operate under severe financial constraints. This situation will require that nurses judiciously use the limited resources available. More than ever, effective delegation will be required in these financially difficult times. Clearly, from what we're seeing, financial access to health care will remain a public policy concern well into the twenty-first century.

DEMOGRAPHIC TRENDS

The above discussion of the driving forces for health care reform mentioned several demographic changes.

Multiple demographic trends are influencing how we deliver health and wellness care to the American people.

CHECKPOINT 2-1

List the two demographic trends that are influencing the changes in patient care delivery models just mentioned in the discussion of health care reform.

1. _____

2. _____

See the end of the chapter for the answers.

Age

A growing percentage of our population is above the age of 65, and the greatest percentage increase will be in the over-85 group (Kaufman, 1993). This trend means that more people with chronic and debilitating conditions require more care than ever before. This demand for services means increases not only in total health care expenditures but in every type of expenditure in every category: more long-term care; more home care; more support services; more unique, community-based wellness services; more health education services (Bergman, 1993); and more training for family members to provide care.

Poverty

Anyone who reads a newspaper or listens to national news coverage hears that the number of poor in this country continues to increase, as has been the case since the so-called Decade of Greed, the 1980s. It is not as necessary to delineate why this is happening as to look at what it means for health care. The poor tend to wait longer to seek health care services and are thus sicker when they do come for care, so they end up using more services. They tend to suffer more violent crimes, so they end up using more services. They tend to have more children born to mothers with substance abuse problems, so they end up using more services. They tend to avoid engaging in preventive health activities because they don't have the money to pay for such care, because they don't know about such measures, and because they don't have the time to engage in such measures, so they end up using more services. Community-based services jointly developed by community and health care professionals are increasing in an effort to create healthier communities (Lumsdon, 1993).

Consumer Involvement

Americans are engaging in healthier behaviors related to smoking, eating, exercise, and stress management. They are also exploring the use of alternative medicine with increasing zeal. Congress, in 1992, passed benchmark legislation that directed the National Institutes of Health to study the effectiveness of alternative medicine therapies.

As consumers increase their involvement in health care decisions, they are becoming more involved in the way health care services are provided in their communities. Families are extremely involved in home health care; for example, relatives and friends are providing about 80 percent of the care for the disabled elderly. In 1997, nearly 1 in 4,000 households was involved in providing home care (Meyer, 1997). Consumers are also demanding more information about health care so they can make informed decisions. Additional consumer involvement is driving a need for more health teaching and advocacy services from the health care discipline that has claimed accountability for delivering this aspect of wellness care—professional nursing. Coincidentally, the pool of nurses is relatively stable, just at a time when the need for expanded services from nurses is increasing.

> Families are extremely involved in home health care; for example, relatives and friends are providing about 80 percent of the care for the disabled elderly. In 1997, nearly 1 in 4,000 households was involved in providing home care (Meyer, 1997).

Value Orientation of the Consumer

The American consumer switched horses in midstream, so to speak, in the early 1990s. Business and news magazines as well as news broadcasts highlight this change quite often. Rather than buying the most expensive item, consumers now want value for the dollar. This doesn't mean they won't spend money for something. But they will only spend to the level necessary to get the value they want. And they are demanding that producers of goods and providers of services deliver higher value at less or at least stable cost. Health care providers are facing this consumer demand as much as Rubbermaid, IBM, or any of the U.S. automakers.

Trends in RN Supply

Baby boomers, the largest age group of this century, aren't getting any younger. As they age, they will also retire from the work force. This won't happen for at least 10 years (about 2008). And, of course, then they will enter that high-usage group called the elderly.

Meanwhile, college enrollments in nursing programs appear to be falling again. Many of those entering nursing now are in their middle adulthood rather than early adulthood, which means they will retire sooner from the RN work force (Brewer, 1997).

Forecasts by the federal government on RN supply and demand seem to vary yearly, so there is no clearly documented trend. However, we are hearing reports from all areas of the country that we do indeed have a nursing shortage. In some states and areas, the shortage is becoming acute. In the state of Washington, the

This means professional nurses must continue to develop and refine efficient and effective patient care delivery models that appropriately use varying skill levels.

State Nursing Association reported that one hospital under their contract had 30 positions for nurses that were going unfilled for months on end. This does not bode well for community health nursing, where the demand for nurses is also increasing. The need for more nurses with education at the BSN and higher levels is a generally accepted trend. If this and other trends we are seeing continue (and we see no reason why they will not), then, clearly, this means professional nurses must continue to develop and refine efficient and effective patient care delivery models that appropriately use varying skill levels.

HEALTH CARE DELIVERY TRENDS

To continue to deliver more health care services for minimal cost-increase prices, providers have been forced to find ever increasingly efficient ways to do so. Now we are moving to a discussion of environmental factors with which you are intimately familiar. Even without health care reform legislation at the federal level, health care providers and insurers have created reforms of their own in an effort to deliver services at much lower rates of increase or even at the same cost. Providers knew that the economy of the United States simply could not sustain the spiraling health care costs of the 1970s and 1980s.

More and more businesses are offering employees options of health maintenance organizations (HMOs) or managed care plans for their health care insurance coverage. In either of these settings, the need to deliver services at a lower cost than previously thought possible is forcing many providers, including hospitals and home care agencies, to rethink how they deliver care. They often must accept significant discounting on their costs to be included in a managed care plan offered by a major employer in a given area. The number of HMOs nationwide is increasing annually. Although HMO premiums are usually higher, they deliver preventive services often not available through traditional health care insurance coverage. But to be competitive in the eyes of the consumer, they also must find a way to deliver their services at a discounted cost. The good news about this is the inclusion of staff personnel in the planning and discussions on how to deliver the same quality care for a lower cost.

Another key trend is the change in the length of stay in acute care facilities. New technologies have enabled the ambulatory care setting to provide more and more services previously only available in a hospital. The same growth in technology often means patients suffer less trauma from invasive procedures that are done in the hospital and are able to go home sooner. In addition to technological advances that have shortened the length of stay for many types of hospital patients, the advent of managing the costs of care has led to shorter and shorter lengths of stay for those patients who still require hospitalization. The patients in hospitals are sicker than 15 years ago, stay a shorter length of time, and require more care while they are in the hospital. A look into the future, however, indicates that hospitals as they are known today may not even exist due to decreasing need

A look into the future, however, indicates that hospitals as they are known today may not even exist due to decreasing need for surgical interventions and the technology to treat patients in a community-based setting (Bergman, 1993).

for surgical interventions and the technology to treat patients in a community-based setting (Bergman, 1993). Patients still require nonacute care after these shortened lengths of stay, which means that home health care, long-term care, hospice care, and other community-based care will continue to grow.

"Policy experts predict that by the beginning of the next millennium, the majority of active nurses will no longer be employed in acute care settings. Instead many acute care nurses will work in a community-based or home care setting" (Schoen et al., 1997). With the enactment of the Medicare program in 1966, home health began its first burst of growth. In 1973, the benefits were extended to cover disabled individuals regardless of age. The increase in covered lives added an additional growth spurt to the home health industry. Home health agencies increased from 1,163 in 1963 to 3,000 in 1979, an increase of 39 percent (Mundinger, 1983). In

"Policy experts predict that by the beginning of the next millennium, the majority of active nurses will no longer be employed in acute care settings. Instead many acute care nurses will work in a community-based or home care setting" (Schoen et al., 1997).

1995, more than 18,000 U.S. home care agencies delivered services to some seven million individuals who required such services because of acute illness, long-term health problems, permanent disability, or terminal illness (Halamandaris, 1996).

As the home health industry has grown, so have the types of agencies offering services. Agencies fall into three general categories: public, nonprofit, and proprietary. The majority of these agencies are Medicare certified—meaning that they provide the full range of services including skilled nursing; physical, occupational, and speech therapy; social work; and home health aide services—and they are reimbursed for those services by the Medicare or Medicaid programs.

- Public agencies: These are government owned and operated. The home health agencies that serve veterans are public agencies, as are most public health departments.
- Nonprofit agencies: The visiting nurse associations are an example of a nonprofit. Some hospital-based home health agencies are also classified as nonprofit. But because the hospital-based agency generally reflects the financial structure of the hospital, it can be either nonprofit or for profit. Most hospice agencies are also classified as nonprofit.
- Proprietary agencies: As for-profit agencies, proprietary agencies may be owned by individuals, groups, or corporations. These agencies, which comprise 43 percent of all certified agencies, frequently offer private duty nursing or extended hourly care as well.

In addition to the agencies listed above, many private agencies offer services from homemaking and companion care to skilled hourly nursing care. These agencies are almost always for profit and are private pay or insurance reimbursed. Long-term care insurance is the usual type involved in paying for these services.

As our population ages, more preventive and/or community-based services for the elderly will be needed (Bergman, 1993). In addition to the changes described above, nursing case management strategies are being employed for health care delivery all across the country.

CHANGING NATURE OF WORK

This chapter started by painting a picture of rapid change in the work environment in the world today. Now it is time to put it in the context of your work world in health care. The 1990–1991 recession and the cuts in defense spending brought about an increase in unemployment across the country. Several things are different about this surge of job cuts nationwide, however. First of all, it is continuing even as the country remains in a vigorous growth economic cycle. Managers and professionals are losing jobs at a rate that has alarmed even the most previously secure professionals—health care professionals. Job security seems to be a thing of the past in all sectors of the economy in America. This bad news comes as companies and organizations flatten their structures in attempts to get rid of the hierarchy. At the same time, mergers and acquisitions are occurring across all industries, even health care.

Specific changes are also occurring in health care that are dramatically altering the work world of the nurse (Carleton, 1997; "Data Watch," 1997; Gerson and Vernarec, 1997; Lewin, 1997). Lengths of stay are decreasing for a variety of reasons. One very frustrating outcome of this change is that nursing personnel have less time in which to get to know their patients. Teaching, discharge planning, and individualizing care are all affected by this shortened time with patients. More procedures are moving to the outpatient setting, and with this shift comes the move of RN jobs to the outpatient site as well. Mergers and acquisitions mean the learning of new organizational cultures as well as procedures and structures. Increasing numbers of hospitals are closing their doors with a consequent loss of jobs, perhaps necessitating a move to a new community in search of a nursing job or a change in type of job within the same community. At the same time, some home care agencies are closing; others are reducing their staff, or restructuring in response to the new financial constraints placed on them by the Health Care Financing Administration (HCFA). For those agencies and facilities that continue to provide services, problem solving will be done with all members at all levels of the organization having input. All of these changes have strengthened the expectation that all workers will play a more active role in decision making in the organization. (That's the good news!) We call this empowerment— and it strikes fear in the hearts of some who feel ill prepared to make those decisions they are now called upon to make (Duck, 1993). The trend toward empowering staff has evidenced itself in nursing departments through shared governance, implementation of quality programs, and the movement toward self-managed units and organizations (Wake, 1990).

> For those agencies and facilities that continue to provide services, problem solving will be done with all members at all levels of the organization having input. All of these changes have strengthened the expectation that all workers will play a more active role in decision making in the organization.

RESTRUCTURING AND REDESIGN

Restructuring and redesigning lessons first implemented in industry are being employed in health care organizations across the country (McManis, 1993). In an effort to find more efficient and effective ways to deliver patient care, many organizations are employing the concept of process redesign or reengineering. Other organizations are looking at patient-focused restructuring. It does not really

CHECKPOINT 2-2

Think back to the section on "Demographic Trends." List the two trends discussed in that section that relate to the use of total quality management (TQM) or continuous quality improvement (CQI) programs in health care organizations.

1. _____

2. _____

See the end of the chapter for the answers.

matter which avenue for this process change is taken. What matters is what is happening: the traditional boundaries of organizations are falling down. Indeed, in the reformed health care environment, our whole concept of what constitutes an "organization" will change as we implement systems thinking to redesign care delivery across the continuum of care (Bergman, 1993). The delivery of care to patients is being accomplished by networks—or teams—of professionals, not individuals, and is a clear indication of the environment in which we will work into the next century (Kiechel, 1993).

Inextricably linked with the introduction of process redesign and changing organizational structures into your work world has been the implementation of total quality management (TQM) or continuous quality improvement (CQI) programs in health care organizations ("The Quality March," 1993, p. 6). Often it is not clear which has come first. The use of TQM and CQI, or any other formalized program to ensure the implementation of a full quality system in an organization, is driven by the increased involvement of consumers/clients/patients in purchasing and using health care services. For home care, strengthening the HCFA-required advisory board is an example of the move to empower the consumer. These consumers, who constitute communities, are demanding increasing value for their health care dollars. And they want continued high-quality outcomes. The use of TQM and CQI has opened the door for nurses to identify more

> Nurses are being challenged daily to use their holistic, systems-focused knowledge base to create the continually changing environment in which they work to provide care for individuals as well as communities.

effective and efficient means by which to provide high-quality, high-value care to their patients. Some are choosing multiskilled workers; some are choosing care partners; some are choosing new forms of old teams. Nurses are being asked in quality meetings to articulate clearly their contributions to the outcomes for the patients and communities they serve. They are being asked to find ways to improve or maintain outcomes for patients or clients without increasing the costs of achieving those outcomes. Nurses are being challenged daily to use their holistic, systems-focused knowledge base to create the continually changing environment in which they work to provide care for individuals as well as communities. Sister Rosemary Donley (1984, p. 6) was exceedingly prophetic in forecasting what the nurse's future work world would look like when she wrote:

> "Third wave nurses will be recruited into positions not for what they do but for what they control, manage, and decide." Nurses in 2000 AD "will not be supertechnicians but professionals who establish parameters of assessment and use information to make clinical decisions."

MATURING OF THE NURSING PROFESSION

This involvement of nurses in creating their new world of work has led to another environmental trend that actually bridges all others. More than any other trend, it has brought about the increased focus on clinical delegation skills for the management of patient care. "Regardless of where RNs work, executives expect RNs to delegate more tasks to lesser trained personnel and to assume more case management and gate-keeping roles" (Buerhaus, et al., 1997). It has brought about the maturing of the nursing profession—like the movement from adolescence to young adulthood.

Each of you is aware that at various stages of our lives we perceive things differently. Those perceptions are filtered through generationally grouped filters. A profession also goes through these stages of development. The corollary runs something like this: As the nursing profession developed, it moved into adolescence, most likely during the mid-1970s. The focus was on establishing an identity as a profession. The profession was greatly influenced by peer behavior, but it was also quite intensely inward-looking and unsure of itself. Primary nursing, interpreted by many to mean that the RN did everything for a patient, was perfect for this phase of development. The search for a unique body of nursing

CHECKPOINT 2-3

List the six major trends that are shaping the world in which you work.

1. _____
2. _____
3. _____
4. _____
5. _____
6. _____

See the end of the chapter for the answers.

knowledge and the quest for autonomy of practice coalesce under the adolescent struggle for identity (Rodgers, 1981).

Now, however, nursing has moved to young adulthood. The profession is fairly certain about its identity. Nursing has a set of values and is ready to test them out in the "real world" on its own. Nurses have come to realize that performing tasks is not the essence of nursing. The nursing process, which requires thinking as well as doing, is part of the profession's set of values, as are holism and systems thinking. But the profession is still learning. It is learning to work with others.

In this learning process, nursing is growing more and more understanding of its own identity. It is increasingly certain of its unique contribution to quality outcomes and the health of the communities. RNs are able to work with other disciplines and other workers on quality teams and task forces and develop new ways to shape their world of work. They are focused less on their own autonomy and more on their patients and communities. Community health nursing has from its beginning been an all RN (usually bachelor-prepared) nursing staff. Over the past 20 years, other disciplines have emerged into community health services. Licensed practical nurses (LPNs) are now used as extenders of RN services, as are nurse aides. As in other arenas of nursing practice, community health nurses are out there as a young adult profession bringing to life the identity established during adolescence.

> The nursing process, which requires thinking as well as doing, is part of the profession's set of values, as are holism and systems thinking. But the profession is still learning. It is learning to work with others.

As the profession ages further, who knows what changes in practice will develop or what exactly professional practice will come to mean. The vibrancy of the nursing profession's young adulthood allows it to continue learning and shapes the understanding it will bring to this learning in years to come. All of this means that more change is yet to come in your work world—change that will be shaped by you as professional nurses, based on the needs of patients and communities. Who knows where virtual reality and the information superhighway will take nursing in its "middle age." That is your world to know and to create!

> Change is always difficult, but nursing has always risen to the challenges encountered along the way, and it will in this situation.

HOME HEALTH CARE RESPONSES
TO THE CHANGES

Ruth I. Hansten, Marilynn J. Washburn, and Virginia L. Kenyon

Given the many changes in our environment, we now have a better understanding of the issues and challenges facing our practice. It does mean that we will all continue to change the way we do things. For some of you it means major shifts in how you think and practice. Cost containment, increased efficiencies, and demand for quality will continue to be a focus. All of this spells more change. Change is always difficult, but nursing has always risen to the challenges encountered along the way, and it will in this situation. When you feel the tendency to adopt the "victim" stance, remember that change is an opportunity to do something different, something new that is better suited to the challenge confronting you and ultimately better for your patients.

If you are "the average nurse" of today, you are 42 years old and have at least 15 years of experience (McCarty, 1992). You have also experienced a fair amount of change during your career and sometimes you probably feel like you have been through a war. Indeed, we are in the middle of a revolution. As former Secretary of Health and Human Services Joseph Califano (1993, p.10) reminds us:

> "Few of us have a greater responsibility or opportunity than the American nurse. Revolutions, like nations, do not drift in a vacuum. They move in a direction. And in the coming years, the opportunity for nurses to help shape the direction of America's health care revolution is enormous."

CHECKPOINT 2-4

List four changes you have observed that nursing has implemented in response to the dynamic environment of health care.

1. _____
2. _____
3. _____
4. _____

With all of this in mind, what changes have been made or are under way in home health care in response to the shifting health care environment? Your list may include some of the following changes:

- planning for discharge and self-care
- implementation of disease-specific clinical pathways
- use of new technologies
- focus on education of client/public
- use of unlicensed personnel

PLANNING FOR DISCHARGE AND SELF-CARE

"Discharge planning is a continuum of care rather than episodic. It begins at admission, if not before" (Long, 1993, p. 168). As the Balanced Budget Act of 1997 is implemented, discharge planning in home health care will become more critical than ever. Gone will be the days when you had 3 to 4 months and 20 to 40 visits to teach a client self-care. Now with the cost caps and visit limits per beneficiary per year, nurses must plan from the beginning of care for the day of discharge. Additionally, they must prepare the client for discharge, particularly if he or she has had services in the past and experienced a longer, more involved plan of care. All care will now have to be streamlined, every visit having preestablished visit content and outcomes. This has placed additional responsibilities on the nurses supervising care in the field to ensure that services are appropriate, efficient, and geared toward acceptable outcomes. Services must be specific to the

acute problems identified, time limited with identified outcomes and an
anticipated date of discharge.

> All care will now have to
> be streamlined, every visit
> having preestablished visit
> content and outcomes.

IMPLEMENTATION OF
DISEASE-SPECIFIC
CLINICAL PATHWAYS

Clinical pathways, or critical paths as they are also called, came into use in the mid-1980s as an interdisciplinary version of standardized medical orders combined with a tracking tool. These pathways were originally implemented in the acute care settings to better manage the DRGs and were used as guidelines for effective planning and monitoring of patients' progress. The literature reveals numerous reports of studies that demonstrate the effectiveness of these plans in reducing lengths of stay in acute settings and achieving desired outcomes in a more cost-effective manner. As the use of clinical pathways increased in acceptance in the acute care settings, other settings—including clinics, long-term care, and home health—began looking at this process as a means to use services better and identify efficient outcomes for patient care. As this move accelerated, organizations began asking, "Can you have pathways that cut across all those settings?" (White, 1993, p. 160). In some settings, primarily HMOs, the cross-settings clinical pathways began to be employed by case managers. Clinical pathways became the backbone of case management, a care delivery system already used extensively in home health care. The type of clinical pathway used more often in home health care is frequently referred to as "Disease Management" (see Disease Management later in this chapter). Examples of disease management and/or clinical pathways used in home health care are shown in Exhibits 2–1 and 2–2.

There are several important points to remember when using critical/clinical paths or disease management for patient care planning. The most obvious is that not all patients will fit neatly into a clinical path diagnosis, co-morbidities being the first that comes to mind. The RN case manager must always assess the patient as an individual, clearly identifying those nursing diagnoses that fit that patient as well as recognizing and dealing with those needs that do not fall into a standard critical path.

Recall that critical path management was first described in engineering and construction to assist in project guidance and control, and as they were introduced into health care are "simple direct timelines that focus on an episode of illness. They are not standards of care nor care plans . . . [but] are at a glance reminders of the predictive (routine) care for a condition or situation" (Carpentino, 1996, p. 6). When a nurse looks only at the critical paths as a guide to tasks to be done, without full assessment of the individual patient, then planning preferred outcomes with

Exhibit 2–1 Disease Management

Shading = Phase I   No Shading = Phase II   Shading/Underlining = Phase I & II

CHF PLAN OF CARE   PAGE ____ OF ____

Phase I: Admit plus repeat visits 2–5   **Phase II: Visits 6–13**

DATE	PROBLEM STATEMENTS:	DATE	INTERVENTIONS: SKILLED NURSING OBSERVATION (SNO) INSTRUCT AND SUPERVISE (I/S) SKILLED NURSING CARE (SNC)	D/C DATE	OUTCOMES: PT/PCG HAS/IS ABLE TO:	TARGET	MET	UNMET	VARIANCE	INITIALS
INIT		INIT		INIT		VISIT				
	☒ Knowledge deficit regarding disease process and symptom management		☒ Assess VS and cardiovascular status		☒ 1. Pt has VS and CV status stable for range at rest.	–	☐	☐	–	
			☒ I/S S/S to report to MD (CHF #1)		☒ 2. Verbalize when to seek appropriate medical help.	–	☐	☐	–	
			☒ I/S use of NTG for angina.							
			☒ I/S S/S of complications of CHF (CHF #2)		☐ 3. Pt has stable weight.	–	☐	☐	–	
			☐ I/S definition and cause of CHF (CHF #5a.b.)		☐ 4. Understanding of disease process and self-care management.	–	☐	☐	–	
			☐ I/S role and rationale for treatment, diet, activty/rest							
			☒ I/S use of weight record (CHF #6)		☒ 5. Demonstrate via daily log weight increases to report to MD.	–	☐	☐	–	
			☐ I/S S/S of electrolyte imbalance and mental status change							
	☒ Inadequate medication management.		☒ SNO/I/S knowledge of med regimen and side effects (CHF #7)		☒ 6. Verbalize understanding of medications, effects, and side effects.	–	☐	☐	–	
			☐ I/S use of med schudule in writing and mediset if needed (CHF #3)							
			☐ I/S adjusting meds according to RX changes.		☐ 7. Adjustment of meds according to RX changes.	–	☐	☐	–	
	☒ Knowledge deficit regarding nurtition/ hydration/ elimination		☒ I/S OK/NOT OK foods for decreased Na diet (CHF #4a.b.)		☒ 8. State, via food choices, understanding of low Na and K rich foods.	–	☐	☐	–	
			☐ I/S in use of small frequent meals and rest after meals.							
			☐ I/S to avoid straining at stool.							
			☐ I/S potassium sources (CHF #8)							
			☐ Take 24° diet history to check compliance/ understanding (CHF #9)							

CLINICIAN SIGNATURE   INITIALS   DATE

PATIENT NAME _____   _____   _____   _____

ID# _____   _____   _____   _____

                               _____   _____   _____

Source: Used with permission of Visiting Nurse Services of the Northwest, Seattle, Washington.

Exhibit 2–2 Disease Management

Shading = Phase I   No Shading = Phase II   Shading/Underlining = Phase I & II

CHF PLAN OF CARE   PAGE _____ OF _____

Phase I: Admit plus repeat visits 2–5   **Phase II: Visits 6–13**

DATE	PROBLEM STATEMENTS:	DATE	INTERVENTIONS: SKILLED NURSING OBSERVATION (SNO) INSTRUCT AND SUPERVISE (I/S) SKILLED NURSING CARE (SNC)	D/C DATE	OUTCOMES: PT/PCG HAS/IS ABLE TO:	TARGET	MET	UNMET	VARIANCE	INITIALS
INIT		INIT		INIT		VISIT ✓ ✓				
	☐ Decreased mobility with inability to perform ADLs		☐ I/S frequent rest periods with elevated feet/legs.		☐ 9. Pt has no acute symptoms with activity.	–	☐	☐	–	
			☐ Evaluate need for HHAide (on admit)							
			☐ Evaluate need for OT: home, bath, kitchen safety; assistive devices/ equipment needs; work simplification.							
			☐ I/S how to take pulse (CHF #10)							
			☐ I/S how to pace activity (CHF #11)							
			☐ Supervise HHAide Q 2 weeks for bathing and personal care.		☐ 10. Manage ADLs independently or supports in place	–	☐	☐	–	
	☐ Increased anxiety due to disease process and potentially inadequate support system		☐ Identify caregiver and support systems.		☐ 11. Decreased anxiety	–	☐	☐	–	
			☐ Evaluate need for community referrals.							
			☐ Evaluate need for MSW; lack of community support systems; pt/pcg issues; coping problems; economic problems.							
	☒ Need for discharge plan to support self-care management		☒ I/S re: discharge and follow-up plans.		☒ 12. Verbalize understanding of discharge plans.	–	☐	☐	–	
			EVALUATE NEW YORK FUNCTIONAL CLASS: ADMIT:_____ RECERT:_____ DISCHARGE:_____							

	CLINICIAN SIGNATURE	INITIALS	DATE
PATIENT NAME _____	_____	_____	_____
ID# _____	_____	_____	_____
	_____	_____	_____

Source: Used with permission of Visiting Nurse Services of the Northwest, Seattle, Washington.

> When critical paths are used in close collaboration with the patient and his or her interdisciplinary care team, with the RN providing for individualization of the total plan of care, assessment, and evaluation of the patient's progress toward preferred outcomes, the results are exciting.

the patient and family becomes less of a focus and task completion becomes the goal. At that point, the patient becomes a cog in the wheel of his or her progress, and the valuable assistance of a critical path becomes a stumbling block to comprehensive, integrated patient care for that patient in all settings.

When critical paths are used in close collaboration with the patient and his or her interdisciplinary care team, with the RN providing for individualization of the total plan of care, assessment, and evaluation of the patient's progress toward preferred outcomes, the results are exciting. Improved quality, shorter episodes of care, better pain control and comfort, and functional ability are some of the documented results (Ireson, 1997). These positive statistics correlate with Grier's work that supports the use of clinical decision-making aids to guide nurses to an improved focus on patient goals or outcomes (Grier, 1976). The message is clear: Use critical paths as guides, but don't substitute them for what nurses do best—assessment, nursing diagnosis, planning, evaluation of the results of interventions, coming full circle to redesigning the plan.

Clinical paths have the following characteristics:

- are a critical guide to track progress and streamline processes in patients whose diagnoses and care can be fairly standardized
- tend to decrease episodes of care and improve resource use
- tend to improve patient and family understanding of the patient's illness and allow for greater patient participation
- are a useful tool to improve communication among the health care team members and the patient and his or her family

Critical paths are not

- a substitute for individualized nursing care plans dealing with all the patient's nursing diagnoses and critical problems
- useful for all patients with many diagnoses and complex care
- necessary for all patients

Critical Paths for the Caregivers

Care paths for the caregivers have also been developed for nurses and their colleagues during times of stress to remind themselves of the need for self-care. *Individualized, specific goals and the steps to achieve the goals include the following:*

- Improve one health habit each week by using stairs instead of an elevator, taking scheduled breaks, drinking 6–8 glasses of water daily.
- Restore interdisciplinary communication by greeting others or listening actively to someone from another discipline.
- Develop career paths by reading a professional journal or joining a committee or task force.
- Learn one new stress management technique per week.
- Develop a new self-image by introducing self and articulating your role to patients and families.
- Support peers by writing a note to someone who did a great job or practicing outcomes-based communication techniques (see Chapter 8).

Care paths transfer skills from quality management processes while using the nursing (scientific) process and are a tool that can be used in personal growth and family life as well as care of patients.

TECHNOLOGY EVALUATION

Technological breakthroughs can be either a blessing or a curse in that we often see the results in increased costs and questionable impact on the outcome of patient care. Some technologies, however, have dramatically improved care in the home. The new, wallet-sized, infusion pumps run by computer chips have allowed patients who would previously have been tied to their IV poles in the hospital or home to return to a productive life, sometimes even return to work. Algineate dressings have had a very positive outcome for wounds and decubitis, sometimes healing old wounds in weeks

> The new, wallet-sized, infusion pumps run by computer chips have allowed patients who would previously have been tied to their IV poles in the hospital or home to return to a productive life, sometimes even return to work.

versus the months previously experienced with gauze dressings. However, not all innovations are this dramatic. As frontline providers, we are continually evaluating the effectiveness of treatment and monitoring the usage of technology with a watchful eye. Costs and benefits of new technology have to be weighed and evaluated more completely than ever before. As the health care dollars are more constrained, nurses will need to be sure the technologies they are applying in the home have the value-added outcomes that justify the expense.

EDUCATION OF THE CLIENT/PUBLIC

Nursing has traditionally focused on the holistic approach of patient care needs, realizing that education for patients is an integral part of their ability to maintain their optimum level of health. As Sister M. Olivia Gowan once wrote:

> "Nursing in its broadest sense is an art and a science which involves the whole patient—body, mind, and spirit; promotes his spiritual, mental and physical health, by teaching and by example; stresses health education and health preservation as well as ministration to the sick" (Hansten and Washburn, 1990, p. 11).

When Lillian Wald began the Henry Street Settlement in 1893, she laid the foundation for today's public/home health. Care was delivered in a holistic manner with an understanding of the clients within their community.

Home health care, with its roots in public health, has always ascribed to the philosophy of treating the whole human being in the context of his or her environment. Whereas public health has traditionally cared for communities, home health has always directed care to the individuals within the community. Individualized plans of care are developed using clinical/critical/disease-specific pathways. Teaching and education of the client regarding the disease process and the care thereof has always been a primary focus of the plan of care. With the change in the Medicare reimbursement formulas for home health care, it will become more imperative than ever that this goal be achieved. Clients, once educated, will be expected to manage their own health care needs with limited intervention from the home health nurse. More emphasis will be on preventive treatment and self-care. Recent changes in the economy of health care delivery are now supporting this position as insurance groups reimburse for preventive treatment and the system shifts from the traditional episodic, crisis-driven medical model to a continuum of wellness supported by preventive education.

GROWTH OF HOME CARE

We are seeing an increasing trend to home health and community nursing, settings where nursing has always been the predominant provider. The growth in this area is so significant that "the Bureau of Labor Statistics forecasts that home-health aide will be the fastest growing job category of all, nearly doubling to 550,000 by 2005" (Richman, 1993, p. 53). Home care is truly nursing's arena, and as the trend increases, nurses will continue to identify this as a successful response to the patient's changing needs. Home care has enjoyed a rebirth of interest as hospitals dealt with the reimbursement realities of the prospective reimbursement system (DRGs, or "*Da Revenue's Gone*") that began in the 1980s, resulting in the discharge of patients as quickly as possible. The acuity of patients within the home increased along with the number of elderly and acutely or chronically disabled. This trend fostered the need to intensify the coordination of care that originated in public health programs at the turn of the century. Driven by increasing acuities and diminishing resources, case management has become more sophisticated in the setting where it had its beginnings.

Home health continues to use a multidisciplinary approach to illness care within the home, employing physical, occupational, speech, and respiratory therapists; social service workers; and nutritionists. Psychiatric care has been provided by RNs or other mental health therapists. Chores and activities of daily living have been provided by homemakers or home health aides. These assistive personnel also may provide transportation, shopping, and other important living maintenance tasks that do not require licensed health professionals. Supervision of unlicensed health care assistants has been a long-term reality for home health care RNs.

In some states, notably Oregon and Washington, specific regulations have been written to guide RNs in supervising unlicensed assistive personnel in such settings as adult family homes or homes for the developmentally disabled. In Washington, a study has been commissioned to evaluate the safety and effectiveness of trained, unlicensed assistive personnel in these settings doing such tasks as rectal suppositories; oral and topical medications; nose, ear, and eye drops; dressing changes; catheterization using clean technique; blood glucose monitoring; and gastrostomy feedings (Washington State, 1995).

As we reform our system and community-based organizations scramble to adapt to the changing configuration of health care, home health providers continue to use the concepts of case management and multiskilled, unlicensed assistive workers to provide care.

> Supervision of unlicensed health care assistants has been a long-term reality for home health care RNs.

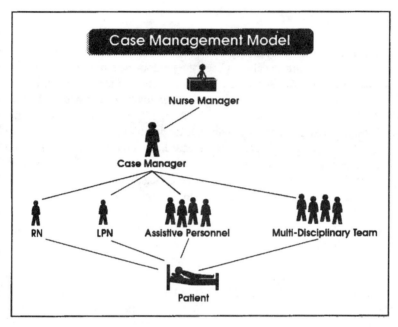

Courtesy of Dennis Burnside, 1998, Omaha, Nebraska

Case Management

The concept of case management involves determining what care is needed, when, and by what provider so that patient outcomes can be achieved with the most effective use of visits and other resources. Home health care has always used this model of service delivery. With the use of critical pathways as a guide, the RN case manager coordinates the services of the multidisciplinary team. As the Balanced Budget Act of 1997 is implemented and the cost-effective use of resources becomes critical, home health case managers will need to focus on which caregiver will be the most appropriate for the clients' needs. This may mean that physical therapists (PTs) will need to use the home health aide to follow through with the exercise routines, a practice used in the past to extend PT services when PTs were in short supply. As PTs became more available, however, the tendency to use the home health aide as a restorative aide decreased. The RN case manager will need to control this aspect of service

> With the use of critical pathways as a guide, the RN case manager coordinates the services of the multidisciplinary team.

> The RN home health case manager must fully exercise his or her role as coordinator and manager, determining who will provide services, when they will be provided, and for how many visits. It will require that he or she fully involves other disciplines in the planning, but ultimately, it will be the case manager's responsibility to "manage the care."

provider selection. The RN home health case manager must fully exercise his or her role as coordinator and manager, determining who will provide services, when they will be provided, and for how many visits. It will require that he or she fully involves other disciplines in the planning, but ultimately, it will be the case manager's responsibility to "manage the care."

Disease Management

Blending the strengths of case management and critical pathways with recognition of the managed care requirements for cost-effective care, discrete populations of patients with special needs are managed with improved efficiency and results in disease management. As Karen Zander (1997, p. 85) so aptly describes it:

> Disease management employs the concepts of critical pathways and care planning to "conceptually and operationally organize care, essentially care of chronically ill people, to achieve lower costs yet optimal clinical outcomes. Disease management is actually case management on the continuum level, with emphasis on prevention and reduction of the risk of exacerbation, hospitalization, and further functional decline/disability."

In the late 1990s, disease management has become a potential savior for managed care providers and has been embraced by others as a way to deal effectively with the chronic outliers who consume so much of our health care resources. Instead of evaluating a specific period of illness, disease management looks at the continuum of care for a patient with a given diagnosis in all settings, then uses the disease to measure cost, from diagnosis of the illness to its end stages, which allows for interesting and helpful studies of how best to treat patients for optimal function, satisfaction, and decreased costs. What a natural place for nurses to lead!

USE OF UNLICENSED PERSONNEL

Care Delivery Systems in Nonacute Settings

As we struggle for meaningful health care reform, there have been changes in care delivery systems in virtually every organization along the health care continuum. Whereas acute care providers, such as community hospitals, once often seemed to set the pace for changes in the care of the ill, now extended care within the home and community has taken a proactive lead in holistic health care of the public. To be able to care, with fewer dollars, for the ever-growing population with temporary or chronic disability, these organizations have adapted the actual methods of providing care in creative ways.

Long-Term Care

For example, many skilled nursing facilities have used a modified functional nursing structure, with an RN leading in care planning and supervision, an LPN (LVN) giving medications and some treatments, and nursing assistants performing hygienic and activities of daily living tasks. With a new emphasis on rehabilitation of their changing client population, they have developed new roles for the nursing assistants. One such role is that of the restorative aide. These individuals receive additional supervision and training related to range of motion, transfers, and other activities, and may work in a team with physical and occupational therapists.

In some states, nursing assistants in long-term care or residential facilities receive additional training to administer oral medications under the supervision of an RN, who evaluates the medication regimen and determines whether the medications should be administered as planned. This function is carefully regulated. Conversations with state board of nursing officials in several states reveal that this practice has been quite effective to date and may reflect a trend (see Chapter 3).

> Whereas acute care providers, such as community hospitals, once often seemed to set the pace for changes in the care of the ill, now extended care within the home and community has taken a proactive lead in holistic health care of the public.

Some extended care facilities that use many nursing assistants have developed the role of "team leader" among the nurse aides. These experienced, skilled assistants have exhibited additional leadership potential and are able to help the RN train, mentor, and evaluate the tasks completed by orientees. Because this group of assistants often exhibits a fair amount of turnover, the creation of this position has also become a means to develop and recognize highly competent, tenured employees.

Some facilities have developed a care triad: an RN, LPN (LVN), and certified nursing assistant. This team is assigned a group of patients, and work is divided among them based on their licensure, job descriptions, and special strengths. In some settings, personnel who were once thought to be "outside" the care team are considered valuable members of the treatment team. Consider an Alzheimer's residential facility and how important it may be for the housekeeper, who often spends a fair amount of time interacting with the patients, to understand current methods of answering questions and directing or helping the residents to their rooms. In other facilities, combining the skills of former environmental services personnel with those of the certified nursing assistant has created a job description for a cross-trained worker who is able to respond to many possible needs. In theory and often in fact, cross-training provides the worker with additional job growth and added potential for individual job mobility, and provides the manager with more productive workers.

RN-led case management has also been used as a very effective method of providing the highest quality care, using all members of the team, within extended care organizations. Just as acute care must focus on discharge planning and effective use of resources, the RN case manager coordinates the care given in the long-term care facility as he or she organizes the discharge plan and after-care with the interdisciplinary team from the present care site to the community. Many acute care organizations have established linkages with subacute, ambulatory, home care and extended care facilities so that one RN case manager oversees the care of a particular patient throughout the continuum.

Ambulatory Care

In ambulatory care arenas, such as physicians' offices, outpatient clinics, adult day care centers, short-stay surgeries, and mental health clinics, assistive personnel are employed much as they are employed in acute and long-term care. Positions and job descriptions are created to adapt to the needs of the organization. Surgical technicians, medical assistants, mental health technicians, and rehabilitation aides are trained and perform according to the specific state's practice codes and organizational job descriptions. Experiments with new types of team approaches and combinations of workers to fulfill specific needs are being conducted throughout the country in order to adapt to health care trends and contingencies.

Group Homes and Assisted Living Facilities

The past 5 to 10 years have seen an explosion of the development of adult family homes and assisted living facilities. These facilities/homes are licensed as "boarding homes," but many of them function like the old skilled nursing facility long-term care floors. As the residents of these facilities "age in place," more and

---

CHECKPOINT 2–5

Which of the following are true descriptions of the case manager role?

a) coordinates an interdisciplinary approach
b) may or may not provide the direct client care
c) uses clinical pathways/disease management pathways to organize care
d) effectively manages resources
e) all of the above

See the end of the chapter for the answers.

---

more of the homes have moved to using assistive personnel to meet the growing needs of the residents. Although it is not yet a requirement in most states that the personnel be certified as it is in the home health and nursing home industry, there is evidence that some states may soon require the use of certified nursing assistants in these facilities as well. The rules are less stringent in these facilities; however, increasingly nurses are being asked to delegate nursing tasks to the assistive personnel hired by the homes. The same rules for delegation apply in these settings as they do in all others where nurses delegate nursing tasks.

WHERE DO WE GO FROM HERE?

We have heard many nurses, particularly those from acute care, respond to the need for clinical delegation skills with the opinion that this is a passing phase and that once reform is implemented, assistive personnel will vanish, leaving RNs to provide all the care once again. We think not. Nor are we returning to the nursing of 30 years ago, to become generalists who assign tasks to other personnel, using the same principles of the work teams of the postwar era. We see distinct differences emerging between the team concept of the past and the current systems. We are responding not to a shortage of nurses (although shortages are cropping up once again in specific areas) but rather to a shortage of professional nursing care. Prescott (1989) describes this as occurring when nurses are too busy performing tasks that do not require their knowledge and skill base. Personnel with the minimal base of knowledge to perform tasks will be used to perform task assignments, not patient assignments.

CHECKPOINT 2–6

Long-term care organizations, such as skilled nursing facilities, step-down units, subacute care, swing beds, nursing homes, and adult family homes have responded to health care trends by developing innovative methods of delivering care. Ambulatory and home health care providers have also adapted their systems. What similarities are evident?

See the end of the chapter for the answers.

Whether you practice in community health or acute care, you will always be involved in working with other people. Not practicing in a vacuum, you will be called on to use your skill and expertise to delegate wisely to the multidisciplinary members of the team, maximizing your resources for the most beneficial outcomes for your patient. As Connie Curran sums it up,

"We can look at our history and realize that being in nursing is being in the patient care business, and being part of the largest group of care givers in this country. That would produce a redefinition of nursing based on the ethics that underlie the profession, some basic competencies, patient advocacy, clinical outcomes, and coordination of other health care workers in a variety of settings" (Friedman, 1990, p. 3120).

ANSWERS TO CHECKPOINTS

2–1. Increase in the number of elderly; increase in the number of poor.

2–2. Consumer involvement; value orientation of the consumer.

2–3. Influence of the 1980s nursing shortage; health care reform; demographic trends; health care delivery trends; changing nature of work; maturing of the nursing profession.

2–5. e

2–6. Use of creative multiskilled job descriptions, case management, varying team configurations, use of all health care workers and disciplines in the delivery of care, linkages throughout the health care continuum, and an ever-present need for the RN to lead, coordinate, and supervise.

REFERENCES

American Hospital Association. 1996. Workers' families to be hardest hit as employer-sponsored health insurance shrinks. News release, September 10.

Bergman, R.L. 1993. Quantum leaps. *Hospitals & Health Networks* 67 (October 5): 28–35.

Blegen, M.A., et al. 1992. Who helps you with your work? *American Journal of Nursing* 92, no. 1: 26–31.

Brewer, C. 1997. Through the looking glass: The labor market for registered nurses in the 21st century. *Nursing and Health Care Perspectives* 18, no. 6: 260–269.

Buerhaus, P., et al., 1997. Future of the nurse labor market according to health executives in high managed care areas of the United States. *Image: Journal of Nursing Scholarship* 29, no. 4: 313–316.

Califano, J.A., Jr. 1993. The nurse as a revolutionary. *Missouri Nurse* 62, no. 2: 10.

Carleton, S. 1997. Health reform rediscovers the patient. *Business & Health* 15, no. 5, supplement A: 4–11.

Carpentino, L.J. 1996. Critical pathways: A wolf in sheep's clothing? *Nursing Forum* 31 (January-March): 3–6.

Chalmers, K., et al., 1998. The changing environment of community health practice and education: Perceptions of staff nurses, administrators and educators. *Journal of Nursing Education* 37, no. 3 (March): 109–117.

Data watch. 1997. *Business & Health* 15, no. 7 (July): 48.

Donley, R. 1984. Nursing 2000, an essay. *Image: The Journal of Nursing Scholarship* 16, no. 1: 4–6.

Duck, J.D. 1993. Managing change: The art of balancing. *Harvard Business Review* 71, no. 6: 109–118.

Friedman, E. 1990. Nursing: Breaking the bonds? *JAMA* 264, no. 24: 3117–3122.

General Accounting Office. 1996. *Children's health insurance in 1994* (GAO/HEHS-96-129). Gaithersburg, MD: US General Accounting Office.

Gerson, V., and E. Vernarec. 1997. Are we squeezing the life out of hospitals? *Business & Health* 15, no. 5, supplement A: 25–29.

Greene, J. 1997. Currents. *Hospitals and Health Networks* 71, no. 19 (October 5): 22–23.

Grier, M. 1976. Decision making about patient care. *Nursing Research* 25, 105–110.

Halamandaris, V.J. 1996. *Basic statistics about home care*. National Home Care Association.

Hansten, R., and M. Washburn. 1990. *I light the lamp*. Vancouver, WA: Applied Therapeutics.

Ireson, C. 1997. Critical pathways: Effectiveness in achieving patient outcomes. *Journal of Nursing Administration* 27, no. 6: 16–23.

Kalnins, I. 1989. Home health agency preferences for staff nurse qualifications and practices in hiring and orientation. *Public Health Nursing* 6(2): 55–61.

Kaufman, N.J. 1993. Selected trends in America: Their impact on health. *Advances* (Newsletter of the Robert Wood Johnson Foundation) Fall: 7.

Kiechel, W. 1993. How we will work in the year 2000. *Fortune* (May 17): 38–52.

Lewin, T. 1997. Hospitals serving the poor struggle to retain patients. *The New York Times* A1, A16.

Long, A. 1993. Discharge planning in critical pathways, lower LOS, better care. *Hospital Case Management* (September): 168.

Lumsdon, K. 1993. Patience and partnership. *Hospitals & Health Networks* 67, no. 24: 26–31.

McCarty, P. 1992. How to keep mature, skilled nurses. *American Nurse* (July–August): 9.

McManis, G.L. 1993. Reinventing the system. *Hospitals & Health Networks* 67, no. 19 (October): 42–48.

Meyer, H. 1997. Home care goes corporate. *Hospitals & Health Networks* 71, no. 9 (May): 20–26.

Mundinger, M. 1983. *Home care controversy: Too little, too late, too costly*. Gaithersburg, MD: Aspen Publishers, Inc.

Murray, T.A. 1998. From outside the walls. *Journal of Continuing Education* 9, no. 2 (March–April): 55–60.

Pathfinders for Seniors Home Page, p. 11, 1998 (Internet access only).

Perkins, K. 1997. Caught in the post-50 insurance gap. *Sacramento Bee* (May 3): A1, A18.

Pew Health Professions Commission. 1995a. *Critical challenges: Revitalizing the health professions for the twenty-first century*. San Francisco: UCSF Center for the Health Professions.

Pew Health Professions Commission. 1995b. *Reforming health care workforce regulation: Policy considerations for the 21st century*. San Francisco: UCSF Center for the Health Professions.

Prescott, P. 1989. Shortage of professional nursing practice: A reframing of the shortage problem. *Heart and Lung* 18, no. 5: 436–443.

Prospective Payment Assessment Commission (ProPac). 1993. *Medicare and the American healthcare system: Report to the Congress*. Washington, DC: Prospective Payment Assessment Commission.

The quality march. 1993. *Hospitals & Health Networks* 67, no. 24: 6.

Richman, L.S. 1993. Jobs that are growing and slowing. *Fortune* (July 12): 53.

Rising health spending makes reform crucial. 1994. *Seattle Times* (January 4): B4.

Rodgers, J. 1981. Toward professional adulthood. *Nursing Outlook* 29, no. 8: 478–481.

Schoen, M., et al. 1997. Home health care nursing past and present. *MedSurg Nursing* 6, no. 4 (August): 230–233.

Smith, L. 1988. The battle over health insurance. *Fortune* 7: 145–150.

U.S. Dept. of Health and Human Services. 1988. *Secretary's Commission on Nursing final report*, Washington, DC: HHS, 1.

Star-Telegram News, June 11, 1998 (Internet based).

Wake, M.M. 1990. Nursing care delivery systems: Status and vision. *Journal of Nursing Administration* 20, no. 5: 47–51.

Washington State. 1995. House Bill. (E2SHB 1908).

White, M. 1993. Providers tackle care pathways beyond the hospital walls. *Hospital Case Management* 1 (September): 160.

Zander, K. 1997. Classic nursing management skills and disease management: Something old, something new. *Seminars for Nurse Managers* 5, no. 2 (June): 85–90.

CHAPTER 3

Know Your Practice:
Is My License on the Line?

Ruth I. Hansten and Marilynn J. Washburn

"I am so tired of those nurses whining about their licenses being on the line! Every time we make any changes around here, someone says something about her license being on the line. I hate that phrase! I don't care what you have to do, but get them some information so they know what the law says about their license status, for goodness sakes!" (home health administrator contracting our services).

We, too, have heard this phrase on numerous occasions, and we share some of the same concerns as the administrator quoted above. However, we recognize the plea for what it is, a cry for help and a sincere statement of concern and fear that the licensure status that allows you to practice as a professional nurse is in danger of being jeopardized by some change in the working conditions or whatever new plan the administration has created for you. The resolution of this situation lies in Adelaide Nutting's statement, "Knowledge is our only working power," (Hansten and Washburn, 1990, p. 66). Nurses must have a fundamental knowledge of the practice act, both the statute and the rules, that governs the practice of nursing in each state. Armed with that knowledge, nursing can better evaluate new care delivery systems and requests from administrators who are focused on effectiveness and efficiency, not necessarily on the standard of nursing practice.

The statement "My license is on the line" has been overused by nurses and in many cases is a "fighting phrase" that triggers a very negative response from many members of the management team. If you are justifiably concerned about the legality of the changes in your practice (and you may very well be!), we cannot emphasize enough that you must support that concern with knowledge of the law that governs nursing practice. Unfortunately, most nurses have received

> "Knowledge is our only working power."

CHECKPOINT 3-1

It is important to know about my nurse practice act because:

a) This information will help me do a better job clinically.
b) It's not important to me; the board of nursing is paid to tell me when something is not legal, so I don't have to worry about it.
c) This law directs my practice and is the legal foundation for what I do as a professional nurse. An understanding of the law and the rules will help me to evaluate the safety and legality of actions I am requested to take by my employer and any other member of the health care team.
d) As long as I pay my fees and keep my license current, that's all I need to know.

See the end of the chapter for the answers.

very little education about the practice act, and educational reforms are seeing nursing trends classes and professional issues classes deleted from many nursing curricula. In addition, practicing nurses of today have not kept themselves informed regarding the current status of the law governing their individual practice. If you have not had the opportunity to receive some information regarding the law of nursing, all is not lost. This chapter will focus solely on the topic of the nurse practice act (specifically as it addresses the issue of delegation) and will provide you with many resources that are readily available to you. Read on!

THE STATE BOARD OF NURSING

Every state in the nation is replete with governing bodies that overlook various professions, occupations, and pastimes. From the board of pharmacy to the board of game and fish, a significant number of agencies are devoted to monitoring our personal and professional behaviors. The board of nursing is one such regulatory agency created by the state government, but most nurses have contact with it only on an annual or biannual basis as licenses are renewed and fees are paid. What does the board of nursing do the rest of the year, when it is not collecting fees?

Many nurses are confused about the purpose of the board of nursing and may find out the hard way that this particular agency is not in existence to advocate for them. Just as the game and fish department writes rules to protect the public from unsafe habits of hunters and other sportsmen, the board of nursing is primarily interested in the safety of the public you serve as a nurse. If you are looking for support and the advancement of nursing practice on a professional level, try one of the professional associations such as the state nurses association. The role of the state nurses association is often confused with the role of the board, when in reality the two are very different. Table 3–1 clarifies some of the basic differences.

> The primary responsibility of any regulatory board is to protect the safety of the public.

Professional Associations

For further information about membership in various professional organizations, you can contact the American Nurses Association (http://www.ana.org.) or the National Association of Home Care (http://www.nahc.org).

Table 3–1 Roles of Boards of Nursing and Professional Organizations

	Board of Nursing	Professional Organization
Membership	Appointed by the governor to regulate practice of nurses in a given state	Based on criteria such as credentials, specialty, geographical location
Fees	None	Membership fees as required by the group, usually annual
Purpose	To protect the safety of the public	Varies with the organization, from networking opportunities for nurses with the same interest, promotion and advancement of the profession, collective bargaining representation, research specific to the specialty
Meetings	Open to the public except for executive sessions, matter of public record, required by law	May be restricted to members or potential members or by invitation only
Communication	Periodic newsletter sent to all registered nurses licensed in the state	Newsletters, faxes, district forums, workshops for education and networking

The Home Care Aide Association of America can also be found under the Web site of the NAHC. This association was established by NAHC in 1990 to "provide a forum for the development of issues related to the work of the paraprofessional in home care and to create a mechanism for legislative and regulatory advocacy on issues affecting home care aide services. . . . to promote national recognition of the essential nature of home care aide services through:

- advocating consistent standards of classification, training, supervision and practice
- advancing legislative and regulatory agenda which supports the effective utilization of home care aide services
- securing appropriate reimbursement from all payment sources"

The state nurses association in your state will also be a good resource for the various specialty organizations. See Appendix A for addresses and phone numbers of your state organization.

CHECKPOINT 3-2

The *primary purpose* of the board of nursing is to:

a) advocate for nurses accused of unsafe practice
b) approve schools of nursing and grant or revoke licenses
c) regulate the practice of nursing
d) protect the public from unsafe practice of nursing

See the end of the chapter for the answer.

Let's take a look at each of the answers in Checkpoint 3–2 to clarify some common misperceptions.

a) advocate for nurses accused of unsafe practice: If you are ever involved in a board investigation as the result of a complaint made regarding your professional practice, you may find that the approach taken by the board is adversarial and not supportive. Remember, this agency is there to protect the public, not you. If there is reason to believe that you are unsafe to the public, it is the board's responsibility to take corrective action and to ensure that the public is protected. Thus, it often does not come across as being "on your side"—indeed, it may not be! Here again, a working knowledge of how the board functions, particularly its disciplinary process, will give you a better understanding of the legal side of your practice.

b) approve schools of nursing and grant or revoke licenses: These are certainly duties of any board of nursing and are methods by which it governs the practice of nursing to ensure public safety. It is important to remember a little history here: Nursing as a profession in the United States did not have licensure until 1903. The first licensing law for nurses was actually passed in Cape Colony, South Africa, in 1891 (Donahue, 1985). After many years of struggle, British and American nurses began to make progress, and lawmakers began recognizing the need to protect the public from inconsistent standards and questionable practices. Prior to this time, a "nurse" could receive education through the mail, attend any one of a growing number of nursing schools with a great variety of curricula, or train "on the job." Sophia Palmer spoke of poorly qualified schools and nursing impostors in her editorial in the *American Journal of Nursing* in 1903: "How long will nurses permit such conditions to exist when only a strong, concerted action is needed to improve the educational standard, to protect the public and nurses themselves against impostors, and to give trained nursing a place among the honorable professions!" (Donahue, p. 375). Shortly after this publication, several states adopted nurse practice acts providing for the standardization of education and the regulation of practice through licensure.

Today it is the duty of the board of nursing in each state to establish criteria and approve schools of nursing that meet those criteria, thus upholding a standard of education. Through licensure and the disciplinary process for revoking or suspending licenses, the board also supports its prime directive to protect public safety. Such regulation of licensure eliminates the risk of impostors and ensures that anyone practicing nursing will have acquired a specific standard of education.

c) regulate the practice of nursing: The process by which each board of nursing regulates nursing practice varies from state to state. Generally, each board is empowered by law to adopt rules or issue advisory opinions concerning the authority of nurses to perform certain acts. Criteria, in the form of standards of conduct, are established by each board and regulated through the investigative process. Powers of regulation extend to schools of nursing and to individual licensees but not generally to institutions or agencies that employ nurses. These groups are generally regulated in other sections of the law. It is not the duty of the board to regulate practice by overseeing what policies an employing agency or institution creates for the employment of a nursing staff. State licensing laws for hospitals and other health care facilities, the Joint Commission on Accreditation of Healthcare Organizations (Joint Commission), and the Health Care Financing Administration (HCFA) are examples of institution-regulating agencies.

d) protect the public from unsafe practice of nursing: The board of nursing is empowered to implement a disciplinary process that ensures the safety of practice. Although the actual system may vary from state to state, the outcome is the same: Nurses found to be practicing in an unsafe manner will be disciplined. Generally, paid staff members working for the board of nursing function in the roles of consultants and investigators. In addition to administering the process of licensure, these staff members receive complaints made by the public or by nursing personnel themselves and begin an investigation. The results of their investigations are then presented to the board members for review and action. Hearings may be involved; the individual nurse may be represented by an attorney (the attorney general's office will represent the board), and the case may be presented to the board in this very formal manner. The board members are empowered to rule on the outcome of the hearing or investigation and to take disciplinary action, usually in the form of (1) issuance of a letter of concern, (2) allowance of practice with limitations, (3) suspension, or (4) revocation of the license.

Lawsuits versus Discipline

There is often confusion regarding the potential action that may be taken against a nurse if there should be a negative outcome to a patient's care. Many times we hear the statement "I might get sued," and we suspect you have heard it too. But you may not be clear about what happens if a nurse is sued. Disciplinary action taken by a board of nursing occurs when a complaint has been made regarding someone's nursing practice and an investigation reveals that the practitioner was indeed at fault. The steps available to the board are as noted above, and they involve measures that will directly affect the nurse's practice in terms of where, when, with what limitations or restrictions, or whether the nurse will be allowed to continue to practice at all. Although the board is represented by the attorney general's office and the nurse may also have legal representation during the hearing, this is not a civil case or a lawsuit. It is indeed possible to be disciplined by the state board and *not* be sued by the patient. Likewise, it is possible to be sued by an unhappy patient and/or family and not have the board of nursing involved at all. The fear of legal reprisal is intensified when you delegate tasks to others, and it can become a significant barrier to effective delegation, because many believe they are accountable for the delegate's actions as well. We will explore this in detail after you take the test later in the chapter (Exhibit 3–1).

Composition of the Board

Now that we have established the significant power of this group of individuals, it is important to know who they are. The composition of the board is defined in statute, with law specifying the number of members appointed to serve on the board and the area of expertise that each individual will represent. This ensures that major areas of practice, from management to education, are represented. It is

CHECKPOINT 3-3

Powers and duties of the board of nursing include:

a) approving schools of nursing
b) granting or revoking licenses
c) regulating practice of the profession
d) all of the above

See the end of the chapter for the answers.

not unusual for the state to require representation from a public member as well, representing the public perspective on nursing practice. The geographical location each member represents may also be specified, again to ensure broad representation of the profession. In addition to the qualifications of each member, the terms of service are also defined, usually ranging from a two-year to a five-year appointment. Appointment of board members is a political decision, usually from the governor's office, and board members are not paid.

Appointed members, defined by law and serving unpaid terms, make up the board of nursing in each state. The board will employ staff members to fulfill its administrative, clerical, and investigative needs. These individuals are hired by the board and do not participate in its decision-making process regarding licensure or other matters. The leader of the personnel will most likely be the executive director or executive secretary. This individual oversees the staff and is present at all board meetings for assistance and administrative support. The executive leader and the president of the board represent each state at the National Council of State Boards of Nursing (NCSBN), a source authority to which we will refer often in this book. Collectively, this group strives for standardization among the states and issues position papers and advisory opinions, commissioning studies and investigations of current practice trends from a national perspective. (See Appendix A for a complete listing of the boards of nursing, including the NCSBN.)

Meetings

The board convenes on a regular basis, from as frequently as monthly to as infrequently as quarterly. Meetings are open to the public, and agendas and locations for meetings are easily available by calling your board office. Attending one of these meetings can be very educational and will quickly familiarize you with the process of the functioning of the board. Some boards offer an "open mike" time when nurses may come forward and address specific practice questions for the board's advice and consideration. This is an excellent time to get to know the members of the board and to establish a very important professional relationship.

Resources

Several resources are at your disposal to help you build your knowledge about the board and the nurse practice act.

The Nurse Practice Act

Nurse practice acts are generally provided when you move to a new state, when you write the exam, or when you request a new license. Depending on the state, the document may be free of charge or may cost a nominal fee. The format will also vary, from a three-volume set in California (RN, LVN, and CNA are all separate books) to a pamphlet overview in Louisiana. Note that registered nurse (RN) and licensed practical nurse (LPN) laws may be included in one document or may be separate, depending on the state. It is also important to be aware that the majority of health care practitioners (physical therapists, pharmacists, respiratory therapists, nursing assistants [NAs], etc.) will also have regulatory documents to govern their practice. If you are delegating to an interdisciplinary team, you will want to be aware of the framework of regulation and discipline for each of these roles.

The age of computers makes it even easier to get the information you need regarding nurse practice acts and regulations. As of this edition, more than 27 states have their own Web page on the Internet, and many more plan to follow. The NCSBN (more on this group later in the chapter) has its own Web site and offers an overview of every state nurse practice act. A new addition to this Web site is the hot link to a site specific to delegation and unlicensed assistive personnel. For the computer savvy, this is an easy way to access specific regulatory language on a national level.

> You can reach the NCSBN at http://www.ncsbn.org.

Board Consultants

Members of the staff may be called consultants or investigators or advisors, and have specific areas of expertise. There may be individuals on staff who advise

CHECKPOINT 3-4

Check the following statements that apply to you:

❑ I have a copy of the nurse practice act for my state.
❑ I know who the members of the board of nursing are.
❑ I have attended at least one board meeting.
❑ I have served on a committee for the board.
❑ I have spoken with one of the staff or members of the board regarding a question I had.

If you checked two or more: Congratulations! You are well on your way to having a solid foundation of knowledge about your practice. If you checked fewer than two: Oops! Call your board of nursing now, and start getting informed!

regarding scope-of-practice issues, impaired nurse programs, nursing school criteria, and so on. These individuals are excellent resources for answers to questions regarding the safety of your working environment and the use of assistive personnel, and they may be of valuable assistance in answering that question that led you to believe your license might be on the line. Consultants or other staff members, including the executive director, often make themselves available to visit schools of nursing, professional association meetings, or health care facilities. They are usually very willing to provide an overview of the law and the duties of the board and to advise on specific questions. They may not issue black-and-white answers, but they will be able to direct you in evaluating your particular situation.

Advisory Opinions

Often the law is written in very generic terms and requires some interpretation. It is usually not possible or practical to write law that speaks to every unique situation that a nurse may encounter. In this case, the board may issue an advisory opinion that further clarifies the law and addresses practice in a more specific manner. In recent years, as the use of assistive personnel has increased, several state boards have issued advisory opinions to offer assistance to the practicing nurse in interpreting the expectations of the law. Since that time, many state practice acts have been changed, and the requirements of the delegating nurse have been more clearly delineated. You may request a copy of any advisory opinion written by the board and are encouraged to do so if you are uncertain about any practice issue. Subjects of advisory opinions may include abandonment, mandatory reporting, acceptance of assignments, and delegating to unlicensed personnel.

Committee Involvement

Within the working structure of any board of nursing is the creation of committees to oversee specific areas of practice. These committees are chaired by a board member and staffed by one of the investigators or consultants employed by the board. Committee members are professional nurses who have an interest in the work of the committee and have expertise in that area. For example, a board may appoint a committee to look at scope-of-practice issues for the advanced practitioner or the legal and legislative interests of nurses in the state. These committees may review a particular part of the rules that is confusing or controversial and may draft an advisory opinion (see above) that is then presented to the board for approval. Prior to legislation (a lengthy process), many advisory opinions were issued on the subject of delegation.

Committee meetings are open to the public and are another source of information regarding what is happening on a state level in terms of nursing practice. Your membership on one of these committees may be an opportunity for you to share your expertise and to develop your leadership and professional skills.

THE NATIONAL COUNCIL OF STATE BOARDS OF NURSING

We have referred to this group often in citing the basic definitions of delegation and supervision. A little background regarding this organization will be helpful in understanding the framework of regulations from a national perspective. As noted previously, this organization has a Web site and can be contacted at http://www.ncsbn.org. It will provide you with an abundance of important information regarding the profession of nursing.

The NCSBN is just that, a national group made up of two representatives from each state's board of nursing, including the District of Columbia and five U.S. territories. Its mission and purpose is to "lead in regulation by assisting Member Boards, collectively and individually, to promote safe and effective nursing practice in the interest of protecting public health and welfare" (revised August 1997, NCSBN Web site).

Major functions of the NCSBN include the development of the NCLEX exams for RNs and LPNs, the competency evaluation for nursing assistants, policy analysis, networking information, and ensuring uniformity in regulation of practice on a state-to-state basis. It also performs research, monitors issues and trends in public policy, and most important, serves as the communication clearinghouse on nursing regulation.

MULTISTATE REGULATION

With the increasing mobility of our practice, nurses often find themselves working across state lines and moving from state to state in a network health system. What laws then govern this multistate practice? Does a nurse need licensure in all states? To respond to these questions, the NCSBN convened a task force in 1996 to gather data and to issue a recommendation regarding further action. In December 1997, the delegates at a special session approved the proposed language for an interstate compact in support of a standard approach to a mutual recognition model for nursing regulation. The ten implementation strategies approved also include the strong recommendation that states do not adopt the compact prior to January 1, 2000. Additional work and development of supportive strategies for the individual state boards will continue at the NCSBN annual meeting in August 1998 (news release, 12/16/97). And on March 14, 1998, Utah became the first state to adopt into law the concept of the mutual recognition of nursing licenses (news release, 4/3/98).

What does this historical statement mean to you? We are one giant step closer to a standardized model of practice, reducing the variations that currently exist from state to state and eliminating the need for expensive licensure in multiple states.

Let's look at why this is happening. The NCSBN cites several reasons, and although the process is not yet complete, significant steps have been taken to begin a national standard of licensure.

Reasons for Multistate Regulation

- New practice modalities and technology (on-line interstate consulting) are raising questions regarding issues of current compliance with state licensure laws.
- Nursing practice is increasingly occurring across state lines.
- Nurses are practicing in a variety of settings and using new technologies that may occur across state lines.

- Expedient access to qualified nurses is needed and expected by employers and nurses.
- Having a nurse demonstrate the same licensure qualifications to multiple states for comparable authority to practice is cumbersome and neither cost-effective nor efficient. *(National Council, 1997)*

THE NURSE PRACTICE ACT

With the advent of multistate recognition, it becomes even more important to have solid knowledge of the nurse practice act for the state in which you are licensed. Because there are numerous references to this document, we believe that it warrants more than a word or two of explanation. Let's start with the basics: The nurse practice act is the general term applied to the law, or statutes, written in each state to regulate the practice of nursing. In fact, it has different names in different states: Wisconsin Statutes Relating to the Practice of Nursing, the Law Relating to Registered Nurses, the Revised Code of Washington, the Texas Administrative Code, and so forth. Whatever the title, this document is the legal framework of practice. It is written through the legislative process, meaning that any changes in the language must be initiated in the form of a bill passed by both the house and the senate and signed into law by the governor of the state. For this reason, the statute relating to nursing is typically very general in terms, allowing for broad interpretation and application over an extended period of time. Changes in law may require several years to enact, depending on the nature of the change and the amount of support or controversy it engenders.

Basic components of the practice act will include:

- the creation of a board of nursing, defining membership and qualifications
- the listing of the powers and duties of the board, including meetings
- the licensure process, including qualifications, fees, renewal, permits, reciprocity
- definition of nursing
- approval process for nursing schools
- authority to adopt rules and regulations

> The statute relating to nursing is typically very general in terms, allowing for broad interpretation and application over an extended period of time.

CHECKPOINT 3-5

The following is one of the major differences between a rule and the law:

a) There are no differences because nurses are disciplined according to the law and the rules.
b) Law is more specific in nature because it must go through the legislative process for approval.
c) Rules are more detailed in nature than the law and must be based on and supported by law.
d) Rules can be written by anyone, and laws must be written by legislators.

See the end of the chapter for the answers.

RULES AND REGULATIONS

Because of the durability of the law, specific areas such as staffing ratios, acceptability of assignments, complete listings of the procedures allowable for nurses to perform, and detailed definitions of such concepts as supervision and delegation are not usually addressed in law. However, the statute enables the board to adopt rules and regulations to clarify and amplify the intent of the law. If you are confused, consider the following anatomical analogy: The law is like a skeleton, providing the framework for the muscle and flesh of the rules. Only rules that have support by statute can be written, but they can be much more specific in nature.

Members of the board of nursing may write rules and will often use committee input to create them. Once written, rules undergo a similar, yet simpler process of promulgation to become official. Many issues that cause concern about whether your license is on the line are addressed in the more detailed rules and regulations. For example, the increased use of assistive personnel has caused most states to

> The law is like a skeleton, providing the framework for the muscle and flesh of the rules. Only rules that have support by statute can be written, but they can be much more specific in nature.

clarify the reporting relationship of these individuals and to be more specific in the definition of supervision as it pertains to the process of delegation. This topic will be explored in greater detail in the rest of this chapter.

THE TEST

We have now spent considerable time building your foundation of knowledge about the state board of nursing, the NCSBN, and the nurse practice act. It's time to put that information to the test and ask you some key questions that will be major determinants of whether your practice with assistive personnel puts you at risk. Please answer the questions given in Exhibit 3–1 as true or false, according to the practice act in your state. Ready?

How did you do? Using statements of the NCSBN and a representative sampling of state practice acts, let's review the answers.

Question 1: FALSE

This brings us to the definition of delegation, a fundamental that will be emphasized many times because it forms the basis of the legal expectations of your role. Dictionary definitions of the term *delegation* include to assign, entrust, or transfer. The NCSBN (1995, p. 2) has issued the following definition of delegation as it specifically applies to nursing:

> Delegation: "transferring to a competent individual the authority to perform a selected nursing task in a selected situation. The nurse retains the accountability for the delegation."

Note the general nature of this definition. Those individuals who are looking for a black-and-white list of what may and may not be delegated will be a little concerned at the apparent ambiguity of this defined process. Take heart! The definition, as with statute, is intentionally generalized to allow you, as the RN, to practice the art of nursing. No authority can begin to cover every unique and specific practice issue that may arise. This definition considers your expertise and knowledge to be guiding factors in your decision of which selected tasks and in which selected situations you deem it appropriate to delegate care. Your primary legal obligation is to ensure the competency of the individual you are working with, and we will explore that issue in detail.

Exhibit 3–1 Test on the Nurse Practice Act

Please answer the following questions as true or false:

____ 1. Once I delegate a task to an unlicensed health care worker, I am no longer accountable for what happens.

____ 2. My state's nurse practice act specifically allows me to delegate nursing care activities.

____ 3. My state's nurse practice act specifies that I must know the competencies and abilities of the person to whom I delegate.

____ 4. My state's nurse practice act states that I may be in violation of the standards of conduct if I delegate tasks to those I have reason to know lack the ability to perform the function or responsibility.

____ 5. If I fail to supervise those to whom nursing tasks have been delegated, I may be disciplined by the state board.

____ 6. If a health care assistant makes a mistake during a task I have delegated, it would mean I could lose my license.

____ 7. Employer policies or directives can relieve me of my responsibility for making judgments about the delegation of nursing activities.

Source: Reprinted with permission from Loretta O'Neill, Ruth Hansten, and Marilynn Washburn, and the Washington Organization of Nurse Executives, © 1990.

> Your primary legal obligation is to ensure the competency of the individual you are working with.

Your primary legal obligation is to ensure the competency of the individual you are working with.

To answer the first question, when you delegate a task to an unlicensed assistant, you remain accountable for the delegation, according to the definition above. What causes concern for many is the concept of accountability and the feeling that "if I am accountable, why delegate in the first place?" The term *accountability* has been applied to the nursing profession liberally and with minimal clarification of its meaning. It is often linked with responsibility, authority, and autonomy, other broadly defined terms that translate to being the one who shoulders the blame if something goes wrong. This is not necessarily the case. Being accountable means being answerable for what one has done (in this case, the decision to delegate the task) and standing behind that decision and/or action. For example, the home health aide (HHA) to whom you delegated the task of obtaining vital signs made an error in the procedure of taking the blood pressure. The HHA is responsible for his or her performance, and you are accountable to the patient for the decision you made to delegate the task and for taking action and correcting the error. As we continue through the remaining test questions, it will become clear just what you are accountable for in terms of patient care.

Question 2: TRUE

Within the statutes or rules of all nurse practice acts is the definition of nursing. Many of these definitions clearly address the function of delegation; others imply the process, as in the following examples. According to Chapter 18.88 of the Revised Code of Washington (1995), "The practice of nursing means the performance of acts requiring substantial specialized knowledge, judgment and skill ... in . . . (3) the administration, supervision, delegation and evaluation of nursing practice." And according to Massachusetts Nursing Regulations (244 CMR 3.00, Section 3.05, Sept. 1996), "The full utilization of the services of a qualified licensed nurse may permit him/her to delegate selected nursing activities to unlicensed personnel. Although unlicensed personnel may be used to complement the qualified licensed nurse in the performance of nursing functions, such personnel cannot be used as a substitute for the qualified licensed nurse." Not only does the language of the law specifically allow the RN to delegate, but in many states the relationship of the HHA is delegation dependent. In New Jersey, for example, the state defines "Homemaker-home health aide: means a person who is employed by a home care services agency and who, under the supervision of a registered professional nurse, follows a *delegated* nursing regimen or performs tasks which are delegated consistent with the provisions of this law" (New Jersey Nursing Regulations: 13:37–14.2). A survey completed by the Montana State Board of Nursing in 1992 revealed that of the 41 respondents (the NCSBN has 62 jurisdictions), 28 have specific language regarding delegation; all the others imply the process within the definition of nursing. Review of the nurse practice acts via the NCSBN Web site in September 1997 revealed 299 citations of the word delegation in more than 35 state practice acts.

Question 3: TRUE

Many state practice acts have adopted language from the NCSBN and specifically address the legal requirement that nurses know the competencies of the delegate. In its paper, "Delegation: Concepts and Decision-Making Process," the NCSBN (1995, p. 1) stated: "Boards of nursing should articulate clear principles for delegation, augmented by clearly defined guidelines for delegation decisions." We anticipate that all states are in the process of promulgating rules that specifically address this area. Here are two examples from states that have already done so. Chapter N 6 of the Wisconsin Statutes and Administrative Code Relating to the Practice of Nursing (1993) states under "(3) Supervision and direction of delegated nursing acts" that "in the supervision and direction of delegated nursing acts an RN shall: (a) delegate tasks commensurate with educational preparation and demonstrated abilities of the person supervised." South Dakota Nursing Regulations (1996) states, in Section 20:48:04.01:01 (General Criteria for Delegation), "(5) The licensed nurse has either instructed the unlicensed person in the delegated task or verified the unlicensed person's competence to perform the nursing task."

Oregon Nursing Regulations get very specific regarding the instruction and documentation of the preparation of the assistant: "Prior to delegating the task, the registered nurse shall do the following: A) teach the unlicensed person the task of nursing care; B) observe the unlicensed person performing the task to ensure that the unlicensed person performs the task safely and accurately; C) leave written instructions for performance of the task for the unlicensed person to use as a reference; D) instruct the

"Homemaker-home health aide: means a person who is employed by a home care services agency and who, under the supervision of a registered professional nurse, follows a *delegated* nursing regimen or performs tasks which are delegated consistent with the provisions of this law."

> Training to develop competency in a delegated task must be provided by the agency or the delegating nurse to ensure safety of the client.

unlicensed person that the task being taught and delegated is specific to this client only and not transferable to other clients or taught to other care providers; . . . K) following teaching and delegating the task, the registered nurse shall document, in writing, that he/she takes responsibility for delegating the task to an unlicensed person and ensures that supervision will occur for as long as the registered nurse is supervising the performance of the delegated task." (Oregon Nursing Regulations: 851–47–030). Ensuring competence through initial direction and/or instruction is an essential part of delegating safely. In a Florida case, an HHA was accused of dropping a quadriplegic patient, with resulting injuries requiring surgery. One of the allegations was the lack of training for the aide by the home health agency. Subsequently, the jury awarded $30,000 (Fiesta, 1994). Training to develop competency in a delegated task must be provided by the agency or the delegating nurse to ensure safety of the client.

Question 4: TRUE

Knowing that the delegate is not competent or prepared educationally and proceeding to delegate the task anyway will certainly be a violation of the standard of practice in any state. All nurse practice acts list specific acts that are in violation of the standard; indeed, this is where you will find the highest degree of clarity! It's quite easy to identify what will get you in trouble. According to Georgia RN Nursing Regulations, Chapter 410–11.02 (1996), the definition of unprofessional conduct is "(h) delegating nursing care, functions, tasks or responsibility to others when the nurse knows or should know that such delegation is to the detriment of patient safety."

For example, as an RN in a home health agency, you assign a temporary rehab aide the task of feeding a stroke patient who has dysphagia but has been progressing nicely with the assistance of speech therapy. You know the aide has had difficulty in the past and in fact can recall one instance when the aide almost caused another client to aspirate part of a tomato. But because your regular aide called in sick, and you have no time to make the visit, and because it's in the aide's job description, you guess he'll just have to learn with practice. WRONG! Don't put your license in jeopardy by making this kind of decision. You will be responsible for the correctness of this delegation, and in this case, the task should not be delegated to this individual. Your choices may include working with the aide, assigning another aide (whom you know to be competent) to feed the patient, or doing it yourself.

Question 5: TRUE

Among the terms commonly defined in every practice act is *supervision*. The NCSBN (1995, p. 2) defines the term as follows: "The provision of *guidance or direction, evaluation* and *follow-up* by the licensed nurse for accomplishment of a nursing task delegated to unlicensed personnel." Note that the italics identify the important components of supervision:

1. *Guidance or direction*—the instructions you provide when first delegating the task: for example, "Please check the blood pressure on Mrs. Jones and report it to me immediately" or "Bathe Mr. Hawley three times this week, on Monday, Wednesday, and Friday during your visit. Use the bath oil Mrs. Hawley has gotten from the doctor. I'll be in on Friday to assess his skin and see how you are doing."
2. *Evaluation*—the decision you make regarding the frequency of checking back with the delegate is based on your judgment of the current situation. It is a defined expectation that you will provide supervision in the form of follow-up with the delegate. In the example above, the home health nurse is "evaluating" the HHA on Friday. He or she may be doing this weekly, or as infrequently as monthly, depending on the circumstances.
3. *Follow-up*—you need to communicate your evaluation findings to those who are in a position to do something about the situation. For example, if you note in your evaluation that the HHA is not using the bath oil as directed, and Mr. Hawley's skin condition is worsening, you will need to discuss this directly with the aide. Florida Nursing Regulations, Rule 59S-14.002 (July 1996), clearly delineates this expectation: "the delegation process shall include communication to the UAP which identifies the task or activity, the expected or desired outcome, the limits of authority, the time frame of the delegation, the nature of the supervision required, verification of the delegate's understanding of assignment, and verification of monitoring and supervision."

Failure to provide either the initial direction or evaluation and follow-up

> Supervision: "The provision of *guidance or direction, evaluation* and *follow-up* by the licensed nurse for accomplishment of a nursing task delegated to unlicensed personnel."

will be interpreted as a failure to supervise the delegate adequately and will be the basis for disciplinary action of the RN, as noted in the New Hampshire Nursing Regulations, Chapter NUR 200, Part Nur 215 Disciplinary Sanctions: "(2) Failure of licensee to supervise individuals or groups required to practice nursing or provide nursing-related activities under supervision."

Supervision may be direct and on-site, with the RN immediately available, as in the acute care setting. It may also be indirect, with the RN still accountable for the supervision of the individual but not physically present at the site of care. In home health practice, community-based settings, and some long-term care facilities, supervision by the RN is indirect. "The nurse who delegates an act to another assumes responsibility for the supervision of the act, whether the nurse is physically present or not" (NCSBN, 1990, p. 2). Chapter 5, Section 1 (1996), of the Maine Nursing Regulations clarifies this well: "Supervision may require direct, continuing presence of the registered professional nurse to observe, guide and direct the nursing assistant; intermittent observation and direction by the registered professional nurse who may only occasionally be physically present; or development of a plan of care, in advance, by the registered professional nurse. In the latter situation, the registered professional nurse must be available for supervision, in person, in the event circumstances arise that cause the registered professional nurse to believe such supervision is necessary."

Just as supervision may be direct or indirect, you will base your decision regarding the frequency of periodic inspection on varying levels of supervision:

1. *Never delegated:* Certain acts, including the assessment, evaluation, and nursing judgment, are never delegated. In addition, some states specify certain procedures that are never to be delegated but can be performed only by the RN. Detailed discussion on this will follow later in the chapter.
2. *Unsupervised:* When an RN is working with another RN in a collegial relationship, he or she is not in the position of supervising the other RN unless the delivery model identifies the relationship through a charge nurse or other designated capacity. For example, when three RNs are working during the week for one home health agency, they are not supervising each other and are not accountable for the fundamentals of supervision unless one of the three is working in the capacity of a charge nurse, resource nurse, or team leader, as defined by the agency.
3. *Initial direction/periodic inspection:* The RN supervises an individual, either licensed or unlicensed, whom the RN knows in terms of competency and has developed a working relationship with over time. A home health nurse in the field may have worked with an HHA for the past year and be confident in meeting with the aide on a biweekly basis for evaluation of the assigned cases.

4. *Continuous supervision:* When the working relationship is new or the RN has reason to believe that the delegate will need very frequent to continual support and assistance, the highest level of supervision is required. A new nurse being oriented to the agency will need to have someone assigned as a preceptor to provide continuous supervision until the new nurse has demonstrated a level of expertise that the supervising RN is comfortable with. An HHA who has just completed his or her training course will need continual supervision throughout orientation until the RN is satisfied with the new assistant's demonstrated level of skill.

It is important to remember that the RN, in assessing the appropriateness of delegation, also determines whether the level of supervision needed to ensure safe practice is indeed available. Again we cite Massachusetts Regulations, General Criteria for Delegation: "(3) The degree of supervision required shall be determined by the qualified licensed nurse after an evaluation of appropriate factors involved, including but not limited to the following: a) the stability of the condition of the patient/client, b) the training and capability of the unlicensed person to whom the nursing task is delegated, c) the nature of the nursing task, d) the proximity and availability of a qualified licensed nurse to the unlicensed person when performing the nursing activity."

CHECKPOINT 3-6

Determine the level of supervision that is appropriate in each of the following situations:

1. A student nurse who is assigned to provide care to two of your patients. Her instructor is in the office but also has eight other students assigned to her.
2. A fellow RN who is working with you and Marge, the area supervisor.
3. A school health aide who has been assigned to work with you at the junior high—this is her first day.
4. A mental health assistant who offers to give the intramuscular medications because he "was a medic in the Army."

See the end of the chapter for the answers.

HCFA GUIDELINES

Home health agencies, like acute care facilities, are governed by a number of regulatory bodies. If the home health agency is providing Medicare services, HCFA has some very specific requirements regarding the organization and its overall functioning. One issue HCFA is very clear on is the relationship of the RN to the HHA or personal care attendant. Supervision is specifically defined, and the frequency of this oversight is also clarified by regulation:

484.36(d) Standard: Supervision

(1) If the patient receives skilled nursing care, the registered nurse must perform the supervisory visit required by paragraph (d)(2) of this section. . . .

(2) The registered nurse must make an onsite visit to the patient's home no less than every 2 weeks.

(3) If home health aide services are provided to a patient who is not receiving skilled nursing care, . . . the registered nurse must make a supervisory visit to the patient's home no less frequently than every 62 days. In these cases, to ensure that the aide is properly caring for the patient, the supervisory visit must occur while the home health aide is providing patient care.

(Interpretative Guidelines-Home Health Agencies, Revised 2/21/95)

Question 6: TRUE, but only if you delegate inappropriately

This question often stumps many of the nurses we work with and is often the basis for their concern about professional responsibility and "their licenses being on the line." In the eyes of the law, you will be evaluated according to the manner in which you delegate a task and the supervision you provide to the delegate. Delegates are responsible for their individual performance of the task they are trained to perform. You cannot assume (and are not expected to assume) responsibility for the personal performance of all individuals on the health care team. Again, we reference the NCSBN (1995, p. 3): "The delegate is accountable for accepting the delegation and for his/her own actions in carrying out the act." The state of Washington has further clarified (in WAC 246-839-010) what is expected of the delegator within its definition of supervision: "Supervision of licensed and unlicensed personnel means the provision of guidance and evaluation by a qualified RN for the accomplishment of a nursing task . . . and the authority to require corrective action."

> Delegates are responsible for their individual performance of the task they are trained to perform.

Due to the controversy and concern voiced by nurses across the country, states are adopting rules that more clearly state the nurse's responsibility in working with other personnel. One of the barriers to effective delegation is the fear that the delegating nurse has regarding his or her accountability for the results of a task performed by another individual. Being clear on where that line of responsibility is drawn will help to remove that barrier and allow the nurse to function at the level of his or her professional education, providing optimum care to the individual. According to Alaska Nursing Regulations: Appendix D (1993): "It is the responsibility of the unlicensed assistive personnel to perform the delegated activities correctly."

Knowing what conditions must exist for that line of responsibility to be drawn is also very helpful when making decisions to delegate. According to Colleen Person from Creative Nursing Management, "Professional nurses who negligently delegate or supervise unlicensed personnel may be subject to a civil liability if a patient is injured, provided the patient can show that:

- the professional nurse had a duty
- she or he breached that duty by failing to act as a reasonably prudent nurse would have
- the professional nurse's conduct caused the harm, or subject of the complaint
- and the nurse's conduct was the proximate cause of the harm" (Person, 1997, p. 12)

Let's discuss the case presented in Exhibit 3–2. What is the RN accountable for in this situation? According to our discussion of the legalities of nursing practice, we know the RN is accountable for assessing the situation and for the decision to delegate. She is also accountable for supervising the delegate by providing initial guidance and direction, evaluation, and follow-up. According to the scenario described, the RN did all of these things.

Did the RN delegate properly? Recalling the regulatory requirements of delegation, you know that the RN delegated properly if she knew the competen-

Exhibit 3–2 A Delegation Case Study

An RN at Cityview Home Health Agency is working with an HHA whom she has worked with for the past six months. On the initial visit she delegates to the HHA the task of taking vital signs, giving particular instruction about Mrs. Avery, a fresh post-op now home with a new AV fistula in her right arm. Mary, the HHA, is instructed to take Mrs. Avery's blood pressure on the left arm, as noted in the care plan. Mary nods in understanding. On the RN's return visit three days later, the RN is approached by Mr. Avery, who says, "I thought the aide was not supposed to take my wife's blood pressure in the right arm. But she insisted, even though my wife complained and said it hurt."

What is the RN accountable for in this example?

Did she delegate correctly?

Is her "license on the line" for working with an incompetent aide?

What is Mary (the HHA) responsible for?

cies of the HHA. Knowing they had worked together for several months, one assumes that she had opportunity to assess job performance and knew that this HHA could perform the job competently.

Is her license in jeopardy? Not at this time. The RN assessed the situation, made a reasonable assignment, and provided initial direction. In the performance of periodic inspection, she has discovered a potentially harmful circumstance. The action she takes now will determine whether she completes the legal expectation of a delegator, that of taking corrective action. The RN must assess the patient's condition, checking the patency of the new fistula, notifying the physician if necessary, and following up with Mary to make certain this does not happen again. (For more on the feedback process, see Chapter 10.)

What is Mary responsible for? According to our legal guidelines, the delegate is responsible for accepting the delegation and for her own actions in carrying out the act. If the patient has been harmed as a result of the improperly placed cuff, Mary is responsible for the damage.

Working with other individuals always poses some risk, but no one individual can provide all of the care that a patient needs. The RN who must rely on the LPN to pass the medications correctly knows that the LPN is responsible for the accuracy of the medication administration and is personally responsible for any error that may be made in performing that act. The physician (the primary delegator on the health care team!) who delegates the administration of the chemotherapy to the oncology nurse knows that the oncology nurse is responsible for performing that act correctly. Understanding our legal boundaries helps us to minimize risks and to function at the highest level of our scope of practice.

Question 7: FALSE

The NCSBN (1995, p. 2) clearly states its position: "It is inappropriate for employers or others to require nurses to delegate when, in the nurse's professional judgment, delegation is unsafe and not in the patient's best interest. In those instances, the nurse should act as the patient's advocate and take appropriate action to ensure the provision of safe nursing care. If the nurse determines that delegation may not appropriately take place, but nevertheless delegates as directed, he/she may be disciplined by the Board of Nursing."

Employee policies cannot override the law and rules of nursing and will not protect the nurse who is following policy but acting outside of the practice act. In fact, several state practice acts are very clear regarding employer policies. For example, South Carolina Nursing Regulations Section 91.1.A (4) states, "The nursing tasks which may be assigned to unlicensed nursing personnel shall be stated in the employer's policies. The training of the individuals and their competencies to perform the tasks shall be verified by the employer." It is clear that the practice act is the ultimate authority by which your performance will be judged. Conflict with an employer may be difficult and unwanted, but as a practicing professional, you will find that it is in your best interests to discuss the differences with the employer. No health care agency can stay in business long by breaking the law or asking its employees to do so. (Refer to Chapter 4 for further discussion of the employer relationship.)

An example of employer policy differences involves the case of the University of Chicago Clinical Research Center (Illinois Nurse, 1993). The employer in this instance had developed a policy allowing unlicensed assistive personnel (UAP) to be delegated the task of drawing blood. Nurses felt this was an unsafe delegation, citing the following concerns: (1) drawing blood involved the administration of heparin; (2) the procedure is a complex nursing task requiring professional judgment, particularly in the Clinical Research Center, where there are frequent blood extractions and the use of long-term indwelling lines; and (3) the RNs were not involved with the UAP or knowledgeable about their skills, training, and qualifications. This conflict posed several risks to the RNs: They could face charges of abandonment for refusing to follow the policy, or they could be disciplined by the board of nursing for supervising a UAP in an undelegatable task. Fortunately, the RNs were willing to be involved in the resolution, and, using the assistance of the Illinois Board of Nursing, they were able to change the employer policy. UAP at this medical center are now delegated "technical" tasks, and nursing is involved in the decision-making process.

> The practice act is the ultimate authority by which your performance will be judged.

THE LPN ROLE

Very little has been said up to this point regarding the role of the LPN. Rules and statutes that have been cited speak to unlicensed personnel in some instances and to both licensed and unlicensed personnel in other instances. During recent years, the role of the LPN has been altered a great deal in response to closer scrutiny and further clarification of the various roles of nursing. It is not unusual to see the LPN role diminished in many areas as functions previously allowed through employer policy have been eliminated or restricted. We have received letters of concern from LPNs who are struggling to understand the "new" restrictions placed upon them, and we feel it is essential for the RN to understand the legal scope of this delegate as well as that of the unlicensed person.

The role of the LPN was created in response to the increased demands for nursing personnel during World War II. Because all of the needs could not be filled with RNs, a new level of caregiver was created that required less education and could be trained faster. Due to the limitations of training, the role of the LPN was defined as being under the supervision of either an RN or a licensed physician, with the understanding that this individual would not have autonomy of practice. During the nursing shortage of the 1970s and then again in the 1980s, in many instances employers expanded the role of the LPN, allowing LPNs to perform functions not clearly outlined within their scope of practice. Assessments, IV medications, tracheal suctioning, and insertion of nasogastric tubes are examples of the procedures that were not previously within the LPN scope of practice. Roles became blurred as employers responded to shortages, and it was not unusual to find an LPN taking an assignment on a hospital unit similar to the RN. And in some home health agencies, LPNs are caring for ventilator-dependent patients, teaching ventilator care, and performing tracheal suctioning. Driven by necessity, little attention has been paid to the differentiation of the roles in some instances, and indeed, many RNs have difficulty articulating the differences between an RN and LPN!

An LPN is still limited in scope of practice, and whether the practice act and the governing board are separate or combined with the RN boards, the limit is still the same. LPN practice is "recognizing and meeting the basic needs of the client, gives nursing care under the direction and supervision of the registered nurse or licensed physician to clients in routine nursing situations" (WAC 308-117-020, Washington).

> In some home health agencies, LPNs are caring for ventilator-dependent patients, teaching ventilator care, and performing tracheal suctioning.

In several states (for example, Colorado and Texas) the LPN is prohibited by law from delegating nursing tasks, and this function is allowed only to the RN. The definition of supervision as described earlier is applicable to RNs working with LPNs, and the need for initial guidance and direction, evaluation, and follow-up of these members of the team must be demonstrated. The difference in the roles of the RN and the LPN should be reflected in policies, job descriptions, methods of assigning, and documentation, no matter what the setting.

> The difference in the roles of the RN and the LPN should be reflected in policies, job descriptions, methods of assigning, and documentation, no matter what the setting.

DELEGATION AND THE NURSING PROCESS

Although the operational definition of delegation is purposefully general, the RN has some guidelines to use when evaluating the decision of whether to delegate. In fact, as some of you will be delighted to know, some very specific statements set forth what may not be delegated under any circumstance. For example, according to the NCSBN (1995, p. 2), "While nursing tasks may be delegated, the licensed nurse's generalist knowledge of patient care indicates that the practice-pervasive functions of assessment, evaluation, and nursing judgment must not be delegated."

The part of the nursing process most readily delegated involves the component of intervention. Tasks, procedures, technical duties, and so forth all fall into this

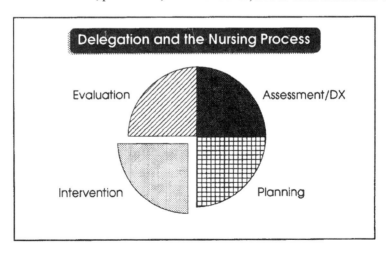

Courtesy of Dennis Burnside, 1998, Omaha, Nebraska

"While nursing tasks may be delegated, the licensed nurse's generalist knowledge of patient care indicates that the practice-pervasive functions of assessment, evaluation, and nursing judgment must not be delegated."

category and are part of the patient's care that may be readily performed by another individual besides the RN. However, as a reminder, the decision is yours to make, and one we hope that you base on each specific situation, considering carefully the patient's response and the outcome you desire. In one setting, you may choose to delegate the task of a clean dressing change to the HHA, knowing that the wound is healing and that the patient has been taught what to observe in the process. In another setting, you may elect to do the dressing change yourself, wanting to assess the skin and teach a family member to look for signs of infection.

Specific limits to interventions that may not be delegated to unlicensed personnel are outlined in each state and vary according to state law. The more common restrictions are similar to those found in the Massachusetts Nursing Regulations: "(5) Nursing Activities That May Not Be Delegated. By way of example, and not in limitation, the following are nursing activities that are not within the scope of sound nursing judgment to delegate:

(a) Nursing activities which require nursing assessment and judgment during implementation
(b) Physical, psychological, and social assessment which requires nursing judgment, intervention, referral or follow-up
(c) Formulation of the plan of nursing care and evaluation of the patient's/ client's response to the care provided

CHECKPOINT 3-7

1. In my state, the LPN (may/may not) delegate selected nursing tasks.
2. At the agency where I work, there (is/is not) a difference in the role of the RN and the role of the LPN according to policy.
3. I (know/do not know) what the limitations of the LPN are in this state.

See the end of the chapter for the answers.

(d) Administration of medications except as permitted by MGL Chapter 94C
(e) Patient/client Health Teaching and Health Counseling."

> Judgment "means the intellectual process that a nurse exercises in forming an opinion and reaching a clinical decision based upon analysis of the evidence or data."

Item (a) in the above list is one criterion that is listed in the majority of nurse practice acts and reinforced by the NCSBN, the limiting factors being any task that requires nursing "judgment" and "assessment." The Montana Nursing Regulations (Rule 8.32.1703, Sept. 1996) states that judgment "means the intellectual process that a nurse exercises in forming an opinion and reaching a clinical decision based upon analysis of the evidence or data."

We would add as a point of clarification that assessment goes beyond the collection of physical data and is really "the initial phase of the Nursing Process which involves the interpretation of the significance of the available subjective and objective data regarding a specific patient situation, performed in order to formulate an individualized plan of care" (Hansten and Washburn, 1995, p. i). Assessment is certainly the cornerstone of home health nursing and the basis for all delegated care.

Many states strictly prohibit delegating the administration of medication, but several states are recognizing that this is appropriate in some settings. Group homes for the developmentally or mentally disabled, community settings for the physically handicapped, group homes for the elderly, and long-term care facilities are all examples of areas where assistive personnel may be allowed to administer medication. Currently, at least 20 states allow medication administration by medication aides in carefully described circumstances (Montana State Board of Nursing, 1992). These carefully described circumstances include the involvement of the RN in training and supervising the assistive personnel. Oregon has devel-

---

CHECKPOINT 3-8

Check the following statements that apply to you:
- ❏ I know what I may not delegate to unlicensed assistive personnel according to my state's practice act.
- ❏ I know which parts of the nursing process I may safely delegate.

oped a very specific training course, as have other states, to meet the needs of very particular populations.

Although we have cited cases in which the practice act is clearly restrictive, it is also important to note the trend toward the creation of task lists that describe those delegatable interventions. The position statement adopted by the Alaska Board of Nursing in 1993 and revisited in 1996 offers a very specific discussion of tasks that may be performed by those without a license. ". . . changes in the levels of health care provided in traditional and nontraditional settings have altered the scope of practice of nursing and its relationship to unlicensed assistive personnel. The unlicensed home care provider may now be involved in procedures such as assisting with medication, intermittent bladder catheterizations and gastrostomy feedings. . . . A license to practice nursing is not required for the repetitive performance of a common task, activity, or procedure which does not require the professional judgment of an RN or LPN and which:

1. is delegated by a licensed nurse
2. frequently recurs in the daily care of a client or group of clients
3. is performed according to an established sequence of steps
4. involves little or no modification from one client-care situation to another
5. may be performed with a predictable outcome
6. does not inherently involve ongoing assessments, interpretations, or decision-making which can not be logically separated from the procedure itself. . . . urinary catheterizations, medication administration (including insulin), and oxygen therapy are appropriate under these guidelines" (Alaska Nursing Regulations, Appendix D).

And finally, HCFA defines the scope of the HHA in its broadest sense:

> **484.36 (c) Standard: Assignment and duties of the home health aide**
>
> **2) Duties.** The home health aide provides services that are ordered by the physician in the plan of care and that the aide is permitted to perform under state law. The duties of a home health aide include the provision of hands-on personal care, performance of simple procedures as an extension of therapy or nursing services, assistance in ambulation or exercises, and assistance in administering medications that are ordinarily self-administered. Any home health aide services offered by

a home health agency must be provided by a qualified home health aide. (Interpretive Guide-lines-Home Health Agencies, Revised 1995)

Although our diagram of the nursing process appears limiting, we want to make certain that you understand that parts of the process of assessment, planning, and evaluation may also be delegated. Once again, the accountability of the assessment rests with the RN, and it is the RN who is best prepared through education and experience to assess the patient.

The accountability of the assessment rests with the RN, and it is the RN who is best prepared through education and experience to assess the patient.

Planning is another area of the nursing process that may invite participation from the other members of the team. HHAs may have the opportunity to spend additional direct time with the patient and may learn information that would assist the RN in best planning the care for the patient while under the care of the agency. An HHA who visits the home three times a week will certainly have valuable input for the RN who makes only a monthly visit.

Evaluation involves the interpretation of data to make judgments regarding the effectiveness of the interventions, and it rests primarily with the RN. Again, the other members of the team may have observations and other information that will assist the RN in the evaluation, but the responsibility for the judgment belongs to the RN. The RN's critical analysis will be necessary to determine if the nursing diagnosis is correct, if the outcomes targeted are reasonable, and if the patient is responding to the interventions that have been performed. This systematic process involves the coordination of all members of the team and requires the organized skill of the RN.

The bar graph in Figure 3–1 illustrates the overlap of the performance of the various components of the nursing process by the four levels of nursing personnel.

An HHA who visits the home three times a week will certainly have valuable input for the RN who makes only a monthly visit.

This study involved the survey of more than 15,000 providers, randomly selected from all states, by the Research Services Division of the NCSBN (NCSBN, 1994). The purpose of the study was to obtain data to delineate the roles of the four levels of personnel and to facilitate the delegation of nursing activities to unlicensed per-

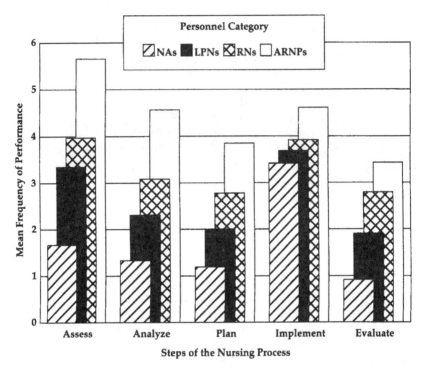

Figure 3–1 Average Mean Frequency of Performance Values for Nursing Process Activity Statements, by Personnel Category. *Source:* Courtesy of the National Council of State Boards of Nursing, Inc., Chicago, Illinois.

sonnel. A complete report of this study was distributed at the Delegate Assembly in August 1994.

The survey demonstrated a specific pattern regarding the performance of the activities of the nursing process. The frequency of each component is ranked as follows:

NAs and LPNs:	implementation, assessment, analysis, planning, evaluation
RNs:	assessment, implementation, analysis, evaluation, planning
Nurse Practitioners:	assessment, implementation, analysis, planning, evaluation

From this study it is apparent that NAs and LPNs report spending more time implementing care, whereas RNs and nurse practitioners spend more time assessing the need and type of care to be given.

CONCLUSION

In this chapter we have discussed the fundamental knowledge of the nurse practice act that is necessary to determine if the delegation you are considering will truly "put your license on the line." Understanding the limitations of your practice act, as well as the purpose and the powers of the board of nursing, are key factors in dispelling the fear of responsibility for the actions of those with whom you work. No single individual can provide all things to all people, and the risks involved in relying on others can be minimized with the knowledge of legal definitions and expectations.

> Obtain a copy of the nurse practice act in your state, request any advisory opinions that have been issued on the subject of delegation, and contact your board of nursing to learn more about the process of ensuring the safety of the public through the regulation of nursing practice.

You are encouraged to seek the resources available to you: Obtain a copy of the nurse practice act in your state, request any advisory opinions that have been issued on the subject of delegation, and contact your board of nursing to learn more about the process of ensuring the safety of the public through the regulation of nursing practice. Better yet—get on the World Wide Web and access the NCSBN Web site, or any number of professional organizations that have a Web page for your continued professional development. It's your license—protect it!

ANSWERS TO CHECKPOINTS

3–1. c

3–2. d

3–3. d

3–5. c

3–6.
1. initial direction/periodic inspection
2. unsupervised
3. continuous supervision
4. never delegated

3–7.

1. The LPN may or may not be allowed to delegate nursing tasks. Check your state's nurse practice act for the correct answer in your state.
2. There is a difference. (There should be!) This difference should be apparent in the job description, the system of care delivery, and the reporting and documentation expectations of the LPN.
3. I do know the limitations of the LPN in this state. (If you do not, do you feel safe in delegating to an LPN?)

REFERENCES

Donahue, M.P. 1985. *Nursing, the finest art.* St. Louis: CV Mosby.

Fiesta, J. 1994. Legal update, 1994, Part II. *Nursing Management* 26, no. 3: 10–11.

Hansten, R., and M. Washburn. 1990. *I light the lamp.* Vancouver, WA: Applied Therapeutics.

Hansten, R., and M. Washburn. 1995. *Land in sight.* Children's Hospital Workshop Syllabus, Seattle, WA, p. i.

Montana State Board of Nursing. 1992. State survey delegation of nursing tasks [letter]. January.

National Council of State Boards of Nursing. 1990. *Concept paper on delegation.* Chicago: NCSBN.

National Council of State Boards of Nursing. 1994. *Preliminary report: Role delineation study of nurse aides, licensed practical/vocational nurses, registered nurses and advanced registered nurse practitioners.* Chicago: NCSBN.

National Council of State Boards of Nursing. 1995. Delegation: Concepts and decision-making process. *Issues* (December): 1–4.

National Council of State Boards of Nursing. 1997. News Release, December 16, 1997.

National Council of State Boards of Nursing. 1998. News Release, April 3, 1998.

Person, C. 1997. Delegation: Risk management implications for nurses. *Creative Nursing* 3, no. 1: 12.

CHAPTER 4

Know Your Organization: What about Where I Work?

HISTORICAL DEVELOPMENT— OR, HOW DID WE GET HERE?

Ruth I. Hansten, Marilynn J. Washburn, and Virginia L. Kenyon

"My manager is always talking about the mission and values of this organization. Big deal. All that means is how much work they can get out of us without paying us any more. They keep changing things and talking about this wonderful quality program at the same time they're taking our jobs and giving them to assistive personnel."

In the previous chapters we have begun to create a foundation of knowledge regarding the legal support you have as a practicing professional. At the same time we have discussed some of the primary reasons for the constant state of change that many organizations are experiencing, with the intention of offering you some basis for understanding what you as an employee might be experiencing. We must now take our assessment one step further and take a clear look at the environment in which you work.

Those of you who are groaning at the idea of a little history, please stay with us as we quickly review organizational development to better appreciate the framework of the health care system as it has evolved today. It is unusual for many of us to question why things are the way they are. For most, if the environment in which we are working is challenging, unfulfilling, or supportive, we don't question the rationale but seek instead to make changes or to be grateful for the job we have and make the best of it. But why are you in a top-down, chain-of-command system? Or if you are in a more progressive style of participative

---

CHECKPOINT 4-1

Are the following statements true or false?

___1. There is only one style of organization, and the administrator always controls the decisions.
___2. There has been little change in the way health care professionals are treated as employees.
___3. Most health care organizations have a mission statement and have always had one.
___4. Unions are involved in all health care facilities and have been since hospitals first opened.
___5. Employer policies are more important than the nurse practice act.

See the end of the chapter for the answers.

---

management, complete with administrative support for multidisciplinary team building, why is your organization making this change? If you are a student, thinking about future career options, what work setting would fit you best?

How did you do with the checkpoint above? As we continue our discussion, keep these questions in mind. We will be reviewing the role of unions, mission statements, and policies in the evolution of the health care system from its humble beginnings to the challenges of today. Most important of all will be the process of delegation as part of your changing work environment and the role the organization plays in the process.

IN THE BEGINNING

If we were to go back before Nightingale's day, we would discover that health care was not an organized system. Hospitals were few, home health care and public health nonexistent, and the women of the family were generally expected to provide the majority of ministering to the sick. Effective medicinal resources were few, and society as a whole had not fully organized its system of work.

The Industrial Revolution, the progression of medicine, and the advancement of technology brought significant changes to the newly forming hospital and public health systems. Almshouses and military and public hospitals offered the only early options for health care outside of the home. With the advent of anesthetics and septic technique, the demand for hospitals increased as physicians no longer found it desirable to perform surgery on the kitchen table, where many patients had demanded it be done. Public health was emerging as a health focus and driving force in the community, Lillian Wald was establishing the Henry Street Settlement, and the frontier nurses were providing care via horseback to women and children living in rural areas.

> Public health was emerging as a health focus and driving force in the community, Lillian Wald was establishing the Henry Street Settlement, and the frontier nurses were providing care via horseback to women and children living in rural areas.

The world continued to change rapidly as transportation made it easier for families to be mobile and industry became more organized in its structure. Salaried management emerged in all industries, and administrators and professors joined the ranks of universities. In hospitals, however, the decision-making power was shifting to the physicians, who were more and more in control of its admissions. Boards of trustees were being replaced by medical boards, who held controlling authority over the administration of the hospital. It was not unusual for physicians to own small, private hospitals and to employ a management team to enact their decisions. As the hospital setting grew and physicians were able to belong to several hospitals, their needs for administrative services increased as well.

Administrators were empowered with increasing authority to oversee the employees, ensuring that the hospital ran smoothly internally so that the physicians could perform their services. Hospital management then followed the mainstream of scientific management principles, and a top-down, controlling approach was embraced.

Public health became a part of government-offered services and was seen as critical for the public health and well-being. Public health and, later, the visiting nurse services began organizing much in the same way the hospitals had organized. It became evident that to manage the care needs of patients and/or the public, administrators were needed. As with the hospital administrators, the community health administrators were empowered with the authority to oversee employees so that the needs of the community and the individual served by these organizations were met. Boards of directors were created to oversee the financial policy issues.

> Public health became a part of government-offered services and was seen as critical for the public health and well-being.

In the meantime, nursing was advancing quickly, organizing nursing schools, setting minimum standards for licensure, and responding to the needs of the people in the community in addition to the institution. Lillian Wald, mentioned earlier, was an exemplary leader in the late 1800s, developing the Henry Street Settlement and advancing the system of public health. Under her direction, the first system for nurses in public schools was created, and nursing services for insurance policyholders were initiated (Christy, 1984). Nursing was defining its role in many arenas outside the hospital, but the hospital remained the benchmark for the health care system.

Hospital development was rapid throughout the twentieth century, responding to many diverse sociocultural events. World Wars I and II, the Great Depression, and the changing face of disease from polio epidemics to demands for organ transplants kept the hospital system in constant turmoil. Public health departments assumed an even greater role in the public's health. Under the public health departments, massive polio vaccination programs were initiated, sewage systems were developed that safeguarded the public's health and prevented epidemics previously experienced in communities across America. The treatment of employees, including nurses, became more controlling, as hospital and public health managers adopted policies and systems to strengthen their control over an internal environment in response to increasing public and federal involvement. Unions found their place in health care after World War II, representing nurses and health care workers alike who fought for employee protection and the insurance of individual rights.

THE UNIONIZED ORGANIZATION AND DELEGATION

Karen A. McGrath

What could unions possibly have to do with clinical delegation? Whether you are considering or already working in a facility where nurses are represented by a union, it is important to understand the role of the union in ensuring a fair and reasonable work environment.

Since before the turn of the century in this country, workers have struggled to assert some measure of control over working conditions. Leaders came from the ranks of employees in a number of trades or industries; they included miners, garment workers, autoworkers, and longshoremen. They understood the workplace and what was needed to prevent abuse and exploitation of employees. They worked to educate and unite workers, to establish equitable wage standards, and to improve the quality of work life generally.

Health care employees are relative newcomers to the union movement. Federal laws, the Railway Labor Act of 1926 and the National Labor Relations Act (or Wagner Act) of 1935, were enacted to protect workers' "right to self-organization, to form, join, or assist labor organizations, to bargain collectively through representatives of their own choosing, and to engage in concerted activities, for the purpose

> Unions found their place in health care after World War II, representing nurses and health care workers alike who fought for employee protection and the insurance of individual rights.

of collective bargaining or other mutual aid or protection" (National Labor Relations Act, Section 7). Until 1974, however, private, not-for-profit health care institutions were exempt from coverage. Individual states passed laws governing collective bargaining rights for public sector employees.

Other laws advancing unionization included the Taft-Hartley Act (or the Labor-Management Relations Act) of 1947, which further defined the rights and duties of both labor and management, and the Landrum-Griffin Act (or the Labor-Management Reporting and Disclosure Act) of 1959, which spelled out the rights of union members. These measures went a long way to eliminate abuses and corruption that had come to light. The American Nurses Association (ANA) and its constituent state nurses associations (SNAs) had since their inception in 1896 been addressing employment standards for nurses, and until the mid-1940s they had achieved only limited success. The approach had focused on educating nurses and consumers about matters affecting the recruitment of qualified nurses. In 1946, the ANA House of Delegates took a bold step by approving a plan for a national economic and security program. A key piece of the program called on the SNAs to act as collective bargaining representatives for nurses. Many of the SNAs began to build their own programs with trained staff to meet this challenge. Today, 26 of 53 SNAs have full economic and general welfare (or labor relations) programs that are responsible for representing nurses in a variety of work settings.

> In 1946, the ANA House of Delegates took a bold step by approving a plan for a national economic and security program. A key piece of the program called on the SNAs to act as collective bargaining representatives for nurses.

In addition to the SNAs, many other unions represent health care employees, including nurses. During the 1970s and 1980s, the economy in the United States began to shift away from the manufacturing sector to a growing service sector. Health care, as a large part of the service industry, became

> Today, 26 of 53 SNAs have full economic and general welfare (or labor relations) programs that are responsible for representing nurses in a variety of work settings.

fertile ground for organizing, and unions looked to bolster shrinking membership numbers by shifting their attention to this arena.

No matter which union a group has selected as its representative, knowing some basic principles will maximize your union experience (if you work in a facility where the employees are represented by a union) and make it work for you and your patients. Remember those key phrases from the Wagner Act: collective bargaining, mutual aid and protection, and concerted activity? They assume people are working together toward a common goal. It begins with a secret ballot election in which an identified employee group decides if, and by which union, it wants to be represented. The group becomes a bargaining unit and proceeds to elect local leaders from within its own membership. The new leaders' task is to seek out and represent the needs and desires of the membership. The union provides experts in labor relations and industry trends and standards to guide and advise the leaders as they negotiate a collective bargaining agreement (a contract) with the employer.

In order for all of this to be successful, the membership has certain rights and responsibilities as well. The union has the legal responsibility to represent all members fairly, and the members are expected to join and support the union they have selected. This is one instance where the old axiom about the house divided truly applies. The union *is* the membership and functions democratically. The members give direction to leaders by participating in meetings and voting on matters of concern. To be an effective member, you must be informed and involved. Your degree of involvement will depend on your own desires as well as other personal and professional demands on your time. Attending meetings, reading the literature, volunteering for committees, and becoming a unit representative are degrees of involvement open to you as a union member.

When dealing with management, the most successful bargaining units are able to demonstrate unity and credibility. An adversarial relationship is not necessary and is often counterproductive to reaching mutually acceptable solutions to problems. Management representatives who recognize and respect the collective bargaining relationship are also most often successful in maintaining a measure of what is known as labor peace. The process lends itself to the popular thinking of participative man-

> The union has the legal responsibility to represent all members fairly, and the members are expected to join and support the union they have selected.

agement: total quality management (TQM) and continuous quality improvement (CQI). The difference in the unionized setting is the balance of power. The assistance of the union in dealing with the management structure is intended to level the playing field.

> One committee that is very important for nurses is the nursing practice committee.

But what does all of this have to do with clinical delegation?

An employment contract typically covers such topics as wages, premium pay for unusual or extra shifts, holidays, vacations, insurance benefits, seniority, work schedules, and a grievance procedure for dispute resolution. In addition, contracts covering nurses very often speak to staffing and patient safety concerns and establish joint labor-management committees designed to open communications.

One committee that is very important for nurses is the nursing practice committee. This committee is composed of nurses elected by members of the bargaining unit who meet from time to time with representatives of nursing administration to discuss issues of concern with policies and procedures affecting patient care delivery. The issues may be raised by either the nurses or managers, are thoroughly researched, and require a written response from administration detailing what is to be done to resolve the issue. In most cases a joint solution can be found.

Let us see how the system works in a practice setting.

Northern Visiting Nurse Service has been experiencing a growth spurt. Referrals are up as patients are discharged sooner, often needing nursing follow-up. Maureen finds herself going home later and more tired, even though she loves home care and still feels professionally challenged. She has been an SNA member since graduation but has never really paid much attention to the contract. The raises have been nice, and she enjoys a fairly good relationship with Jean, her supervisor.

A memo from the Director of Patient Care Services warning about the excessive use of overtime results in increased grumbling in the office, and Maureen is worried. Jean's response is that the directive is from upstairs and there is nothing she can do. Posted on the bulletin board, next to the overtime memo, is the list of bargaining unit officers. The same day, Maureen locates the chairperson and asks if the union can do anything about the mounting pressure. She expresses her frustration with an administration that appears to have lost touch with the facts of direct care. John is very understanding and reports that nurses have been calling him all day.

As they talk, it becomes apparent that the problems are sicker patients requiring more time, more paperwork, and orienting new nurses without an adjustment of workload. John invites Maureen to a meeting of the bargaining unit to discuss the issues. She is able to repeat her concerns, and John leads a discussion of possible solutions to be presented to administration. At the next labor/management meeting, John presents the issue along with a time study done by several of the nurses. Administration's initial response is that the nurses just have to dig in and bear with it until the new nurses are able to make visits independently. John continues to discuss the solutions developed by the group, concentrating on the enormous amount of paperwork required. As he describes the different forms and their purposes, it becomes clear that some contain redundant information and are simple enough that clerical employees could transcribe the information from reports that the nurses complete. The nurses have calculated that approximately one hour per day is spent by nurses on an activity that could be done by current clericals, saving the agency a significant amount in overtime costs or lost visits. The director is impressed and commits to examining the issue further, looking at the paperwork to determine if a report is really needed and, if so, who could fill it out. John reports that Maureen will head a bargaining unit task force to examine the agency's preceptor program with a goal of maximizing the orientation experience while being sensitive to the workload of the preceptors. The director states that she is eager to see the results.

As you can see, the presence of a union is not a guarantee that employment is secure and that no changes in your practice will ever be made. Selecting a union can be important, but it is not enough. As with any process, you have to make it work. It is a little like buying a car. Without one, you may take a bit longer to get around, but it does not do any good just left to sit in the garage. For managers, having a union is not a sign of failure. It can provide a vehicle for discussion and change. A contract provides structure that everyone can understand and work with to resolve problems.

ASSESSING THE HEALTH CARE ORGANIZATION

Ruth I. Hansten, Marilynn J. Washburn, and Virginia L. Kenyon

As you can see, the presence of a union is not a guarantee that employment is secure and that no changes in your practice will ever be made.

THE NONUNION ENVIRONMENT

If you aren't in a union environment, never fear! In many states or locales, nurses are not represented by a union, nor do they feel a need for one. When management practices in a participative fashion, with true empowerment of all staff, such as in shared

CHECKPOINT 4-2

1. Union representation
   a) is available in all states
   b) is required in all hospitals
   c) has always been available for health care employees
   d) relies on membership participation to be effective
2. Being a member of a union
   a) means that I will always have a job
   b) is required by my licensure
   c) provides me with an additional opportunity to join with fellow employees in an organized fashion to discuss working conditions with management
   d) is prohibited by my nurse practice act
3. I can be involved in changes in care delivery that result in my need to delegate nursing care by
   a) being an active union member and attending nurse practice committee meetings
   b) participating in the management of my (nonunion) work setting by attending staff meetings and serving on committees and task forces that plan changes in care delivery and staffing
   c) keeping myself informed and updated on trends in nursing practice
   d) all of the above

See the end of the chapter for the answers.

governance or self-directed work teams, staff nurses' concerns are equally important and valued. Wise administrators develop staff through education and encourage autonomy in decision making regarding patient care. Wise staff become involved in committees or task forces (whether union or not) that develop policies and procedures and plan for innovative practice that will ensure quality and cost-effective care. "Organizations are realizing that they are in partnership with their workers in delivering health care" (O'Grady, 1992, p. 178). And it is your responsibility as a professional nurse to uphold that partnership.

Whether the facility or agency you work for has union representation for its employees is only one part of the picture. Several factors must be assessed as we continue our knowledge of the organization.

THE MISSION STATEMENT

Today's health care facility/agency carries with it the history of intensifying social demands and the increasing involvement of federal policy. The focus of any health care organization must shift from a singular perspective to a systems approach or global perspective on patient and client needs. Traditional roles and traditional management techniques will no longer be effective in the reformed system. Organizational systems are emerging in which the employees are truly valued members of the team and in which it is believed that the employee is responsible to think and achieve. With this major shift in premise is the need to begin at the root of the organization—the mission statement.

Having received a wake-up call from a public that has loudly voiced its dissatisfaction with the health care system, organizations are reexamining their values and mission statements to make certain they are guiding the shift from a product emphasis to a service approach. Mission statements of the early hospitals in the mid-1800s focused primarily on religious and moralistic objectives. It was not unusual for a hospital to identify its mission as one of providing homes for the orphans or the poor and creating a Christian environment. The advent of surgery and the relief of acute illness caused many hospitals to redefine their mission in terms of medical objectives, and the emphasis shifted from a moral stance to the treatment of disease and injury (Starr, 1982, p. 158). Mission statements that looked much like those of the early hospitals also directed Visiting Nurse Organizations across the nation.

The health care organization of today has broadened its perspective, integrating the social, moral, and medical objectives in a more holistic expression of the mission of the institution. For example:

> St. Mary Medical Center is a community of people working together to provide a broad spectrum of high quality health care services to residents throughout Southeast Washington and Northeast Oregon. Faithful to the tradition of the Sisters of Providence since 1879, the mission of St. Mary Medical Center is to continue its leadership role in offering these services in a Christian atmosphere, respectful of the dignity and worth of each individual, with special concern for the poor and oppressed (St. Mary Medical Center, 1993).

> Organizational systems are emerging in which the employees are truly valued members of the team and in which it is believed that the employee is responsible to think and achieve.

The components of quality, cost-effectiveness, and accessibility are common to most mission statements today. Most will also include a component relating to the employee, and the statement may look something like this: "To promote the continuous professional growth of each employee within a supportive environment." Stephen Covey said it best when he suggested a universal personal and professional mission statement: "To improve the economic well being and quality of life for all stakeholders" (Covey, 1991).

In addition to a mission, the statement may include a "vision," a direction or focus for the organization. This may specifically outline an area of the community, an aspect of service to be provided, or a specific age group to be emphasized, as in this statement from an East Coast hospital: "As part of a regional health system, we specialize in quality, family-centered services, with emphasis on a continuum of care for those adults 50 years of age and older. We will be an active partner in improving the health of the communities we serve."

The mission statement may also be supported by a list of "values," those fundamental beliefs that form the framework of the culture of the organization. Diann Uustal has done extensive work in the area of values, specifically as they relate to nursing. She states that "values provide a frame of reference through which we integrate, explain and appraise new ideas, events and personal relationships" (1985, p. 105).

One example of supportive values that we particularly appreciate is found in the mission statement of Health People, Inc., a private-duty home health care organization:

Guiding Principles and Values

The following reflects the guiding principles and values that will determine policies and procedures for Health People:

- An Obsession for High Quality Customer Service and Continuous Improvement
- Team Member Participation in Company and Self Improvement
- Self Responsibility for Team Work, Professionalism, and Success
- Respect and Dignity for Fellow Team Members and Clients
- Absolute Confidentiality and Discretion Regarding Client and Company Information
- Flexibility in Balancing a Productive Work Schedule with Family Responsibilities
- Ethics and Integrity Are a Foundation of Our Company

(Health People, Inc., 1997)

In meeting the demands of the changing times, we are encouraged by mission and values statements that address the involvement of the employee. As Toffler (1990) pointed out, in this time of continued turbulence, organizations depend more on their workers for success than on any other single factor. Support through the mission, the values, and the culture of the organization will be essential for you in understanding and safely implementing the process of delegation. This foundation is critical in making certain that nursing continues to be actively involved in decisions and changes that directly affect the patient, particularly in the redesign and addition of personnel for the delivery of care.

Congratulations! You've made it this far, and we promise you that the following discussion will be firmly focused on contemporary issues (except for a brief reminder of history!).

By now you know that we are emphasizing the importance of the nursing process and continually applying it to our discussion of delegation. A clearer understanding of your organization, or the one in which you will work, requires the assessment of several factors that directly affect you in working with, delegating to, and supervising other health care workers.

Knowing the answers to the questions in the four major areas of assessment outlined in Exhibit 4–1 will help you practice professionally and safely, to the

---

CHECKPOINT 4-3

Knowledge of the mission and values of my employing facility is important because:

a) They are not important because no one follows them anyway
b) I'm not sure, because I have never seen the mission statement
c) They clarify the basic premise of the agency and will enable me to assess what value the organization places on employee involvement, particularly in redesigning the care delivery system
d) The mission will tell me if I'm in the right place and if I need to join a union to improve the working conditions

See the end of the chapter for the answers.

Exhibit 4–1 An Assessment of a Health Care Organization for Support of the Delegation Process

Yes	No	
		Organizational Structure
___	___	1. Is there an organizational chart?
___	___	2. Are there clearly defined reporting systems for RNs supervising delegates?
___	___	3. Is there sufficient communication among the various units?
___	___	4. Is the mission visible to everyone and is it followed?
___	___	5. Are there interdisciplinary committees in which RNs participate?
		Quality
___	___	1. Is a quality program currently in place?
___	___	2. Does the model focus on outcomes?
___	___	3. Is it supported by management *and* staff?
___	___	4. Are nurses actively involved in the process?
___	___	5. Do RNs participate in determining the criteria for measuring quality?
		Safety in Practice
___	___	1. Are the policies directly affecting nursing evaluated for their consistency with state regulations?
___	___	2. Do RNs have responsibility and autonomy for continually appraising the care delivery system and implementing changes as needed?
___	___	3. Is time allowed for the RN Case Manager to adequately meet with all the members of the team to discuss and plan care?
		Educational Resources
___	___	1. Are unlicensed assistive personnel adequately trained and oriented (using validated competencies and measurable outcomes)?
___	___	2. Is there a system for providing additional skill development for assistive personnel when the need is identified by an RN supervising an employee?
___	___	3. Are RNs offered frequent educational opportunities to develop supervisory skills?
___	___	4. Is there a documentation process for establishing competency in all skills required by the job description?
___	___	5. Is there a mentorship or preceptorship program for all new licensed personnel?
___	___	6. Is information regarding new changes in health care and health care regulations, including the nurse practice act, readily available?

Source: Reprinted from R. Hansten and M. Washburn, Know Your Organization, *Clinical Delegation Skills*, p. 94, © 1998, Aspen Publishers, Inc.

fullest potential of your license. A brief discussion of each area should be helpful in completing your knowledge base.

THE ORGANIZATIONAL STRUCTURE

Whether the setting in which you work is part of a hospital system or any one of a number of community-based health care facilities/organizations, there will typically be an organizational chart that describes the reporting relationships of personnel. Although traditional frameworks are continually changing, we have not found a substitute for the "snapshot" provided by a chart showing the titles of positions and/or departments/units and their relationship to everyone else in the agency. This chart serves only as a road map of the agency: It may identify landmarks but will not describe everything about each location. Unlike earlier organizational charts that demonstrated the traditional top-down hierarchy, today's chart may resemble the one in Figure 4–1 or Figure 4–2. The changes noted in the new organizational structure reflect several major changes occurring in the home health environment: mergers, changes in the reimbursement formulas, implementation of the Outcome Assessment Information System (OASIS) data collecting requirement, and, with the increased competition, the need for a more business development focus.

Although the chart may provide the framework for the agency, it leaves several questions unanswered. You will need to further assess the degree of RN participation on committees, particularly collaborative practice and interdisciplinary committees, which may not be represented on any chart. These informal groups may be very instrumental and powerful in planning changes in personnel and care delivery.

CHECKPOINT 4-4

Knowing the organizational chart of the employing agency can tell me

a) everything I need to know about the chain of command
b) nothing, because my facility does not have a chart
c) the framework of the reporting relationships of units/departments/or supervisors
d) the committee I should join to discuss delegation

See the end of the chapter for the answers.

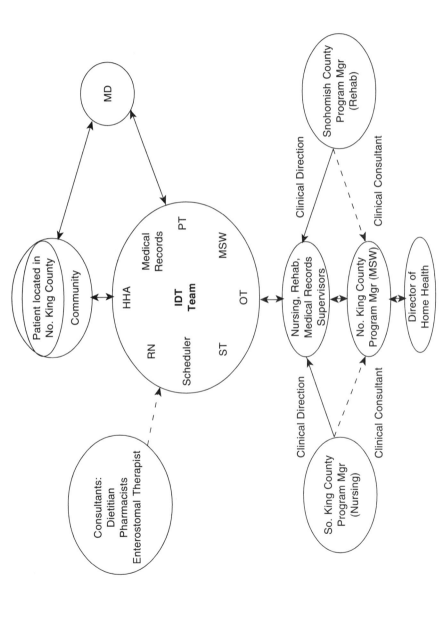

Figure 4–1 1990s Organization Chart. *Source:* Courtesy of Community Health Network Development, Seattle, Washington.

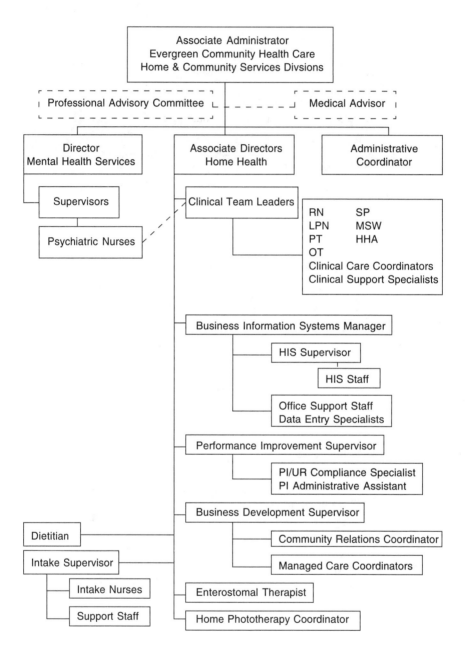

Figure 4–2 Evergreen Community Home Health Organization Chart. *Source:* Courtesy of Evergreen Community Home Health, Kirkland, Washington.

As we discussed in Chapter 3, and will review in subsequent chapters, when an RN delegates, he or she is responsible for supervising the delegate and taking any corrective measures that may be necessary as a result of the delegate's performance. Clearly defined reporting mechanisms and systems that facilitate the fulfillment of this responsibility of the RN are necessary ingredients for the organization that expects the RN to delegate nursing tasks.

THE IMPACT OF REDESIGN

If you've been practicing in health care during the past decade, you have no doubt experienced at least one redesign process. Increasing costs, consumer demands, changes in insurance coverages, and an aging society are all contributing factors to the ongoing movement toward a more cost-effective delivery system. And because nurses make up more than 60 percent of the care providers in this system, it is not surprising that we are seriously affected by any organization's efforts to change the way care is delivered. One of the most common forms of redesign has been the increased use of unlicensed assistive personnel (UAP). "Ninety-six percent of 1,455 RN respondents to *American Journal of Nursing* survey reported working with UAP, and two of every three RNs favored this practice" (Bernreuter, 1997, p. 49).

With this steady increase in the use of UAP, are nurses satisfied? Are there any significant improvements in care? Numerous studies have been done but with little statistical significance, unfortunately. Limited sample sizes, lack of comparison data, and untested instruments led to the recommendation that "empirically rigorous studies be designed to measure costs, nurse and patient satisfaction and care outcomes before delivery models incorporate UAP" (Barter et al., 1997).

A survey completed through the *American Journal of Nursing* in March of 1996 involved more than 7,000 hospital nurses who cited numerous negative comments. The greater use of UAP is a cause for concern when coupled with decreasing lengths of stay, increasing acuities of patients, and changing technology. Declining morale and increasing readmissions, work-related injuries, and nosocomial infections add to the overall negative impact of a rapidly changing environment in which the use of assistive personnel is only a part of the total picture. (Unfortunately, we know of no studies that have been

> "Ninety-six percent of 1,455 RN respondents to *American Journal of Nursing* survey reported working with UAP, and two of every three RNs favored this practice" (Bernreuter, 1997, p. 49).

> No matter what the system, the RN will still need to lead the team, coordinate the care, and delegate the work to those most appropriate to perform it.

conducted in the community health arena regarding the perception of nurses and the use of unlicensed personnel.)

So, the jury is still out, but it's busy measuring and standardizing the data for more effective analysis of the impact of all of this. No matter what the system, the RN will still need to lead the team, coordinate the care, and delegate the work to those most appropriate to perform it. Even though the study cited is from the acute care setting, much of the findings can be applied to the community health setting where nurses must rely more than ever on the home health aide to keep them informed of the changing conditions of their patients. More and more nurses will need to delegate tasks to other health care providers. Many states are beginning to recognize this increasing need to delegate and are beginning to enact laws to that end.

In the state of Washington, clarification of what a home health aide can and cannot be delegated in terms of medication administration has been clearly delineated in law (see Exhibit 4–2). It is important that you know the laws of the state you work in, particularly what you can and cannot delegate. Every state is different. If you are a nurse who has transitioned from the acute care arena to home health, you may be uncomfortable with delegating so much to unlicensed staff. In home care, however, you have little choice.

THE QUALITY PROGRAM

As the Joint Commission has moved into the community health arena, many of the principles applied in the hospital settings were applied to community health. Outcome parameters became the focus, with the requirement for quality improvement activities in the agencies. Agencies are required to demonstrate not only the outcomes, but the participation of all members of the health care team in the collection, analysis, and interpretation of the data. Corrective actions based on the analysis are required, with specific steps to be taken and timelines identified for correction to occur. The change from a

> If you are a nurse who has transitioned from the acute care arena to home health, you may be uncomfortable with delegating so much to unlicensed staff. In home care, however, you have little choice.

Exhibit 4–2 Clarification of Delegation of Medication Administration

BE IT ENACTED BY THE LEGISLATURE OF THE STATE OF WASHING-
TON:

{+ NEW SECTION. +} Sec. 1. A new section is added to chapter 69.41 RCW to
read as follows:

Individuals residing in community-based settings, such as adult family homes,
boarding homes, and residential care settings for the developmentally disabled,
including an individual's home, might need medication assistance due to physical
or mental limitations that prevent them from self-administering their legend drugs
or controlled substances. The practitioner in consultation with the individual or his
or her representative and the community-based setting, if involved, determines that
medication assistance is appropriate for this individual. Medication assistance can
take different forms such as opening containers, handing the container or medication to the individual, preparing the medication with prior authorization, using
enablers for facilitating the self-administration of medication, and other means of
assisting in the administration of legend drugs or controlled substances commonly
employed in community-based settings. Nothing in this chapter affects the right of
an individual to refuse medication or requirements relating to informed consent.

Sec. 2. RCW 69.41.010 and 1996 c 178 s 16 are each amended to read as follows:

As used in this chapter, the following terms have the meanings indicated unless
the context clearly requires otherwise:

(1) "Administer" means the direct application of a legend drug whether by
injection, inhalation, ingestion, or any other means, to the body of a patient or
research subject by:

(a) A practitioner; or

(b) The patient or research subject at the direction of the practitioner.

(2) "Deliver" or "delivery" means the actual, constructive, or attempted transfer
from one person to another of a legend drug, whether or not there is an agency
relationship.

(3) "Department" means the department of health.

(4) "Dispense" means the interpretation of a prescription or order for a legend
drug and, pursuant to that prescription or order, the proper selection, measuring,
compounding, labeling, or packaging necessary to prepare that prescription or
order for delivery.

(5) "Dispenser" means a practitioner who dispenses.

(6) "Distribute" means to deliver other than by administering or dispensing a
legend drug.

(7) "Distributor" means a person who distributes.

(8) "Drug" means:

(a) Substances recognized as drugs in the official United States pharmacopoeia,
official homeopathic pharmacopoeia of the United States, or official national
formulary, or any supplement to any of them;

continues

Exhibit 4–2 continued

(b) Substances intended for use in the diagnosis, cure, mitigation, treatment, or prevention of disease in man or animals;

(c) Substances (other than food, minerals or vitamins) intended to affect the structure or any function of the body of man or animals; and

(d) Substances intended for use as a component of any article specified in clause (a), (b), or (c) of this subsection. It does not include devices or their components, parts, or accessories.

(9) "Legend drugs" means any drugs which are required by state law or regulation of the state board of pharmacy to be dispensed on prescription only or are restricted to use by practitioners only.

(10) {+ "Medication assistance" means assistance rendered by a nonpractitioner to an individual residing in a community-based setting specified in section 1 of this act to facilitate the individual's self-administration of a legend drug or controlled substance. It includes reminding or coaching the individual, handing the medication container to the individual, opening the individual's medication container, using an enabler, or placing the medication in the individual's hand, and such other means of medication assistance as defined by rule adopted by the department. The nonpractitioner may help in the preparation of legend drugs or controlled substances for self-administration where a practitioner has determined, in consultation with the individual or the individual's representative, that such medication assistance is necessary and appropriate. Medication assistance shall not include assistance with intravenous medications or injectable medications.

(11) +} "Person" means individual, corporation, government or governmental subdivision or agency, business trust, estate, trust, partnership or association, or any other legal entity.

(({- (11) -})) {+ (12) +} "Practitioner" means:

(a) A physician under chapter 18.71 RCW, an osteopathic physician or an osteopathic physician and surgeon under chapter 18.57 RCW, a dentist under chapter 18.32 RCW, a podiatric physician and surgeon under chapter 18.22 RCW, a veterinarian under chapter 18.92 RCW, a registered nurse, advanced registered nurse practitioner, or licensed practical nurse under chapter 18.79 RCW, an optometrist under chapter 18.53 RCW who is certified by the optometry board under RCW 18.53.010, an osteopathic physician assistant under chapter 18.57A RCW, a physician assistant under chapter 18.71A RCW, or a pharmacist under chapter 18.64 RCW;

(b) A pharmacy, hospital, or other institution licensed, registered, or otherwise permitted to distribute, dispense, conduct research with respect to, or to administer a legend drug in the course of professional practice or research in this state; and

(c) A physician licensed to practice medicine and surgery or a physician licensed to practice osteopathic medicine and surgery in any state, or province of Canada, which shares a common border with the state of Washington.

continues

Exhibit 4–2 continued

(({- (12) -})) {+ (13) +} "Secretary" means the secretary of health or the secretary's designee.
Passed the House February 13, 1998.
Passed the Senate March 4, 1998.
Approved by the Governor March 20, 1998.
Filed in Office of Secretary of State March 20, 1998.

Source: Reprinted from Certification of Enrollment Substitute House Bill 2452 Chapter 70, Laws of 1998, 55th Legislature, State of Washington.

process focus to an outcome focus forced some major changes in how organizations functioned. The first organizations to face the changes were the hospitals.

Responding to market changes and increased competition for the patient, more health care agencies shifted their focus to emphasize a service approach. The race was on to improve systems and to streamline the delivery of care in any way possible.

Unfortunately, many nurses report that they have not been included in the loop when it comes to quality improvement programs. They remain ignorant in many cases, not fully understanding and certainly not participating in the new programs that have resulted in many of the changes that directly affect nurses.

Let's briefly review the change in quality focus and see where it has taken us so far. When the Joint Commission created its Agenda for Change in the late 1980s, one of its major guiding concepts fostered the rapid growth in a new idea of quality. Driven by increasing consumer demands to demonstrate results and value for the dollar, the Joint Commission stated that "continual improvement in the quality of care should be a priority goal for a health care organization" (1990, p. 2). The opinion was expressed that the assurance of quality was an unrealistic expectation and that a continuing effort to improve quality was more achievable. Greater emphasis was and will continue to be placed on outcomes rather than on the structure or process for attaining those outcomes.

Home health care has weathered some high-profile fraud cases, so efforts at monitoring quality on the part of HCFA and other agencies such as managed care organizations have redoubled. Because increased Medicare and Medicaid funding cuts coupled with financial surveillance have placed more pressure on home health agencies to streamline costs, quality out-

> Home health care has weathered some high-profile fraud cases, so efforts at monitoring quality on the part of HCFA and other agencies such as managed care organizations have redoubled.

> "Smart and savvy use of outcomes that measure the what, why and how of a clinical procedure, patient education, compliance, psychosocial, and cultural aspects, and the environment of care can fill the gap that utilization and functional outcomes miss" (Conway, 1998, p. 25).

comes become crucial, particularly from the perspective of the on-site care providers. Besides the usual annual surveys by federal and state governments, state annual Medicaid assessments, home health agencies must deal with accreditation surveys. But do these surveys actually reflect quality of patient care?

In the mid-1990s HCFA and the Colorado Center for Health Policy and Services Research in Denver developed a 75-plus item assessment performance measurement program known as OASIS, which is being implemented in 1998. Focusing on the patient's functional status is essential, but in addition, "smart and savvy use of outcomes that measure the what, why and how of a clinical procedure, patient education, compliance, psychosocial, and cultural aspects, and the environment of care can fill the gap that utilization and functional outcomes miss" (Conway, 1998, p. 25).

Although all this rationale for the shift in emphasis to results, or outcomes, makes a lot of sense, the point must be made that success for any health care improvement plan will require the involvement and support of all employees, as well as commitment from management. Involvement is a major issue, and nurses will need to seek out that involvement if it is not readily offered. Decisions made that affect the delivery of patient care in an attempt to improve the quality of the outcome must include the nurse executive, stipulates the Joint Commission standard. Through this standard, nursing leaders have received the support for integration into health care facilities' administration and now have an opportunity to involve staff nurses in all clinical improvement efforts, including the creation and use of assistive personnel. Participation on your part is essential. We have spoken with numerous nurses who have not been involved in their quality program and then question the credibility of the data when the survey results are posted. "Yeah, but they don't post the *real* data," has been a comment heard too often. If you want to know the real truth and suspect there is not an accurate reporting, or that what's really important is not being measured, get involved.

EDUCATIONAL RESOURCES

We have repeatedly noted that the RN is accountable for ensuring the competency of the individual to whom he or she delegates any nursing task. To fulfill that

CHECKPOINT 4-5

Are the following statements true or false?

1. The emphasis on quality is now on structure and process.
2. CQI stands for continuous quality improvement, a tool used to facilitate the monitoring of outcomes and look for ways to improve them.
3. The Joint Commission does not support the involvement of nursing in quality improvement efforts.

See the end of the chapter for the answers.

responsibility, certain factors must be in place. Employers who do not provide for the adequate screening and orientation of employees are placing themselves and their patients at risk. RNs need to assess the agency for such tools as skills checklists, performance-based job descriptions, periodic update and renewal of specific skills, and provision of continuing education. Accrediting agencies (the Joint Commission, Osteopathic Association, etc.) and regulatory bodies (the state department of health) have various requirements to ensure competency of employees.

Once hired, personnel need to be oriented, with a plan for evaluating their performance and skill levels at periodic intervals. The RN must make certain this process is in place to provide the supervision that is required of the delegate. What department is responsible for overseeing the orientation process? Are nurses involved in precepting or mentoring? This is a time-consuming responsibility, and not one that nurses have traditionally been trained in, so the availability of preceptorship training is valuable and demonstrates the importance the agency places on the program. New employees who are expected to perform on the day of hire and are not partnered with anyone are placing everyone at risk.

Education of home health aides has been handled creatively at some home health agencies. Encouraging the nursing assistants to use all of their senses to gather data, linking their work to positive patient outcomes, has been more successful.

Agene Parsons, former director of quality improvement and education for a large agency managing 140 agen-

> Encouraging the nursing assistants to use all of their senses to gather data, linking their work to positive patient outcomes, has been more successful.

cies, developed training and checklists to encourage use of all the senses, as well as intuition, as home health aides work with patients (Parsons, 1998). Cozby-Germany Home Health in Grand Saline, Texas, has a chronic obstructive pulmonary disease inservice developed by Shonna DeFoy that helps staff recognize the rationale for such interventions as small, frequent meals; bathing in a way that increases circulatory flow; and mucus removal (DeFoy, 1998). These types of organizational supports and tools enhance the UAP's ability to be the eyes, ears, nose, and hands of the RNs working in that agency, thus assuring quality outcomes and decreasing anxiety of nurses and patients alike.

In addition to the focus on training of the UAP, RNs who are experiencing changes in their roles also need training. According to a survey in 1995 by the American Organization of Nurse Executives and the Veterans Health Administration, "more than 80% (of the nurse executives) said their nurses had taken on new responsibilities in care management and supervision of nonlicensed support staff" (Davis, 1996, p. 5). And in an extensive review of studies that measure the impact of unlicensed personnel, Krapohl and Larson observed, "Several studies noted the RN's need for additional expertise in supervision and delegation" (Krapohl and Larson, 1996, p. 109).

States have also recognized the need for additional training of the RN in the area of delegation. For example, the state of Washington has developed a nurse delegation program for nurses who practice in the community and in some of the state-run institutions. Nurses who wish to delegate in specific areas must take the delegation course before they are approved by the state to provide nurse delegation. The very important issue, then, is education. Make sure you take steps to get the information you need to organize, plan, coordinate, and supervise the care of your patients.

CONCLUSION

We have taken a detailed look at how to assess the organization in which you work in terms of its "delegation-friendliness." Certain factors, such as the policies that define reporting relationships and staffing levels and the measures taken to validate the competency of employees, are critical to the success of the RN in practicing delegation. Also critical to the success of the delegator is his or her level of involvement in the organization. Participation on committees and task forces, whether union or not, is an important component of professional control over changes in patient care.

States have also recognized the need for additional training of the RN in the area of delegation.

Simply understanding why the organization is managed the way it is and why decisions are made is not enough. The RN has a real opportunity to shape practice in the working environment by being actively involved in assessing, planning, and evaluating the decisions made regarding the delivery of patient care. Support for this involvement comes from the regulating and accrediting bodies, as well as from the progressive movement of quality improvement programs. Missions and values are the driving forces of the assessment, and congruency with the professional values of the practicing RN will assist in attaining a satisfying partnership from which the patient benefits.

ANSWERS TO CHECKPOINTS

4–1.
1. false
2. false
3. true
4. false
5. false

4–2.
1. d
2. c
3. d

4–3. c

4–4. c

4–5.
1. false
2. true
3. false

REFERENCES

Barter, M., et al. 1997. Registered nurse role changes and satisfaction with unlicensed assistive personnel. *Journal of Nursing Administration* 27, no. 1: 29–38.

Bernreuter, M. 1997. Survey and critique of studies related to unlicensed assistant personnel from 1975–1997, Part 2. *Journal of Nursing Administration* 27, no. 718: 49–55.

Christy, T. 1984. Portrait of a leader: Lillian Wald. Pages from nursing history. *American Journal of Nursing*: 84–88.

Conway, M. 1998. What does the future hold for home care? *Continuing Care*: 25–35.

Covey, S. 1991. *Principle centered leadership*. New York: Summit Books.

Davis, S. 1996. RNs take on more managerial duties. *Reengineering the Hospital* 3, no. 3: 5–6.

DeFoy, S. 1998. Teach best practices for care of COPD patients. *Homecare Education Management* (June): 91–93.

Health People, Inc. 1997. Mission statement. 10900 NE 8th St., Bellevue, WA 98004.

Joint Commission on Accreditation of Healthcare Organizations. 1990. *The Joint Commission's agenda for change*. Oakbrook Terrace, IL: Joint Commission, 2.

Krapohl, G., and E. Larson. 1996. The impact of unlicensed assistive personnel on nursing care delivery. *Nursing Economics* 14, no. 2: 99–110.

O'Grady, T. 1992. Of rabbits and turtles: A time of change for unions. *Nursing Economics* 10, no. 3: 177–182.

Parsons, A. 1998. Prepare staff to use all of their senses. *Homecare Education Management* (June): 95–96.

Starr, P. 1982. *The social transformation of American medicine*. New York: Basic Books.

St. Mary Medical Center. 1993. Mission statement. Walla Walla, WA.

Toffler, A. 1990. *Powershift*. New York: Bantam Books.

Uustal, D. 1985. *Values and ethics in nursing: From theory to practice*. Greenwich, RI: Educational Resources in Nursing and Holistic Health.

CHAPTER 5

Know Yourself: What Personal Barriers Must I Overcome To Realize the Benefits of Effective Delegation and Teamwork?

Ruth I. Hansten and Marilynn J. Washburn

> *"I am new to home health nursing and I just can't get over being so alone out there, hoping that those home health aides and LPNs are doing the right thing! What do I need to learn to be a good leader of a team that's spread around all over the city?"*

Delegation in any clinical setting is essentially a complex interaction of very personal relationships. Your relationship and communication with your patients and their families, your supervisor, your coworkers, and those you supervise are absolutely fundamental to provide safe and effective care for those you serve. But your relationship with yourself is the cornerstone of the process. Your own thought processes and the words you say to yourself, your "self-talk," determine your ability to perform the delegation process. Your progress along the journey from novice to expert as a practitioner, your experience, and your internal personal barriers also affect your ability to work effectively with others in a team. The thoughts expressed above show that the transition from acute care to expertise in home care has not yet occurred, and this nurse's supervisory skills may not yet be adequately developed.

THE TRANSITION FROM HOSPITAL-BASED CARE TO A SEAMLESS HEALTH CARE SYSTEM

Nurses throughout the United States in all areas of practice have expressed their concerns about the delegation process and their ability to supervise other personnel. Their anxieties are a product of several realities: the remarkable interpersonal nature of and risks inherent in the delegation and leadership process, personal barriers known to each individual, and lack of experience or education regarding delegation in the clinical arena. Often compounding the personal barriers surrounding the team leadership role is the fact that many nurses first recognize the need to delegate in response to comprehensive changes in their organizations. For nurses in acute or ambulatory care, the whole idea of delegation then becomes tainted with the anger and fear surrounding the changes the nurses are experiencing. Many of them have chosen to leave acute care and enter other settings as a refuge from the increasing acuity and pressures of the hospital environment.

In home care, delegation to families and nursing assistants or chore workers has been common for decades, but the numbers of novice nurses entering community settings has increased rapidly (Figures 5–1 and 5–2). From 1989, when 94 percent of all working registered nurses (RNs) were employed in acute care and a mere 1.9 percent in community settings, data of October 1997 reveal that the ratio has changed to 73.5 percent to 10.1 percent (National Council of State Boards of Nursing, 1998). According to the Federal Bureau of Labor Statistics, the number of RNs working in home care increased 49 percent from 1993 to 1995, while the number of nurses working in hospitals decreased from 66 percent to 60 percent (Anderson, 1997, p. 2). Present projections show that RNs (in general) will experience a 21 percent increase in job growth from 1996 to 2001; during those

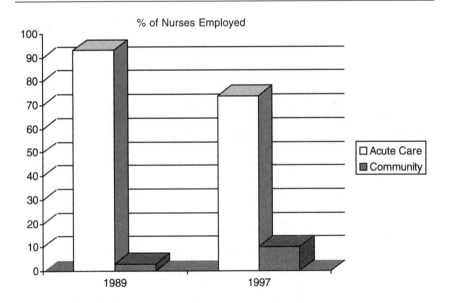

Figure 5–1 More Nurses Working in Community Settings.

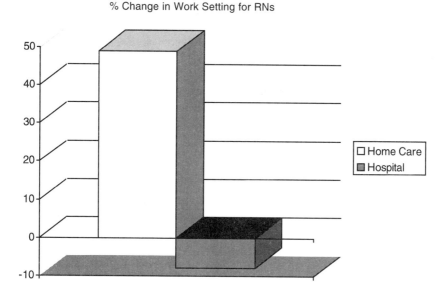

Figure 5–2 Percentage Change in Work Settings for RNs, 1993–1995.

same years, home health aides (HHAs) and personal care and home care aides will enjoy 85 percent and 76 percent growth in employment, respectively. (Bureau of Labor Statistics Report, December 1997). Buerhaus and Staiger (1997, p. 314) identified the increasing shift of nurses from acute care to community settings since 1990, correlating elevations in employment data with those states with more managed care. In the late 1980s and early 1990s, the increase in RN employment in home health was described as "explosive," ranging from 20 percent to 30 percent; at the same time, national spending on home care grew at a rate of nearly 14 percent per year (1994) and has been described as "the second fastest growing component of personal health expenditure" in 1996 (Buerhaus and Staiger, p. 318). As 1999 approaches, payment limits and Medicare cuts have been stunting the potential growth of home care, but from this data, we still expect that flocks of new nurses, whether new graduates or those migrating from other settings, will need to master delegation and supervisory skills.

The expectation of the new millenium in health care is that nurses are the leaders, the thinkers, and the coordinators, while remaining "doers" in some capacity. The health care system walls will become transparent (at present, the walls seem too high for many patients to scale!), and the patient and his family's experience of care should be seamless, receiving service from various care providers without difficulty. To create a system for the twenty-first century that

The expectation of the new millenium in health care is that nurses in all settings must be the leaders, the thinkers, the coordinators while retaining their expertise as "doers." The primary tool of leadership is the nurse herself.

reflects these goals, nurses must be able to grasp the experience of the patient in all arenas. In the 1990s, nurses overlap acute care, ambulatory, and home health practice. Examples are those nurses who work in labor and delivery and postpartum part-time, teaching at ambulatory clinics, while working in homes as lactation consultants. Nurse-managed managed care organizations enjoy success as nurses provide care across the continuum to and from acute and home settings. Development of a comfort level and expertise in supervising others, in leading a team, will continue to be necessary wherever the primary sites of practice.

To become the best leader, supervisor, and coordinator, the nurse must learn to use herself or himself as a primary tool. We looked at "therapeutic use of self" in our nursing theory training, but now we are asking nurses to apply that therapy to themselves. As Pierre Charron stated in 1601, "The most excellent and divine counsel, the best and most profitable advertisement of all others, but the least practiced, is to study and learn how to know ourselves. This is the foundation of wisdom and the highway to whatever is good. . . . God, Nature, the wise, the world, preach man, exhort him both by word and deed to the study of himself" (Charron, p. 1). With this in mind, let's examine what preparation is necessary before making a career move to the community setting.

THE MOVE FROM ACUTE CARE TO COMMUNITY-BASED SETTINGS

To those readers who are experienced community health nurses: don't skip this topic! You are often the preceptors or teachers who help orient new nurses to their community-based jobs. Unfortunately, some nurses aren't able to adjust well within the time limit expectation, and find themselves

"The most excellent and divine counsel, the best and most profitable advertisement of all others, but the least practiced, is to study and learn how to know ourselves. This is the foundation of wisdom and the highway to whatever is good. . . . God, Nature, the wise, the world, preach man, exhort him both by word and deed to the study of himself."

CHECKPOINT 5-1

The authors have tried to establish that I need to know myself better to be a better nurse. Why should I care about this?

a) I need to understand my own learning needs if I plan to enter home health practice.
b) As a leader and supervisor, I use myself as a role model for positive interaction with all those on my team.
c) Understanding my personal barriers allows me an opportunity to overcome them, as they will surely get in my way as I practice.
d) If I can work more effectively with others, I'll feel better about work and about myself, and the care for my clients will be improved.
e) It makes me uncomfortable to read all this "self-awareness" hogwash, and I am waiting for someone to play New Age music while we discuss it. I'd rather remain unaware and collect my paycheck each week anyway.

See the end of the chapter for the answers.

returning to acute or long-term care where their comfort level is restored and stress is (somewhat!) relieved. This leaves the already besieged home care nurses with increased patient loads and higher acuity but without the assistance needed in the form of developing relief staff. So what's in it for you to understand how to make that transition work? Coworkers who provide excellent care and remain in your agency long enough to carry a full patient load effectively! Students or those contemplating a move to home health: this information will assist you in your transition and may encourage you to choose home health with a clear direction for your adjustment period.

In some settings, the orientation process is conducted in four weeks or less (O'Neill and Pennington, 1996 p. 3) as experienced nurses enter the community setting. Some agencies expect as little as two weeks' orientation before competent practice is expected (Murray, 1998, p. 57). However, a survey of home health nurses showed that experienced nurses who were adapting to the new practice arena still felt unprepared after six months of employment (Murray, p. 57). Many nurses stated that they had little understanding of the differences between home health and hospital nursing prior to making the change. O'Neill and Pennington's discussions with home care supervisors revealed that they perceive the minimum time of transition from acute care to home care is six months (p. 64).

Before we discuss the positive reasons that draw nurses to home health nursing, let's first explore the realities of what's stressful about the transition. As you read the stressors and adaptations that are required, keep the faith: there are compelling reasons to survive and thrive after the transition period!

Stressors:

- Dealing with limited access to peer support and equipment
- Feeling isolated because of decreased opportunities for professional interaction
- Relinquishing traditional nursing responsibilities to families or other caretakers
- Documenting for reimbursement
- Supervising all nursing care
- Functioning autonomously
- Heavy paperwork demands
- Increased patient responsibility without adequate back-up
- Demanding or dissatisfied clients or families
- Difficulty in communicating with other professional caregivers
- Uncertainty regarding patient safety, needs
- Getting lost when trying to locate a client
- Frequent schedule changes
- Feeling a lack of control in the home situation

Adaptations:

- Adjusting to performing nursing care on the patient's turf
- Adapting equipment and procedures to the home environment
- Making decisions without the presence of other health care team members
- Managing time effectively
- Becoming clinically competent in a variety of practice areas
- Becoming accountable for practice
- Supervising others well

- Learning to assess environmental and psychosocial characteristics of the patient and family as well as physical needs

How does this translate into real life situations?

- The authors can recall some chagrin while doing a dressing change on a knife wound when there was a knock on the door. "It's the FBI! Open the door!" "I have only one pair of sterile gloves and I am doing a dressing change, would you please wait?" Adaptability and flexibility are important in different ways than in acute care.
- Counseling a family that refuses to quit a three-pack-per-day cigarette habit when the asthmatic child is suffering from it brings anger and frustration, and the need to confront our own value systems and the lack of control we may experience when care outside the walls of acute care becomes challenging.
- Attempting to arrange extra visits for a patient who desperately needs them to remain supported and nonabusive, but confronting difficulties in obtaining financial reimbursement because the nurse's intuition that child abuse is occurring or that the family is at risk does not constitute adequate documentation. The accountability and responsibility weigh heavily as nurses try to meet regulatory requirements and documentation so that patient needs are met and the agency is reimbursed.
- Visiting a pediatric patient on a ventilator, an unstable alcoholic diabetic elderly patient, an AIDS patient, a failure to thrive infant, a pulmonary rehab patient with chronic obstructive pulmonary disease, a debilitated multiple sclerosis patient, and a newly discharged psychiatric patient all on one day shows the wide variety of expertise needed by a nurse who may have been an orthopaedic nurse for decades.
- Finding dog or cat feces on the floor of the bedroom of the bedridden—and hearing from the son or daughter who gives the care that "everything is fine"—challenges the home care nurse's ability to assess the psychological and social aspects of care giving along with the education and support systems needed to keep the patient in a safe home setting.

Indicators of Success

What qualities in a nurse would predict a smooth transition to home care? A study by Bryan et al. (1997) indicates that proficiency in

- wound care and dressings,
- knowledge of community resources,
- diabetic education,
- patient and family advocacy,
- communication with third-party payors, and
- neonatal care

indicates a preferred knowledge base and skill set for early proficiency in the home.

In the same study, critical care nurses perceived themselves to be able to function proficiently in either arena (Bryan et al., pp. 35–44).

Requirements for success in clinical case management include:

- expert assessment skills
- knowledge of community resources
- outstanding organizational skills
- ability to supervise others
- persistence to advocate for patients' needs (O'Neill and Pennington, p. 62)

A Canadian study of public health nurses indicated that as little as 20 percent of the nurses' time is now spent in direct patient care. These patients are now high-risk two thirds of the time rather than one third a few years ago. The remainder of the nurses' time is spent in "coordinating referrals, consulting with other agencies, and trying to help people mobilize their own resources" (Chalmers et al., 1998, p. 112). Additional predictors of success based on skills that nurses themselves have identified included not only the factors delineated by the above studies, but also

- high level of technical competence
- telephone triage and assessment skills
- counseling skills
- ability to deal with psychological needs, stress, group process
- understanding of legal issues
- group process and development skills
- effective management skills (Chalmers et al., p. 113)

Again, on an international level we discover that nurses in Japan have identified their learning needs for the transition to a community setting:

- interviewing and counseling
- interpersonal communication
- high-technology home care
- independent decision-making (Ushikubo et al., 1995, p. 973)

A study of executives in home care settings revealed that short stays and increasing acuity of patients in the home necessitates nurses being skilled in the areas of "palliative care, pain control, patient education, chronic illness monitoring, case finding, and surveillance . . . RNs should learn how to effectively delegate activities to LPNs and aides" (Buerhaus and Staiger, p. 318).

Benefits to Overcoming the Challenges

If all this adjustment and learning must occur when nurses enter the home setting or transfer from other arenas to community nursing, why bother to become a nurse in the community setting at all? Those of you who are experienced home nurses will certainly have an answer for the novices in your setting. Take a moment to reflect on why you chose (or are planning to interview in) a community setting:

_____
_____
_____

We remind nurses across the country that we all seek fulfillment in our work. But when the inevitable challenges of the work setting occur (and they will in *all* work settings), satisfaction comes from our connection with our purpose. The tasks can be checked off a "to do" list, but the "why" of what we do is paramount, and that purpose is in the results we facilitate with those we serve.

Nurses tell us the reasons they make the home or community arena their career choice and stay there:

- autonomy and independence in nursing practice
- scheduling flexibility
- satisfaction with peers and supervisors
- involvement in agency decision-making (Cumby and Alexander, 1998, p. 42)
- increased personal interaction with patients
- ability to see the outcomes or results
- getting to really "know" your patients (Anderson, p. 2)

Lucille Joel, editor of the *American Journal of Nursing,* reminded us during Nurses Week 1998 that

> "It is easier to see our uniqueness as nurses when we are not distracted by the glitter and glitz of high technology, an unwieldy bureaucracy, or the oppressiveness of the medical model. In many ways ... community practice has allowed each of us to 'remember why we became a nurse.'"

Results, relationships, and the responsibility keep community health nurses doing their essential work for the health of our nation.

The proud heritage of community health nursing is not lost on those who continue to practice proudly today, on park benches and homeless shelters, being involved in solving social and health problems that have been ignored by society at large. These nurses celebrate when tuberculosis treatment is successful and fewer cases are reported because a bartender agreed to give a regular customer his medications each day, when a prostitute mother kicks crack, when an elderly patient dies comfortably holding her beloved's hand, when a grandmother learns how to care for an infant with significant disabilities, when chemotherapy treatment allows a patient a few more months so he can enjoy his son's graduation. Results, relationships, and the responsibility keep community health nurses doing their essential work for the health of our nation.

For those readers who are considering this career route, or those who need to be reenergized, we recommend reading *Opening Doors, Stories of Public Health Nursing* and *Nursing: The Finest Art* to experience the stories of those who led us as nurses into the community and those who are currently practicing. (See Recommended Reading at the end of the chapter.)

Based on our discussion in this chapter, after consulting the results of Exhibit 5–1 (Test Yourself), which areas have you identified to be weaknesses or barriers to community health practice?

List them below:

_____

_____

_____

_____

_____

Exhibit 5–1 Test Yourself

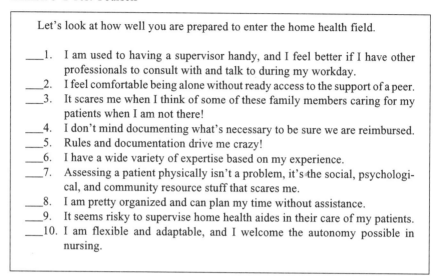

Let's look at how well you are prepared to enter the home health field.

____1. I am used to having a supervisor handy, and I feel better if I have other professionals to consult with and talk to during my workday.
____2. I feel comfortable being alone without ready access to the support of a peer.
____3. It scares me when I think of some of these family members caring for my patients when I am not there!
____4. I don't mind documenting what's necessary to be sure we are reimbursed.
____5. Rules and documentation drive me crazy!
____6. I have a wide variety of expertise based on my experience.
____7. Assessing a patient physically isn't a problem, it's the social, psychological, and community resource stuff that scares me.
____8. I am pretty organized and can plan my time without assistance.
____9. It seems risky to supervise home health aides in their care of my patients.
___10. I am flexible and adaptable, and I welcome the autonomy possible in nursing.

If you checked the even statements in Exhibit 5–1, you are well on the way to being prepared for the community setting. These are your strengths. If you checked the odd statements, or few of the even statements, you've identified some of the weaknesses you'll need to confront as you enter your new work environment.

Consider how you might meet these learning needs. Begin now to educate yourselves on these issues. If you've been focusing on one area of clinical expertise in your present job, and if care of pediatric or neonatal patients is a weak area, for example, you may decide to study a current pediatric nursing text. You may discuss with your supervisor or preceptor those areas of concern you've identified. Use the assertiveness formula in Chapter 8, "How Can I Communicate so That the Work Gets Done Right?" to articulate clearly what you need to do yourself, and what support you would like from your supervisor, to become competent in your new area of practice.

EXPLORING OTHER BARRIERS

As you completed your first self-assessment in Exhibit 5–1, what was your answer to statements 3 and 9? How comfortable are you with the need to be a manager and a supervisor of others?

It's not uncommon for us to teach delegation skills to nurses throughout the country and find at the end of the workshop that several people have not absorbed a word we said. We've discovered that these folks are so caught up in their negative feelings and fears about the changes occurring in their organization that they've been unable to listen. We recommend that they spend some time considering their personal barriers to delegation in some detail.

When you think of delegating to other health care workers, what feelings/ thoughts enter your mind? Write them down now as you reflect.

_____

_____

_____

Personal feelings about allowing unlicensed health care workers to perform care in the home, or about the changes in health care itself, are often barriers to effective clinical delegation. But many other personal barriers may be present within each nurse. Some of these may be related to past experiences, whether from undergraduate education, life experiences, training, or clinical realities nurses have faced during their career. Let's examine these and determine which may be operational in your own life.

Take the self-assessment quiz in Exhibit 5–2 to determine how much these barriers challenge you in a supervisory role.

Look at the items with which you agreed or strongly agreed. These will most likely be your highest barriers. Those that are marked "unsure" may also crop up as problems for you in learning and implementing clinical delegation skills.

Let's dissect each of these in more detail.

Barrier 1: Risk Aversion

We certainly aren't advocating that you take risks with your patients' lives! However, when we delegate to others, there is always some risk.

> You cannot absolutely guarantee that the delegate will not err (just as you may err yourself) or that all will be completed exactly the way you'd prefer. Following the delegation process correctly will minimize the negative aspects of the inherent risk.

Think about the risk involved in not having assistive personnel available to help you do the work. Think about the patient who is without adequate family support and would not receive necessary care without home health aides. There's some risk there as well.

Exhibit 5–2 Delegation Self-Assessment

Answer the following with Strongly Agree (SA), Agree (A), Unsure (U), Disagree (D), or Strongly Disagree (SD).

___1. I hate risk: I don't think risk of any kind should be present in health care delivery.

___2. It's very difficult for me to trust the people I work with. How can I be sure they'll do what I want them to?

___3. Letting go of the tasks I like to do is impossible for me. I get all my positive feedback from doing my clinical tasks exceptionally well.

___4. There's so little I can control about my daily work that I find it very difficult to lose the control I have by doing it all myself. How can I control others enough to be certain everything is done my way?

___5. I find that overcoming my old habits of "doing it all myself" is more difficult than giving up (choose one) cigarettes, or chocolate, or fine wine. Giving up things that are comfortable for me and are a part of my daily life is not my cup of tea.

___6. I feel very little achievement when someone else does the nuts and bolts of the care. I want to do that myself so I can feel the satisfaction of crossing tasks off my list.

___7. If everyone else does the tasks on the care plan, I'm confused about what's left for me to do.

___8. When I try to plan my day, I am often lost. I could use some help with organizing my work so that I can get my home visits done!

___9. I do all the work in my area better than most people. I am an expert clinician and I would hate for the clients to receive an "inferior" product if I am not the person actually performing that care.

___10. I really hate to make people mad when I assign them work. I'd rather do it myself than give a bad assignment to one of the aides.

___11. There are few people who work as hard as I do. I often find myself with the most challenging assignments. I rarely ask for help. I am often doing overtime because I take the most involved cases.

___12. I am uncertain about what can be delegated to whom in the home setting. The roles are unclear, and I'm not comfortable with the state regulations and rules.

___13. I hate to even think about delegating care to anyone else!

___14. If I don't do the tasks I'm used to doing, I wonder if I will still be a *real* nurse. I've worked too hard to become a clinical "has-been."

___15. I've never seen or worked with anyone who is a good delegator. I wouldn't know what it's like.

Source: Reprinted from R. Hansten and M. Washburn, Know Yourself, *Clinical Delegation Skills*, p. 127, © 1998, Aspen Publishers, Inc.

Barrier 2: Being Able To Trust Others

We aren't encouraging you in any way to trust implicitly all the people with whom you work or even those within your personal life. It doesn't make sense; this blind, trusting approach allows charlatans and con artists to take advantage of the elderly, for example.

> In delegating aspects of care to others, some degree of trust must develop. Delegates must trust that you'll be there to help with problems. You must be able to trust delegates to do what they say they will and to communicate changes in patient condition.

How does trust develop? In all relationships, trust develops from risking enough to establish the relationship and then by experiencing the objective results of your relationship. If your expectations are fulfilled, you begin to develop an image of that person as one who can be trusted. When one problem occurs in which that trust is violated, it's difficult to regain the same ease of communication and positive relationship. For example, Pat, an LPN (LVN) had been working with Jo, an RN, for several weeks, and during that time Jo had always telephoned physicians promptly for changes in orders. This time Pat thought that Mrs. Smith's condition was worsening quickly when at the patient's home and called Jo. Jo, however, did not call the physician promptly to discuss the changes in condition. Even though Jo may not have considered the changes important enough, the message given to Pat was loud and clear: She didn't think that Pat's input was important. It will take a long time for Jo to regain Pat's trust.

When we talk to assistive personnel (and we do this nearly every week), we hear that they would truly appreciate some respect for what they do and some discussion about what you expect of them. As a nursing assistant wrote in a letter to the editor of the *American Journal of Nursing,* "Just because the 'numbers' and 'mix' are correct doesn't mean the patients are getting good care. Some RNs are very defensive when an unlicensed person dares to tell them something should be done about one of their patients; others are too busy discussing their social life to be bothered about the patients. Some lack experience, some are burned out, some just shouldn't be RNs" (Robbins, 1997, p. 17). Sounds like there's room to develop trust on both sides!

Barrier 3: Letting Go of Some of the Amenities or Technical Tasks

Letting go of those tasks that have been important to you in the past is difficult but necessary for growth to occur.

> Is it reasonable to expect that our nation is willing
> to pay, for example, $20 per hour for you, as an RN,
> to perform personal care when someone else can
> be paid $10 per hour to do the same work?

In an era of limited resources, yours must be used to the fullest extent. If you aren't performing the professional role of the RN, who is? When we lead a seminar, a nurse occasionally will remark, "But I *like* to do the baths and linen changes! That's why I went into nursing!" If that is true for you, it's time to think about why you are in this profession. Is there anything within the *professional* role of the RN that would also give you some satisfaction? For example, if you became an RN because you wanted to help people or to make a difference in people's lives, then you can certainly do a better job using all your skills, beyond the merely technical to the intellectual. (For more information, review Chapter 6 regarding the PTA model.)

Barrier 4: Fear of Loss of Control

Nurses would like to be able to control a lot more about their work. We can't control what kind and acuity of patients are referred to our agencies. We can't control our caseloads or what infectious disease may strike our communities. At the beginning of our shift, it's difficult to know how our best-laid plans may be upset by the inevitable human factors we may encounter. So we try to control everything we can.

> We can only control ourselves and our own be-
> havior, including the decisions we make when
> delegating.

When we delegate care to others, we can't control their every move. No one expects that we will be able to control our coworkers like robots. However, as we now understand the process of delegation more fully, we know that we can control how we delegate: how we assess ourselves and our barriers; how we appraise the strengths, weaknesses, motivation, and preferences of our delegates; how we match the task to the delegate; how we communicate; and how we evaluate and give feedback to those we supervise. There is more control than we expected!

Barrier 5: Overcoming Old Habits

As we've already discussed, the rate of change is increasing at a dizzying speed. It's probably more difficult to change the way we work than to change some of our personal habits. We often spend more time at work than with our families!

> "Doing it all myself" sometimes seems like the best way to make certain it is done correctly. But when there isn't enough of you to go around, when it's impossible for you to "do it all," give yourself a break. Try to use the delegation process.

Just as some nurses find it is easier to give up that piece of cheesecake after lunch little by little, some nurses find that overcoming the old habits engendered by former care delivery systems may be done in stages. If you decide to "go cold turkey," remember to be kind and supportive to yourself and those with whom you work.

Barrier 6: Needing To Cross Tasks Off a List

If you were recently an acute care nurse who moved from task to task at an ever-increasing speed, you may see care planning for more long-term outcomes for each patient or your community as less concrete and, to some, less satisfying. If you see this as one of your barriers, begin to focus on processes or outcomes rather than tasks. Nurses have stated that this strategy has helped them overcome the nebulous feeling of having achieved very little each day. And when clients or patients achieve a goal with your help, celebrate it as a team. The outcome for the patient or family is the most important achievement of the entire team!

Barrier 7: If I Don't Do What I'm Used to Doing, What's Left for Me To Do?

This barrier is closely related to Barriers 3, 5, and 6. If you've delegated tasks and can't see the implications of your professional role, we recommend that you read the discussion of the PTA model in Chapter 6. Also, think about those things that you've wanted to complete but have been unable to because you've had to deal with so many details of care before (Patient education? Emotional support? Coordination of all health care disciplines? Family conferences? Long-term planning? Communication with other professionals?).

> Begin to think about how you add value in your organization. Why are you needed? Why does the Chief Financial Officer of your agency think that the correct complement of nurses must be present to ensure that patients receive optimal care? (Or

does he or she think it would be just fine to hire more hands in the form of additional unlicensed personnel, with no clue of the value of a nurse?) Why does a physician sigh with relief and state, "Thank goodness I refer my patients to this agency instead of any other! The nurses here really make the difference!" (What difference do you make?) We are convinced that the most important jobs you do, those that make a difference to the patients' end results and the care they receive along the way, have to do with those things *only* a registered nurse can do.

Barrier 8: Needing Help with Organization of Work

We know you recognize the phenomenon: a nurse who is excellent at performing discrete tasks or processes but has difficulty seeing the forest for the trees. He or she may be unable to break down the overall work to be done into manageable pieces. Learning to be more organized is difficult; however, we've seen some successes. If this is a barrier for you, talk to the nurses you find to be the most organized. Ask them to show you how they divide up their work. Sometimes one worksheet or method of organizing will work better for one nurse than another. Keep asking until you find one that makes sense to you. Often a visit with your manager or clinical instructor will be useful. He or she may even authorize some time to shadow or work with someone who is efficient in delivering care. Many home care agencies use a tickler file type of organization so that you can easily keep track of which patient needs to be visited when. Use maps to plan the best routes to save travel time.

Barrier 9: The Supernurse Syndrome

It's great to know you are out there caring for us and our families! Being an expert in your area and being extremely conscientious about your work are certainly positive qualities. However, it is tough for a supernurse to let others grow in their skills. After all, those served may not receive the highest quality of care while others are developing their skills.

Unfortunately, supernurses cannot be everywhere at all times, particularly in this environment of cost containment. Supernurses who find themselves

> unable to delegate will also become overwhelmed and burned out as they try to "do it all." Now you are dealing with a whole community. That's almost more than the real Superman can attempt!

If you are a supernurse, find some examples of care given by others that are satisfactory, maybe even good. Keep looking for those examples so that you will feel less guilty about the care you can't deliver alone.

Barrier 10: Wanting To Be Liked

Who will be happy to take the assignment of the abusive patient who is throwing stool around and needs constant pericare? Which nurse wants to manage the case of the patient with multiple personalities who likes to talk about child abuse exploits? If you are the person in charge of making those types of assignments, you wonder what will happen if you assign your best friend to care for these challenging patients. What will he or she slip into your coffee at the next staff meeting? Will anyone ever ask you to go out for social time after work?

> One of the most difficult aspects of being in a supervisory position is the struggle over this question: Is it more important to be liked or to be respected?

You, through your nurse practice act and by virtue of your job description, must take a leadership role. Would you rather "like" your supervisors and leaders or respect their decisions and leadership abilities? Think about how others earn your respect. Respect is generally earned through performing supervisory duties faithfully. You have been entrusted to ensure that patient/client/resident care is the highest quality possible. Making the best assignment for the "difficult" patient should not be based on who will be the most angry and vengeful. It should be based on the best match of assignment and delegate.

Barrier 11: The Supermartyr Syndrome

> We've started a new group, Supermartyr Nurses Anonymous. It's a 12-step program, and the first step is to announce, "Hi, my name is Mary, and I'm a supermartyr nurse!"

Identifying the problem yourself is the first step. However, ask any of your coworkers: They already know who the supermartyrs are. (Some of them may have used your need to be needed and indispensable by giving you extra work!) Ask your coworkers to help you limit yourself to doing what is reasonable and what is performed by others with your job description. You must take care of yourself so that you can take care of others. (For additional information, see *The Nurse Manager's Answer Book*, Hansten and Washburn, 1993, Chapter 16, on codependency.)

Barrier 12: Uncertain about Rules, Regulations

Nurses who don't want to delegate may be those who are still unsure about what is included in their roles and job descriptions. They may also worry about "putting my license on the line" when working with unlicensed caregivers. There are two main strategies for dealing with this barrier.

First, get some education. After you've read the information in this book, call your state board and get a copy of your nurse practice act. Ask questions of the board staff. Ask your facility to have a speaker from the state come to discuss your concerns.

Second, clarify roles within your organization. Ask to have a staff meeting to clarify who is supposed to be doing what. Find out what the assistive personnel may expect of you as well. What do they think their roles are? Where are you all in agreement? Where is there confusion? This is one of the most essential points for overcoming barriers to delegation. Clarify expectations. This discussion often goes beyond who should do what task and ends up discussing such things as being called by name, being asked with a please and a thank-you, and who really should call for supplies or take all the morning diabetics.

As you clarify roles, you may also find you need to develop a skills or evaluation checklist for each role. We've seen many of these used to assist in overcoming the barrier of confusion about roles.

Barrier 13: Denial

Some of you may not even want to think about delegation! If this is the case for you, or for some of your coworkers, it will be pretty difficult for you to learn how to supervise effectively. We suggest that you are remaining in the denial stage of the grief process. Continue to read on as we evaluate the potential benefits you may reap as you learn how to delegate effectively. It's pretty tough to work in home care and not delegate. We don't know of any agencies where this would be true.

Barrier 14: Am I Still a Real Nurse When I Delegate?

Many nurses continue to harbor this fear even as they continue to do an expert job of delegation and supervising others. Because we have experienced this fear ourselves as we entered supervisory, management, and executive roles, we have struggled with the uncertainty and concerns about remaining "clinically expert."

The first step in overcoming this barrier is to consider why you went into nursing. When we ask this question, we get a wide range of answers. Think now about why you decided to be a nurse.

My reason for becoming a nurse was

_____

_____

_____

Is this still your reason for being a nurse? Does it fit with your current job position and practice setting?

_____

Now define for yourself what nursing is.

_____

_____

_____

Can you still fulfill your definition of nursing, and the reason you went into nursing, if you ask someone else to do some of the tasks?

For example, if you went into nursing to make a difference in other people's lives, and to you nursing is a profession that uses the nursing process (assessment, nursing diagnosis, planning, intervening, and evaluating) in a holistic manner with patients, families, and social systems to aid the individual and his or her significant others to move toward their own definitions of health or wellness, then certainly you can use the help of others in performing your duties. We as nurses have done that since the days of Florence Nightingale.

We've discussed most of the potential obstructions to delegation and have focused on personal barriers. Look at Exhibit 5–3 and determine your most sterling qualities. These strengths will give you the needed boost to expand your delegation skills and bridge your barriers.

If you still think nursing is doing the tasks, it's time to think about what else may satisfy you within your new or emerging role. If you must still perform all the care to feel fulfilled, consider why you are doing your job. You won't feel fulfilled from the tasks that you do but from why you perform your professional role.

Exhibit 5–3 Assessing Strengths

____ I understand my job description as well as the roles of those who assist me.
____ I have studied the state nurse practice act and feel certain about its regulations.
____ I am highly organized in doing my work.
____ I am ready to overcome some old habits and learn some new ways of working.
____ I look at nursing with a broader perspective than "tasks."
____ I am willing to take some careful, calculated risks and slowly gain trust by supervising the assistive personnel.
____ I am cognizant of my own strengths and weaknesses, and I am asking for feedback from my coworkers about my "supernurse" or "supermartyr" tendencies.
____ I have delegated before, and it has been a great learning experience for me.
____ I am focusing more on being worthy of my coworkers' respect than on being liked by everyone.
____ I have learned from some excellent role models, or I can be a role model myself because I am already expert at this skill.
____ I am willing to learn!
Source: Reprinted from R. Hansten and M. Washburn, Know Yourself, *Clinical Delegation Skills*, p. 136, © 1998, Aspen Publishers, Inc.

Barrier 15: No Role Models

We have asked groups of nurses how many of them have had excellent role models in the delegation or supervisory process, and very few have acknowledged delegation mentors. Perhaps this is because nurses weren't looking for this skill in others when it seemed less important. Perhaps it is because some nurses determined that other nurses were highly organized, or efficient and effective, or just that things always went well but didn't connect clinical delegation skills with the end-product: better patient care. Or perhaps expert nurses are out there who can't find the time to mentor others. Often in the home setting we aren't able to witness the excellent supervisor nurse because we are so isolated.

If you don't have a role model, never fear! You will have all the information you'll need to be successful.

DETERMINING THE POTENTIAL BENEFITS

Each nurse may have a barrier or two to conquer, and all have multiple strengths they can use to overcome those barriers. Think about how we evaluate the problems or needs of our clients and families. We identify their strengths for coping and use them in our plan of care. Often the plan of care includes education and practicing new skills. That's our plan for you as you learn (or refresh your memory) about the process of clinical delegation.

To mobilize the energy to leap over these barriers, nurses need to visualize what's waiting on the other side of the wall. What outcomes can be expected?

If you are able to overcome your barriers or at least prevent them from being a stumbling block on a daily basis, and if you become an expert at delegating and supervising others, what will the potential benefits be?

Potential Benefits to Expert Delegation and Supervision
- _____
- _____
- _____
- _____
- _____
- _____

When we began to educate nurses about delegation, we completed informal qualitative research with nurses from all areas of care delivery who had been delegating to assistive personnel for some time. We asked them what benefits had been realized from learning to delegate well. They told us the following had occurred:

- More time for myself
- Personal growth
- Empowerment and growth of the assistive personnel
- Making better use of my brain power and assessment skills
- More time for professional nursing (educating patients, emotional support, coordination of care, planning, and communication with other professionals and family)
- Less stressed out with "doing it all"
- More sense of team and support of each other
- Collegiality
- Someone to help gather data and be my eyes, ears, and nose in the home
- Better job satisfaction

We have personally worked with organizations that have implemented new care delivery systems or have merely improved the delegation skills of their RNs, and they have found the following benefits:

- Patients are happier when they don't have to "bother" the RN for minor requests and when they know that someone is available to help them.

- Families are beginning to recognize the impact of professional nursing practice on their family member.
- Organizations remain solvent from fiscally responsible use of resources.
- Physician and staff satisfaction improves as nurses are able to multiply their effectiveness and improve their communication with each other, as evidenced by positive responses on nurse and physician satisfaction surveys.
- Nurses with some physical disabilities can continue to be clinically involved in a supervisory capacity.
- Nurses understand the full scope of their professional responsibilities and implement their role across the continuum of care, including practical, appropriate care pathways/plans and evaluation of care.
- Better planning along the continuum of care occurs, resulting in decreased lengths of stay in inpatient settings, fewer readmissions for care in any setting or agency, and more effective and efficient use of resources.
- Better communication between health care disciplines (because RNs have time to coordinate care); care planning is individualized and meaningful because all members of the team gather and share data, resulting in appropriate use of other disciplines' talents, streamlined home care, and fewer errors.
- Charting reflects the patient status accurately.
- Better patient outcomes: achievement of the individualized outcomes the patient and team have agreed on as goals at the beginning of their relationship.

Whether the potential bonuses materialize in your work area will be determined, in large degree, by the energy you put into delegating effectively and making the system work the best for you and your patients.

CONCLUSION

> Delegation is a complex process that includes the scientific nursing process, critical thinking, and excellent communication skills. As the initiator of this process, your abilities are fundamental to the success of working in a team.

As uncomfortable as it may be (for all of us!) to contemplate yourself objectively, your ability to act effectively as an RN is enhanced by self-analysis and self-understanding. Recognizing personal emotions or beliefs that inhibit leader-

CHECKPOINT 5-2

This section has allowed nurses to evaluate themselves as an integral part of the delegation process. You have determined:

1. learning needs or personal barriers that may inhibit a smooth move into the home health setting
2. other barriers to delegation and supervision
3. your strengths related to your ability to delegate effectively
4. potential benefits to overcoming the barriers

Have you determined how to deal with your emotional barriers and those of your coworkers? Have you chosen strategies to overcome your barriers to delegation, using your strengths to overcome the obstacles? Keep visualizing the potential benefits for you and for your patients. After all, the bottom line is delivering quality care to those we serve, achieving the outcomes we've planned together.

ship will allow you to be clear about what's in the way and will free you to focus on the benefits of overcoming those barriers. What's in it for all of us? Improved morale, better teamwork, and better patient outcomes. It's worth it!

ANSWERS TO CHECKPOINT

5–1. a, b, c, d are correct. If you chose "e," we regret not including a CD of appropriate music to accompany this chapter!

REFERENCES

Anderson, A. 1997. Loving attention to patients is an attraction for nurses moving into home care. *Memphis Business Journal* (June 16–20): 1–3.

Bryan, Y.E., et al. 1997. Preparing nurses to change from acute to community based care: Learning needs of hospital-based nurses. *Journal of Nursing Administration* 27, no. 5: 35–44.

Buerhaus, P., and D. Staiger. 1997. Future of the nurse labor market according to health executives in high managed-care areas of the United States. *Image: Journal of Nursing Scholarship* 29, no. 4: 313–319.

Bureau of Labor Statistics Report, December 3, 1997. *http://stats.bls.gov.news.release/ ecopro.nws.htm* pp. 1–4.

Chalmers, K., et al. 1998. The changing environment of community health practice and education: Perceptions of staff nurses, administrators, and educators. *Journal of Nursing Edication* 37, no. 3: 109–117.

Charron, P. 1601. Wisdom, bk. 1, preface. *The Columbia Dictionary of Quotations* is licensed from Columbia University Press. Copyright © 1993 by Columbia University Press.

Cumby, D., and J. Alexander. 1998. The relationship of job satisfaction with organizational variables in public health nursing. *Journal of Nursing Administration* 28, no. 5: 39–46.

Donahue, M. 1985. *Nursing: The finest art.* St. Louis: Mosby.

Hansten, R., and M. Washburn. 1993. *The nurse manager's answer book.* Gaithersburg, MD: Aspen Publishers, Inc.

Joel, L. 1998. Remember why you became a nurse. *American Journal of Nursing* 98, no. 5: 7.

Murray, T. 1998. From outside the walls: A qualitative study of nurses who recently changed from hospital based practice to home health care nursing. *Journal of Continuing Education in Nursing* 29, no. 2: 55–60.

National Council of State Boards of Nursing. 1998. National Council studies employment rate, work setting of newly licensed nurses. *Issues* 19, no. 1: 7–9.

O'Neill, E., and E. Pennington. 1996. Preparing acute care nurses for community based care. *Nursing and Health Care: Perspectives on Community* 17, no. 2: 62–66.

Robbins, A. 1997. Letter to the editor. *American Journal of Nursing* 97, no. 7: 17.

Ushikubo, M., et al. 1995. Educational needs of home health care nurses. *Nippon Koshu Eisei Zasshi* 42, no. 11: 962–974.

Zerwekh, J., and J. Primomo. 1992. *Opening doors: Stories of public health nursing.* Olympia, Washington State Department of Health.

RECOMMENDED READING

Donahue, M. 1985. *Nursing: The Finest Art.* St. Louis: Mosby.

Zerwekh, J., and J. Primomo. 1992. *Opening Doors: Stories of Public Health Nursing.* Olympia, WA: Washington State Department of Health.

Also visit the Bureau of Labor Statistics home page on the internet for current projections for the home health labor market. (http://stats.bls.gov)

CHAPTER 6

Know What Needs To Be Done: If I Delegate All My Tasks, What's Left for Me To Do?

Ruth I. Hansten, Marilynn J. Washburn, and Virginia L. Kenyon

Mary is the Branch Director of a large home health care agency. She is making Monday morning rounds of her departments to get a report of the weekend and any issues that might have come up. She asks the supervisor who was on call for the weekend for a report. The supervisor appears very frazzled and reports that they got seven new referrals over the weekend; two of the aides didn't show up for their scheduled shifts at two different clients' homes; the infusion case opened the Friday before went sour, requiring the on-call nurse to spend the entire weekend making repeated trips to the home to assist with the infusion pump; and she didn't have enough nurses to see all the new patients. The Branch Director asks her if there is anything she can do to help. The supervisor replies that she really doesn't see what the Director can do; what they really need is more on-call staff on the weekends to handle the heavy workload.

In the example above, the supervisor had a general idea of what needed to be done but had not done an organized assessment of what was really happening on the weekend. Without a plan, she could only react to the issues as they arose and she was unable to prioritize the workload. Consequently, she could not ask for the required help far enough in advance to meet the need. The result was a feeling of chaos and frustration that could be felt by all the staff working the weekend. The patients will certainly have sensed this feeling as the nurse and/or aide rushes through the visit and scurries off to the next appointment.

The process of working with other people successfully requires knowledge of the total picture, knowing what needs to be done in terms that are clearly defined.

> The process of working with other people successfully requires knowledge of the total picture, knowing what needs to be done in terms that are clearly defined.

Not everyone is organized by nature, and certainly we are not all equally endowed with the ability to see the whole picture. Fortunately, there are steps to take that will assist us in developing these skills. In this chapter we are going to discuss those steps by first exploring a model that delineates three major aspects of the nursing role. We will then discuss planning objectives for optimal conditions and the process of prioritizing those objectives when conditions and resources are limited in some way.

Despite all of our attempts and the multitude of systems created to date, nursing has not been carefully contained within a list of items that are to be done. In fact, as Marie Manthey challenges, "Good nursing care. It's so simple, we all know it. The picture is brilliantly clear. But what are its boundaries? When can any nurse say, 'This patient has had enough nursing care'? The question seems almost sacrilegious. The answer seems to be, 'Never!' There is always one more thing a good nurse can think of to do for someone who is ill" (Manthey, 1991, p. 27). Yet, resources *are* often limited, and boundaries must be set. Not having the ability to be all things to all people all the time, we must begin to define what needs to be done by first defining the role of professional nursing.

DEFINING THE ROLE

Looking at the brief 100-year history of our profession, we can cite countless examples of nursing's amoeba-like progression. Many of us have heard the comment, "Get a nurse to do it if no one else will!" Throughout history, nursing has willingly taken on work that no one else was willing to do. From drawing blood in the home and running it to the nearest lab, rising at 2 in the morning to tend to a home patient's infusion pump that isn't working, to picking up the groceries and prescriptions for a patient, nursing has been there to meet the need. As a result, we lack clear definition of what we do. Further, we are now training others

> Despite all of our attempts and the multitude of systems created to date, nursing has not been carefully contained within a list of items that are to be done.

and delegating to them tasks that have been a part of our scope of practice. Without a finite definition of our role, the idea of delegating any part of it invokes fear in many as they ask the question, "If I delegate all of these interventions, what's left for me to do?"

> Studies have been done that assist us in finding some delineation to our role.

Studies have been done that assist us in finding some delineation to our role. One of the most promising studies to date has resulted in the Nursing Interventions Classification. The result of five years of research under the Iowa Intervention Project, the taxonomy is a listing of 336 nursing interventions, with standardized descriptions of each (McCloskey and Bulechek, 1992). Various work sampling studies indicate that registered nurses (RNs) spend time as follows: 27.5–32.8 percent on direct patient care, 41.8–45 percent on indirect care activities, 15 percent in unit-related activities, and 13–20 percent in personal time. For purposes of these studies, the following category descriptors were used:

- *Direct care:* All nursing care activities performed in the presence of the patient and/or family, such as assessment, medications, treatments, and procedures. Included was time spent communicating the plan of care, teaching patients/families, intervening, and evaluating.
- *Indirect care:* All activities done away from the patient but on a specific patient's behalf, including communicating to others on the team, giving reports, gathering supplies, and preparing equipment and medications.

CHECKPOINT 6-1

As we've discussed so far, working successfully with others involves understanding what needs to be done in terms of the total picture and planning how that can be accomplished by delegating to the members on the health care team.

I can begin to do this by:

a) defining and clarifying *my* role as a professional nurse
b) relying on the supervisor to assist when things get tough
c) doing all things myself, meeting all of the patients' needs as they occur
d) letting members on the team do all of the work so that they can advance

See the end of the chapter for the answers.

- *Agency-related activities:* Activities for general maintenance of the agency such as clerical work, ordering supplies, attending meetings, and running errands.
- *Personal activities:* Activities not related to patient care, including meals, breaks, children's school events, personal phone calls, and socializing with coworkers.
- *Documentation:* All activities associated with documenting, reviewing, or evaluating patient condition and care, including the review of all patient data, correlation of interdisciplinary data and nursing judgment, and the action of documenting (Urden and Roode, 1997).

THE PTA MODEL

Consider looking at the nursing role as made up of three areas of practice in what we will call the "PTA model." In this model (Exhibit 6–1), nursing provides *P*rofessional, *T*echnical, and *A*menity care to a given group of patients or clients. Whether the setting is acute, long-term, or community care, the nurse can be described as functioning in one of these three areas. Let's look at this more closely to see what is meant.

Amenity

During the past decade, this area of our role has received heightened attention as health care as a business became the issue and executives sought an element that would give them a "leading edge" over the health care facility down the street. The "service mentality" was developed and promoted, and we educated our "consumers" to expect Nordstrom-style treatment. Those who could afford to redesigned their service delivery systems to be more customer focused and friendly, and hired marketing personnel to assist them in "going the extra mile." Patient questionnaires were designed to help us measure performance in terms of how friendly the nurse or home health aide was, were they punctual, did the office staff address their concerns when they called, were their concerns addressed satisfactorily. The quality of our amenity ser-

> Consider looking at the nursing role as made up of three areas of practice in what we will call the "PTA model." In this model, nursing provides Professional, Technical, and Amenity care to a given group of patients or clients.

Exhibit 6–1 Examples of Professional, Technical, and Amenity Care

The PTA Model	Professional "The Whole Picture"	Technical "Expert Skill Level"	Amenity "The Extra Touch"
Example 1	discharge planning	passing medications	changing linen
Visible to	colleagues	physicians/patient	patient/family
How Measured	length of stay	medication errors	patient surveys/ letters
Example 2	diabetic teaching in the home setting	giving insulin injection	fixing a snack for the patient's family
Visible to			
How Measured			
Example 3	medication instructions	changing a dressing	changing ice water
Visible to			
How Measured			
Example 4			
Visible to			
How Measured			

Source: Reprinted from R. Hansten and M. Washburn, Know What Needs to Be Done, *Clinical Delegation Skills*, p. 154. © 1998, Aspen Publishers, Inc.

vice is highly visible to management and marketing, in terms of patient surveys, letters to the administrator expressing thanks or dismay, and gifts of boxes of chocolates for the nurses. These were signs we had done our job well. The subtle education of the patient and family to expect the "amenities" of care was complete. This expectation extends to all areas of health care, from the 24-hour on-call staff readily available to assist at any time of the day or night to taking the elderly client to a doctor's appointment and taking notes so the family is kept aware of the client's condition. (We think these amenities are nice touches and very important when you are ill, or aging, or experiencing a significant event in your life—but a note of caution should be made that this is not the primary function of the RN.)

> The "service mentality" was developed and promoted, and we educated our "consumers" to expect Nordstrom-style treatment.

> Examples of our technical expertise include cannulating a vein, catheterizing a child, irrigating the Blakemore tube, balancing the hemodynamic monitor, and giving a painless injection.

Technical

This is an obvious area of the nursing role, and one we take pride in and fight to maintain. Examples of our technical expertise include cannulating a vein, catheterizing a child, irrigating the Blakemore tube, balancing the hemodynamic monitor, and giving a painless injection. These technical tasks are highly visible and their outcomes easily measured, making their performance obviously important. Quality improvement monitors, incident reports, medication error analyses, and patient complaints tell us how well we are performing in this area of our role. Physicians see the outcomes of these technical interventions and measure our effectiveness by the number of incidents they must deal with and the number of complaints from family members when the orders to change their loved one's dressing three times daily have not been carried out.

The two areas of "amenity" and "technical" contain many tasks that are readily delegated to other personnel. It does not take an RN to take the client to the doctor's appointment, walk the dog in a long-term care center, or clean the bathroom. And the increasing numbers of health care technicians offer many willing hands to be trained to perform the majority of our technical duties. Licensed practical nurses (LPNs/LVNs) pass meds, change dressings, and start IVs in some states, and patient care assistants are also passing some medications, completing glucose tests, drawing blood samples, and providing all of the hygienic care required. With so much of our role clearly being done by others, what is left for the RN?

Professional

This part of our model presents the greatest degree of difficulty for many nurses. Answers to this question involve attitude, image, and the number of years of education the nurse has completed. Yet we are not seeking to describe how we attain or present this part of our role, but rather what comprises the very heart of RN practice. What can you do, and do well, that cannot be delegated?

What ensures a high-value experience for the patient that is both efficient and effective? We hope you are saying to yourself that it is the implementation of the nursing process! For it is through your educational foundation, your ability to make assessments and plan the care, that you can effectively coordinate the efforts of the health care team and evaluate their effect. This collaborative coordination is essential to the successful functioning of any health care delivery system and cannot be eliminated or replaced. Tasks may be performed by anyone trained to do them; it is your ability to critically identify the need and evaluate the outcome that remains when all else is delegated. According to the National Council of State Boards of Nursing (NCSBN), delegation means "transferring to a competent individual the authority to perform a selected nursing task in a selected situation. The

> Tasks may be performed by anyone trained to do them; it is your ability to critically identify the need and evaluate the outcome that remains when all else is delegated.

nurse retains the accountability for the delegation" (NCSBN, 1995, p. 2). Retaining that accountability through the implementation of the nursing process as we coordinate the entire picture of our patients' needs is the very core of our professional role.

Why do we find it difficult to articulate the professional component of our role? Realize that we tend to measure what we value. The inverse is also true: we value what we measure. Notice that in the above description of the professional area of practice we have not described any tools of measurement or discussed the visibility of performing the nursing process. As nurses, this is an area where we need to place more emphasis and not continue to allow others to dictate our practice in terms of measurement and value. Clinical errors and patient surveys have been our standard measurement tools in the past, keeping us at a task-oriented technical and amenity level of practice. However, beginning efforts are being noted as more nurses are tracking the impact of their case management and translating outcomes into terms that are highly visible to physicians, patients, the general public, and administrators alike. We must continue to shift our focus from those easily identified and measured parts of our role and understand that "there is a growing gap between the organization's need for nursing to assume an enlarged role in the redefined care delivery system and the traditional task-oriented role decreed by influential elements of the medical profession" (Hanrahan, 1991, p. 35).

CHECKPOINT 6-2

Complete examples 2 through 4 of Exhibit 6-1, providing your own examples of professional, technical, and amenity care, noting who it is visible to and how it is measured.

See the end of the chapter for the answers.

Implementing the nursing process is relatively easy to describe on paper and to other nursing personnel. However, it is not visible in the same manner as giving a bath, changing a dressing, or starting an IV. It is visible only when connected to outcomes, when the whole picture of the patient's care is evaluated in terms of whether the plan of care was achieved in a timely fashion and no untoward results occurred. It is visible only when we make the connection, when we call attention to the fact that the duration of care for a specific critical pathway has decreased by four weeks due to consistent nursing planning and coordination of the care. It is visible only when we note inappropriate readmissions to an acute care facility or the home care agency. It is visible only when we research the connection between our continuous teaching of diabetic foot care and the decrease of lower limb amputations among diabetics. Our professional visibility does not come from checking a task off a "to do" list but from our continuous education of our publics regarding the outcomes of our interventions. Carol Lindeman, former Dean of Oregon Health Sciences, reminds us, "Health care systems don't need a nurse who knows how to do those old routines. And more than that, they don't care how the person does something, as long as it produces the outcome" (Lindeman, 1996, p. 8).

Yes, there is much to be done after you have delegated tasks to the other members of the team. What remains clearly defines you as an RN, and is the "heart" of our profession. As Adelaide Nutting challenged us so many years ago, "Perhaps, too, we need to remember that growth in our work must be preceded by ideas, and that any conditions which suppress thought, must retard growth. Surely we will not be satisfied in perpetuating methods and traditions. Surely we will wish to be more and more occupied with creating them" (Donahue, 1985, p. 366).

Beyond the Nursing Process

In addition to the overall coordination of patient care, which comes through the comprehensive nursing process of assessment, planning, intervening, and evaluating, other aspects of what RNs do are worth mentioning. Consider this scenario: The patient is in a clean bed, has a clean body, is relatively comfortable, has the right IV infusing at the right rate, has eaten the appropriate diet, has ambulated around the house, and has had his dressing changed. What is there left to do? Some nurses will jokingly respond, "Take a break!" And deservedly so,

> Our professional visibility does not come from checking a task off a "to do" list but from our continuous education of our publics regarding the outcomes of our interventions.

for it is the coordinated efforts of the RN that have created such a complete and happy patient. However, a few aspects of care are not yet part of this picture. Discharge planning, referral to community resources, and patient/family teaching are essential functions of the role of the RN. Remember the list of functions that cannot be delegated? (See Chapter 3 for a review.) As Massachusetts Nursing Regulations remind us, "It is the responsibility of the qualified licensed nurse to promote patient/client education and to

> In addition to the overall coordination of patient care, which comes through the comprehensive nursing process of assessment, planning, intervening, and evaluating, other aspects of what RNs do are worth mentioning.

involve the patient/client and when appropriate, significant others in the establishment and implementation of health goals. While unlicensed personnel may provide information to the patient/client, the ultimate responsibility for health teaching and health counseling must reside with the qualified licensed nurse as it relates to nursing and nursing services" (MNR, 244CMR 3.00 Registered Nurse and Licensed Practical Nurse, Section 3.05, 1996).

Intentional Caring

When we ask nurses to describe what they do as RNs to provide value to the organization, they invariably respond, "I *care* for the patient." When you think back on a lot of marketing hype and those cute little items sold exclusively for nurses, you will remember that nurses give "TLC." (Remember the little red heart, or the bear with the banner declaring "Nurses give TLC"?) This "tender loving care" has been an essential aspect of who we are as nurses, just as much as the cure imperative has been for physicians. If we are to make visible this essence of nursing, we must have some definitive form of measurement. Nurse researchers have begun to build a database using measurable and identifiable actions to define caring. The Denver Nursing Project, funded by both state and national sources, is an example of measuring the impact of caring on patients with human immunodeficiency virus. In her discussion of this research and other actions related to caring, Karen Miller, RN, PhD, offers this definition: "Caring, then, may be defined as

> Discharge planning, referral to community resources, and patient/family teaching are essential functions of the role of the RN.

> "Caring, then, may be defined as intentional action that conveys physical and emotional security and genuine connectedness with another person or group of people.

intentional action that conveys physical and emotional security and genuine connectedness with another person or group of people. Caring validates the humanness of both the care giver and the cared for" (Miller, 1995, p. 29). This deliberate and planned intervention is the cornerstone of what RNs do; without physical and emotional security, a patient will not progress, cannot learn, and cannot move on successfully to the next level of independence within the health care continuum.

GETTING THE JOB DONE

Whether we are providing professional, technical, or amenity care, we must first establish what needs to be done. In our example at the beginning of this chapter, the supervisor of the home health care agency noted several issues that needed attention but was not certain how or by whom these issues would be resolved. What needs to be done in this example, and in every situation you face, is no different than the nursing process. (There seems to be no substitute for the nursing process—what a wonderful tool!) Let's take a look at how it applies here.

I. Assess

In any situation, whether in an outpatient clinic, a dialysis center, a home health agency, or wherever you practice, the first step in getting the job done is to assess the situation. You need as much data as possible to plan effectively what goals you can achieve, both for this shift and for the long term. Take a look at the information available. You may not be the one getting the information, but you must be the one to interpret what it means. Recall that in Chapter 3 we defined assessment from the

CHECKPOINT 6-3

Identify three optimum outcomes you might focus on at the beginning of your day.

RN perspective as "the initial phase of the nursing process which involves the interpretation of the significance of the available subjective and objective data." From a critical thinking standpoint, you must be able to integrate your personal experience and assumptions with the facts presented to you to begin to determine potential and realistic outcomes. The foundation of any plan begins with a thorough and complete assessment. In home

> From a critical thinking standpoint, you must be able to integrate your personal experience and assumptions with the facts presented to you to begin to determine potential and realistic outcomes.

care that includes not only the physical and psychosocial but the environment for safety factors and support systems available to the client. Failure to assess all these areas adequately and plan based on your findings could ultimately affect the outcomes for your client.

Consider the following example of what can (and does) happen when staff focus not on outcomes but solely on tasks. This is a true story from years as a home care nurse and administrator and is, unfortunately, a classic example of what can happen in our hurried world of health care. As you read, ask yourself what assumptions have been made and what data have been overlooked in the ongoing assessment of this patient.

Mr. Jones was a severe chronic obstructive pulmonary disease client being cared for in his home by the home care nurse. He has had numerous hospitalizations over the past 18 months due to repeated lung infections. His home care nurse has been with him since he was admitted to the agency and was the primary nurse seeing him although, because of the increased visit load the past 10 months, several other nurses also have been seeing him. Each infection had set Mr. Jones back and he never fully gained back his strength before he had another one and landed back in the hospital. His weight had dropped from 176 to 143 and his endurance now was limited to walking from the bedroom to his living room chair and back. His nutrition was declining secondary to his poor endurance and his appetite decreased with his endurance. As his nutrition declined so did his general health, including the integrity of his skin. Consequently, he had developed several sores on his buttock and the back of his hand. He was obviously in a downhill slide. On a supervisory visit with the primary nurse, it was discovered in reviewing the plan of care with the nurse and the family that the filters in and nebulizer cups for the nebulizer had never been cleaned in the entire 20 months since the client had first started using it at home. Appropriate instructions were given regarding the cleaning of both. Unfortunately for Mr. Jones, the appropriate actions came too late and he died a couple of months later secondary to congestive heart failure related to his extensive lung disease.

Although many factors affect the
nurse's decision as to how time is spent,
none of these factors is as significant as
the primary need to make all decisions
based on clearly defined outcomes that
are supported by thorough assessments.

"Fail to plan, plan to fail."

II. Plan

Often we are so anxious to begin the day that we do not recognize the value of
planning. Remember that old adage Mom taught you (or was it an old nursing
professor?), "Fail to plan, plan to fail." When you are tempted to skip this step and
just jump right into the tasks at hand, be aware of the price you will pay in terms
of feeling disorganized, moving from one job to another, and reaching the end of
the day with no clear sense of achievement. As little as 15 minutes at the beginning
of any day reviewing the clients you will see and looking at the planned outcomes,
determining what can be reasonably done and by whom, will be much more
effective than gathering your charts for the day and heading out. (Further
discussion of the communication process in delegation will be covered in Chapter
8.)

This planning step applies to all settings where you may be employed, from
extended care centers where the emphasis is on long-term planning, to the
ambulatory surgery center where you must consider the list of scheduled cases for
the day and plan for who will be assigned to the patient, to the home health setting
where there is much planning to be done to maximize the amount of time spent in
each visit. Once again, focus on outcomes, on the results of your actions, not the
actions themselves. Set your optimal goals by looking at what your ideal outcomes would be if you had no limitations: All patients/clients receive safe care, all
medications and treatments are given on time and discussed with all patients to
increase their knowledge and understanding of their care, all documentation is
completed accurately, everybody completes their visits (no overtime or visits not
done), and so on. These are very general outcomes; you should have specific
outcomes related to the patient population and setting in which you are working.

Once you have agreed to set aside the time to plan, a word or two must be said
about the process. (Are you surprised? You didn't think we would just leave you
to plan on your own, did you?) Planning requires not only determining outcomes
but realizing that some prioritization must occur if resources are not unlimited.
We propose the following steps.

1. Get the global picture: Don't limit yourself to just your assignment, but have
an understanding of what fellow team members are also expecting to accomplish
during their visits for the day. For instance, do you know what cases the other
nurses on your team are carrying and what cases the physical therapist will be

seeing today? Do you need to coordinate visits? On a skilled care unit in a long-term care facility, be aware of the assignments of the other team members on the floor, not just your assigned rooms. Expanding your awareness of the expectations of the other workers in your area will help you to offer assistance when you have time or to know who might be called on to help you, and to foster a sense of teamwork instead of isolation. The worst words we can ever hear (or

> Expanding your awareness of the expectations of the other workers in your area will help you to offer assistance when you have time or to know who might be called on to help you, and to foster a sense of teamwork instead of isolation.

speak!) are "It's not my patient." Establishing a global picture implies that we have an awareness of what's happening around us, not just with the patients in our immediate caseload.

Often the perception or the mood of the work setting is colored by the events of the previous week. If a patient you are seeing at home has had a family dispute with one or more of his children, the tone for the subsequent visit might be strained. An awareness of the events of the previous week will lend a better understanding to the "whole picture." Understanding that although the events of the previous day or week have ended, feelings carried over are now affecting the information shared will help you plan and present that needed information in a way that most benefits your client. The weekend call coverage for a visiting nurse may leave a very lengthy message regarding the noncompliant attitude of a patient and his refusal to complete the medication regimen, but your phone call on Monday morning reveals a much calmer patient who is willing to talk about his IV therapy and consider completing the treatment plan. Beware of self-fulfilling prophecies—get the whole picture and make your own assessment so that you can plan your care effectively.

2. Set optimal goals: Decide what you really want to achieve during this time in your work setting, given the best possible conditions. (No one is late to work, staffing is adequate, everyone is ready to work together, and so on.) As in our discussion above, focus on outcomes, not on creating a laundry list of tasks to be done. What do you want to be the results of your professional efforts today? Remember, every action you take is a subtle form of education to your public (whether it is the physicians you work with, your fellow team members, the patients, or patients' families and visitors). What is the best impression you can make and the clearest message you can send regarding your professional ability?

3. Decide what is reasonable to expect: Part of planning involves being able to anticipate events and determine potential responses. What happens if a patient "crashes," or one of the home health aides becomes ill, or you receive three

> Part of planning involves being able to anticipate events and determine potential responses.

unexpected referrals? Given limited and changing resources, what is reasonable to expect will be accomplished today? How do we let go of the ideal and optimum outcomes and be "okay" with less than the best? Can we give ourselves permission to do less than the optimum, and under what conditions is this acceptable? (See Chapter 3 for a discussion on policies and procedures in working with limited staff.)

4. Set priorities: Given limits to the resources we work with—supplies, staff, and time—we must be able to determine those outcomes that are essential to achieve, and prioritize our work. We can do this effectively by evaluating each desired outcome according to the following criteria:

- *Life threatening*—Has the patient proven to be a risk to him- or herself and others, therefore requiring placement in an alternative environment? Has the patient demonstrated a labile response to medication, thereby requiring more frequent visits than the plan of care has established?
- *Essential to safety*—Have you received the latest training regarding universal precautions, and do you take the time to practice them to protect your safety as well as that of your patient? Does the patient weigh 200 pounds and require two people to assist in moving or can the patient be safely transferred with a transfer belt? Does the family need to be instructed in how to do a 24-hour observation routine because of a recent fall by the patient?
- *Essential to the medical/nursing plan*—do the vital signs need to be monitored every visit when there has been no significant change for the past month? Is the monitoring of intake and output essential to the outcomes we have established for this patient? Does the lab work that has been ordered on a weekly basis reflect the best therapeutic evaluation for this client? Is the type of dressing ordered the most appropriate for the client at this point in his recovery? Are the exercises the most appropriate at this time?

By asking these types of questions, we can often further assess the work to be done and prioritize according to the reasonable goals we have set. Failing to take the time to ask these questions continually keeps us in the task-oriented, technical- and amenity-based roles of our position and does not allow us (or the patient!) to benefit from what we do best. We can continue to keep ourselves very busy, getting tasks done, not delegating appropriately, and therefore depriving the patient and our employer of the skills we are most needed to provide. It may seem far easier to cross the daily insulins, dressings, and blood draws off a list than to assess the need for these interventions, plan who will do them, supervise the

---

CHECKPOINT 6-4

Prioritize the following tasks based on the desired outcome of providing safe and effective care for Mr. Bailey, a 68-year-old total hip replacement who is one week post op, alert and oriented, and stable. He has been home for two days. Use the criteria (L) life threatening, (S) safety, (E) essential to medical/nursing plan, and (N) nice to do, but not a priority.

___1. change the IV cassette containing a required vasodilator
___2. instruct patient and family regarding care of the IV site
___3. monitor vital signs every visit
___4. assist with obtaining transportation to the doctor's appointment
___5. assist patient with exercise regimen after discussion with physical therapist
___6. order and obtain a walker for the client

See the end of the chapter for the answers.

---

interventions, and evaluate their effect. However, because we are the professional nurses accountable for the total patient care for a given group of individuals, implementing the nursing process while delegating tasks to others is our primary responsibility.

III. Intervene

For many years, our focus has been on systems and processes, supported by criteria of the Joint Commission on Accreditation for Healthcare Organizations (Joint Commission) and state regulations. Beginning in the late 1980s, the Joint Commission developed its Agenda for Change, noting there would be a shift in emphasis from systems and processes (tasks and how they are completed) to an emphasis on the outcomes of the service provided. Further support came from quality management programs: Total Quality Management (TQM) and Continuous Quality Improvement (CQI) replaced the traditional Quality Assurance (QA) monitoring departments found in most organizations. This change has intensified our need to be continuously aware of the cause-and-effect relationship our interventions have on the patients for whom we provide care. Successful practice requires that we as nurses change our focus too, always looking at the process outlined above: setting goals, realizing limits, prioritizing, and then implementing the plan, always with the patient's desired outcomes as our guide.

Job Analysis

With outcomes at the top of our list, having completed the above steps to the process, we are ready to put the plan into action. Armed with priorities, we must determine who can best carry out the interventions necessary. This can be done by completing a quick "job analysis." (A note of caution here, so that we don't lose you entirely in a wave of disbelief—we know how busy you are on the job and realize that you will not have the luxury of spending precious time completing a job analysis when there is work to be done. However, as you are reading this book, there is time to learn and understand the technique so that you can quickly apply the principles in your work setting, making the most of the resources you have by delegating appropriately.) Supervisors often tell us that this is one of the most difficult skills to master and that if there were some way to help nurses to organize their work and base the completion of that work on the resources available by getting the right person to do the job, they would be amazed. So although a job analysis sounds like something out of a personnel manual, we encourage you to read on to learn perhaps a new method for mastering that skill.

Giving a bath is only a task and can be done by anyone if the focus is only on the task. What is the outcome desired by giving the bath? Is it to make the patient feel more comfortable? Is it to assess the condition of the skin and to provide an opportunity to assess the patient more completely? Is it an opportunity to teach a family member how to complete range of motion exercises while also giving a bath? Knowing the desired outcome of the job to be done will have a significant effect on the selection of who should perform the task.

Current analysis of the work done by an RN has revealed that significant time is spent in performing tasks that could be performed by someone else who does not have the knowledge and skill of the RN. Redesigns in care delivery are therefore focusing on isolating those functions that only an RN can perform and grouping the remaining tasks to be done by assistive personnel with minimal training. In many instances, the assistive person is then given a patient assignment with designated delegated tasks to be accomplished.

A job analysis involves the following basic steps:

> Armed with priorities, we must determine who can best carry out the interventions necessary.

1. Break the job or jobs into parts: For example, if the job to be done is to start an IV, are there any parts to the process? Assembling the supplies, getting the proper IV solution from the supply room before going to the home, starting the IV, monitoring the administration, teaching the patient and family about the IV, and documenting the procedure are all parts of the job.

2. Evaluate the job in the following terms:

a) Knowledge: What kind of knowledge is necessary to do this job? In the example of starting the IV, one needs to know the type of equipment required, how to use it, basic anatomy and physiology to select a site, the policy of the facility regarding the procedure, the potential effects of the fluid to be administered, and the physician's orders regarding rate and method of administration.

b) Skills: What skills are required to perform this task? Starting an IV requires the ability to be organized (having all supplies on hand before starting the insertion makes the process smoother!) and psychomotor ability to insert the cannula into the vein and attach the tubing.

c) Personal traits: What personal traits (personality characteristics) would be helpful? The ability to remain calm, appear confident, explain the procedure to the patient, and be reassuring is certainly helpful in starting an IV on anyone.

3. Match the job and the delegate: Given the analysis of the required knowledge, skills, and personal traits, who is the best person on the team to perform this job? In the case of starting an IV, the RN would be best qualified. However, the answer may change if the setting changes—consider a renal dialysis center where technicians have been trained to access a dialysis cannula, or a radiology department where the radiology technician starts an IV for the administration of contrast media. In these instances, the technicians are performing a task with a specific,

---

CHECKPOINT 6-5

Perform a job analysis of the following:

1. Assessment of infection log and tracking data:
   a) knowledge?
   b) skills?
   c) traits?
   d) who would do this job?
2. Teaching insulin administration to an insulin-dependent 60–year-old diabetic who lives alone:
   a) knowledge?
   b) skills?
   c) traits?
   d) who would do this job?

See the end of the chapter for the answers.

predetermined outcome and have been taught the skill of IV insertion and the potential complications of their specific application. The RN, however, will be more knowledgeable regarding the continual administration and monitoring of IV medications and fluids for therapeutic interventions. Once again, consideration of the outcome desired is essential in making the decision of who performs the task.

The core of health care reform involves this very basic process of job analysis. As Virginia Trotter Betts, President of the American Nurses Association, states, "Whether it is in primary healthcare services—which can be safely and appropriately delivered by qualified nurses—or acute and critical services which require the experienced judgment of a registered nurse, the success of health care reform will depend in part on matching the right provider to the need" (American Nurses Association, 1993, p. 3).

Let's see how the whole process of job analysis can be applied to the example given in Exhibit 6–2.

Exhibit 6–2 The East County Satellite

You are the senior RN working in the East County Satellite Home Health Office. The satellite manager, an RN, had emergency surgery on Saturday and will be out for the next two weeks. You are asked to take over and run the office. There are 42 patients on caseload with varying visit schedules and needs. One RN case manager is on vacation and the other two have very little room in their schedules. You have one LPN who works occasionally for the office. You will not be able to see your usual caseload this week as you will be in the office managing.

I. Assess What Needs To Be Done

Assign cases based on care requirements to assure the physical and emotional needs of the clients are met. There are 3 bid dressing changes, 2 infusion cases, 6 daily insulins, and 15 clients with personal care needs as well 18 clients with various visit needs. In addition, there has been a client complaint that needs a follow-up and an employee counseling session that was already scheduled.

II. Plan

a) *The global picture*—All 42 patients have a visit schedule established based on their particular needs; however, two clients will need extra visits this week because of new orders for blood draws. The client complaint is from Mrs. Smith. The aide is scheduled to be with Mrs. Smith from 9 PM until 9 AM. She is supposed to be awake so she can help her to the bathroom at night. Mrs. Smith states that she has caught the aide asleep on at least three occasions and she always leaves before 8 AM but has Mrs. Smith sign for the full shift until 9 AM. Your counseling session is with Cara, a longtime aide whose work performance the past month has greatly deteriorated.

b) *Optimal goals*—to provide appropriate and effective nursing and personal care to all clients on the caseload per their visit schedule, setting aside time to

continues

Exhibit 6–2 continued

> investigate Mrs. Smith's complaint and adequate time to counsel Cara regarding her work performance.
>
> c) *Reasonable to expect*—there will probably be at least six to eight new referrals during the week. In addition, one of the IV cases has been difficult to manage because of the family dynamics, so additional time may be needed by the nurse to resolve some of the family issues. This has been your case, so you will need to orient the relief nurse to the case.
>
> d) *Set priorities*—staff all visits and shifts using an acuity of highest need for who will be seen, e.g., infusion cases, daily insulin, dressing changes, CHF rehab. Plan aide visits also by acuity of need, e.g., incontinent clients, recent post-ops, disabled wheelchair-bound clients. Call Mrs. Smith to verify your information, ask the aide for her side of the story, then take appropriate action. Counsel with Cara.
>
> ### III. Intervene
>
> a) *Break the job into parts*—(1) schedule all visits and shifts; (2) handle the complaint; (3) counsel the aide; (4) assign new cases as they come in.
>
> b) *Consider knowledge, skills, and personal traits of available staff (a job analysis)*—review the individual skills checklists for all staff working for the week. Identify personal preferences and strengths of the RNs, LPNs, and aides.
>
> c) *Match the job to the delegate*—assign all existing and new IV cases to Sara. She has the most experience and tends to handle them best. Call the LPN and assign her the insulin and daily dressing cases for the week. She has demonstrated expertise in these two areas and likes to do them. Assign bath visits based on aides' experience and whether they have seen the client before. Attempt to maintain continuity of care.
>
> ### IV. Evaluate
>
> Check daily with all the in-house and field staff to be sure that visits are being made and shifts staffed. If some of the staff are feeling overwhelmed, discuss their issues with them and do joint problem solving. Check back with Mrs. Smith to be sure that her complaint was handled to her satisfaction and the planned remedy met her need. Check with Cara to see if there is anything more you can do to assist her as she strives to correct her performance.

DECISION-MAKING MODELS

Matching the right provider to the need, whether or not it is part of health care reform, is an essential component for safe delegation. Numerous tools have been developed to assist the RN in deciding who does what. Similar to the job analysis described previously, these models provide a road map for thinking and offer a guide to making the appropriate legal and safe decision of what to delegate.

In its 1995 newsletter, the NCSBN suggested a framework for decision making to ensure patient safety in receiving delegated care. Its seven-step process is covered in Exhibit 6–3 and offers a basic yet comprehensive pathway for evaluating the steps taken in delegation.

Exhibit 6–3 NCSBN Delegation Decision-Making Process

I. **Delegation Criteria:**
    A. Nursing Practice Act
        1. permits delegation
        2. authorizes task to be delegated or authorizes nurse to decide delegation
    B. Delegator qualifications
        1. within scope of authority to delegate
        2. appropriate education, skills, and experience
        3. documented/demonstrated evidence of current competency
    C. Delegatee qualifications
        1. appropriate education, skills, and experience
        2. documented/demonstrated evidence of current competency

Provided that this foundation is in place, the licensed nurse may enter the continuous process of delegation decision making.

II. **Assess the Situation:**
    A. Identify the needs of the patient, consulting the plan of care.
    B. Consider the circumstance/setting.
    C. Ensure the availability of adequate resources, including supervision.

If patient needs, circumstances, and available resources (including supervisor and delegatee) indicate patient safety will be maintained with delegated care, proceed to III.

III. **Plan for the Specific Task To Be Delegated:**
    A. Specify the nature of each task and the knowledge and skills required to perform it.
    B. Require documentation or demonstration of current competence by the delegatee for each task.
    C. Determine the implications for the patient, other patients, and significant others.

If the nature of the task, competence of the delegatee, and patient implications indicate patient safety will be maintained with delegated care, proceed to IV.

IV. **Ensure Appropriate Accountability:**
    A. As delegator, accept accountability for performance of the task.
    B. Verify that delegatee accepts the delegation and the accountability for carrying out the task correctly.

continues

Exhibit 6–3 continued

If delegator and delegatee accept the accountability for their respective roles in the delegated patient care, proceed to V.

V. Supervise Performance of the Task:
  A. Provide directions and clear expectations of how the task is to be performed.
  B. Monitor performance of the task to ensure compliance to established standards of practice, policies, and procedures.
  C. Intervene if necessary.
  D. Ensure appropriate documentation of the task.

VI. Evaluate the Entire Delegation Process:
  A. Evaluate the patient.
  B. Evaluate the performance of the task.
  C. Obtain and provide feedback.

VII. Reassess and Adjust the Overall Plan of Care As Needed.

Source: Used with permission of Columbia Swedish Medical Center, Professional Nursing Practice, Englewood, Colorado.

Many organizations have also created tools to support the RN in making decisions regarding who can do what. Columbia Swedish Medical Center in Colorado, created the pathway in Figure 6–1 to assist in decision making.

The American Association of Critical Care Nursing supported the decision-making process with its framework of factors to consider, first created in 1990 (Evans, 1991, p. 17a). We offer it here as a good review of the more important questions to consider before delegating a task to anyone. Refer to Exhibit 6–4.

Yet another tool for decision making has been developed by Margaret Conger, Associate Professor at Northern Arizona University in Flagstaff. Her Nursing Assessment Decision Grid was developed originally to teach nursing students effective delegation decision making. Since 1993 she has been gathering data to validate the effectiveness of this model and has noted significant difference in students who have completed the module. Through the use of vignettes and a step-by-step guide or analysis, students are taught to apply a logical sequence of questions to a given situation (Conger, 1997). We will not include the entire module here, but Exhibit 6–5 presents the grid developed to provide ongoing reinforcement in the clinical setting. Similar to other models, this one asks a series of questions that will assist you in determining if it is safe to delegate a given task to another member of the team. Regardless of the setting you work in, the models cited above will serve as a good guide.

Last, but not least, we present a rather simplistic but very effective approach for deciding what tasks you are prepared to "hand off" to another member of the team. Since 1990, we have borrowed from the mnemonic of the five rights of medication administration (you remember—the right medication, right time, right route, right patient, right dose?). The Four Rights of Effective Delegation (Washburn, 1991) include consideration and determination of four major areas as described in Figure 6–2.

RN DELEGATION DECISION TREE

RN Cannot Delegate

1. Initial assessment of patients
2. Evaluation of collected data
3. Nursing judgment
4. Patient/family education/evaluation
5. Nursing diagnosis/nursing care plan

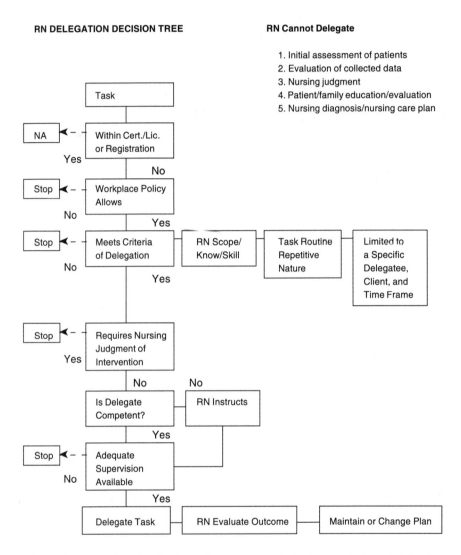

Figure 6–1 RN Delegation Decision Tree. *Source:* Used with permission of Columbia Swedish Medical Center, Professional Nursing Practice, Englewood, Colorado.

Exhibit 6–4 Factors on Which To Base a Decision To Delegate: The American Association of Critical Care Nurses

> - **Potential for harm:** What is the particular nursing activity's potential for harm?
> - **Complexity of the nursing activity:** What psychomotor and cognitive skills are required to perform a particular nursing activity?
> - **Required problem solving and innovation:** If a problem is suspected, does it require individualized problem solving to achieve a successful outcome?
> - **Predictability of outcome:** How predictable are the outcomes of a nursing activity?
> - **Extent of patient interaction:** Will delegating a nursing activity increase or decrease the amount of time a critical care nurse can spend with a patient and the patient's family?
>
> *Source*: Data from *Heart & Lung*, Vol. 20, No. 1, p. 19A, © 1991 American Association of Critical Care Nurses.

Exhibit 6–5 Delegation: When Is It Safe? To Whom Can I Delegate? Questions To Ask Yourself

> **What Nursing Tasks Need To Be Done?**
>
> For each, consider:
>
> | | | |
> |---|---|---|
> | YES | Within partner's skill level? | NO |
> | YES | Partner has documented performance? | NO |
> | Delegate to technical nurse | | Retain by professional nurse |
>
> **What Problems Are Present?**
>
> | | | |
> |---|---|---|
> | NO | Any unstable problem? | YES |
> | NO | Any teaching needs about new medications, procedures? | YES |
> | NO | Patient motivated to work on problem? | YES |
> | Delegate to technical nurse | | Retain by professional nurse |
>
> *Source:* Data from M.M. Conger, *The Intersystem Model: Integrating Theory and Practice*, p. 245, © 1997, Sage Publications.

The Four Rights of Delegation

Right Task:
- Within the scope of practice
- According to job description
- On the shared task list
- Based on desired outcome

Right Person:
Assess competency by:
- Certification/licensure
- Job description
- Skill checklist
- Demonstrated skill

Right Communication:
The Four Cs of Initial Direction:
1. Clear
2. Concise
3. Correct
4. Complete

Right Feedback: the Reciprocal Process
- Ask for teammate's input FIRST.
- Recognize his or her effort.
- Get the teammate's solution to the problem.

Figure 6–2 The Four Rights of Delegation. *Source:* Copyright © 1991, Marilynn J. Washburn.

Using these four criteria as a guide, decision making can become a little easier and more clear. It is also important to note that the NCSBN (1995) used this approach as well, adding a fifth right, that of the right circumstances. Its recommended list looks like this:

- **Right task:** one that is delegatable for a specific patient
- **Right circumstances:** appropriate patient setting, available resources, and other relevant factors considered
- **Right person:** right person delegating the right task to the right person to be performed on the right person
- **Right direction/communication:** clear, concise description of the task, including its objective, limits, and expectations
- **Right supervision:** appropriate monitoring, evaluation, intervention, as needed, and feedback

Making Assignments

Another important part of implementing your plan involves making assignments to the members on your team. This is a skill that generally is not taught, but rather is learned "on the job." (See Exhibit 6–6 for a sample plan of care involving a team assignment.)

Institutional policies and Health Care Financing Administration (HCFA) criteria provide the starting place for making assignments in home health care.

HCFA Regulation 484.36(c) Guidelines: The aide assignment must consider the skills of the aide, the amount and kind of supervision needed, specific nursing or therapy needs of the patient, and the capabilities of the patient's family.

HCFA Regulation 484.36(C): Assignment and duties of the home health aide.

(1) *Assignment.* The home health aide is assigned to a specific patient by the registered nurse.

Written patient care instructions for the home health aide must be prepared by the registered nurse or other appropriate professional who is responsible for the supervision of the home health under paragraph (d) of this section.

(2) *Duties.* The home health aide provides services that are ordered by the physician plan of care and that the aide is permitted to perform under State law. The duties of a home health aide include the provision of hands-on care, performance of simple procedures as an extension of therapy or nursing services, assistance in ambulation or exercises, and assistance in administrating medications that are ordinarily self-administered. Any home health aide services offered by a HHA must be provided by a qualified home health aide. (HCFA Interpretive Guidelines for Home Health Agencies, revised 2/21/95.)

Exhibit 6–6 Sample Plan of Care Involving a Team Assignment

CLIENT NAME (LAST, FIRST) Doe, John		CLIENT NO. 1186	CASE MANAGER Susie Caregiver
SHORT TERM GOALS	Provide for personal care needs. Wound healing and complications. Increase strength in lower extremities	LONG TERM GOALS	Return to indep. functional status.

CLIENT PROBLEMS/ NURSING DIAGNOSIS	INTERVENTIONS/ APPROACHES/ ACTIONS TO BE TAKEN	EXPECTED OUTCOME/ RESPONSE	CLIENT OUTCOME (Sign and Date)
1. Decrease function secondary to fx. (L) hip	1. Walker while up (ordered)	*Ambulate safely	
	2. PT to initiate PT program—Inst HHA re: same, visit 1x wk x 6 wk.	*Increased strength and endurance	
	3. HHA daily x 14d for personal care, vs, daily exercises, meal preparation	*Personal care and nutrition needs will be met	
2. Potential for wound infection	1. RN visit 2x wk x 2 to monitor incision site for s/s infection, inst client and family in same	*Wound will heal without complications	
	2. Monitor general conditions and progress toward goals		
3. Depression/grief secondary to recent loss of husband	1. MSW to visit x3 to provide counseling/ referral to approp. resource as needed	*Depression/grief will decrease	

REVIEW DATE SIGNATURE/INITIALS							

SIGNATURE/TITLE _____ DATE _____

Source: Courtesy of Health People, Inc., Bellevue, Washington.

CHECKPOINT 6-6

What other factors do you consider when making assignments?

Hopefully, you included some of the following factors in your criteria:

- *Location:* No one likes to be running from one end of the territory to the other if it can be avoided. This has traditionally been a major criterion for making assignments, and it is still used today because some offices cover large geographic areas.
- *Continuity of care:* As rapidly as patients are moved through any system, it is essential that some degree of sameness be provided. If you had the patient yesterday, it would be nice to care for him or her again today. This is more than a nicety; familiarity with the patient assists in planning and evaluating his or her progress. Continuity of staff in terms of team composition is important for the same reasons; developing working relationships with a consistent team member makes it easier to plan and delegate work. Too often, the person making assignments is only concerned with the numbers of patients or clients assigned and not with protecting the integrity of the team. The assistant who worked with Mr. Jones yesterday may be assigned to another set of patients today to "make the assignments work. You will spend part of your morning bringing the new assistant up to speed on the clients she has been assigned as well as being sure that she has appropriate directions to each of the clients' homes."
- *Personal preference:* It is nice if we can all have the opportunity to do what we prefer, and hopefully you have matched your preference with your job setting. If diabetic care is your thing, you probably are more skilled in this area and would be best taking diabetic clients. Beyond this, we all have certain geographic areas where we prefer to practice (see Chapter 7, "Know Your Delegate"), and considering this when making an assignment is beneficial to the patient and the employee.

> Continuity of staff in terms of team composition is important for the same reasons; developing working relationships with a consistent team member makes it easier to plan and delegate work.

- *Acuity system:* Most agencies employ a system for determining the acuity levels of all patients so that the work may be distributed more equably among the team. We have yet to find a perfect system, and we continually emphasize that this is a dynamic, not a static environment, with continual changes in patient needs that must be met consistently. Be wary of the importance that is placed on any system; it can be a very divisive tool as members of the team argue about how many "high-acuity clients" they were assigned. It can also be a very useful tool for monitoring staffing needs and the changing demands of the patient population.

- *Care delivery system:* Whether your work setting uses a case management system, primary care, team nursing, or any one of a number of new systems being created, this will influence how assignments are made. As with continuity of care, this criterion may be quickly forgotten as we struggle to make certain everyone has an equal load. We have observed situations where assignments are made on a next-on-the-list basis, which does not take into account the skills, needs, or constraints of the individual you are assigning. A system like this leads to frustrated staff carrying unequal workloads and contributes to staff burnout.

Even if you neither currently work in a home care setting nor ever have the opportunity to make assignments, it is a good method for "getting the global picture" and understanding what your colleagues experience. It is also an excellent tool for prioritizing and performing a job analysis so that you become more skilled at matching the job to the delegate.

IV. Evaluate

Okay, so you've taken the time to assess the needs, plan and prioritize the outcomes, and implement your plan through careful job analysis, matching the job to the delegate, and making the assignment based on specific criteria. Wow! What's next? The final step of the nursing process as we know it involves evaluating what we've done. Considerable discussion will be provided on this topic (see Chapter 11) as it relates to the process of delegation. What needs to be covered here relates specifically to evaluating whether we did the right things (effectiveness) and did them correctly (efficiency).

Once again, the true measure of our success goes back to the outcomes we determined to be our goals in the first step of our assessment. Did we achieve what we set out to do? (You would be amazed at how many nurses do not ever ask the question!) We wonder—if you never stop to evaluate your outcomes, how do you ever know if you have achieved them? How do you measure success? Or, to put

---

CHECKPOINT 6-7

Would you delegate these tasks to an unlicensed caregiver?

1. Helping a stable patient walk
2. Evaluating patient response to pain medication
3. Collecting intake and output data on the patient
4. Calling the physician for medication orders
5. Assisting in ADLs with a homebound 70-year-old
6. Feeding a two-year-old recovering from a spica cast application

See the end of the chapter for the answers.

---

it one more way, we took the time to determine where we were going; shouldn't we take the time to determine if we got there?

The use of two criteria, effectiveness and efficiency, makes our evaluation process simple. Let's look at efficiency first (because we know this to be a term met with disdain by many nurses). Every nurse realizes the importance of doing things correctly. Few professions carry as serious consequences of an incorrect procedure or intervention as health care does. Unlike manufacturing or the provision of retail goods and services, health care deals directly with people's lives, and mistakes carry a high price. Doing things right is tantamount to every nurse's professional standard and receives the appropriate emphasis in all of our training. Beyond the correct performance of a procedure, however, is another question regarding efficiency: Did the right person do the job? We have repeatedly stated that "things ain't the way they used to be," and this certainly applies to the resources available to us as health care providers. It is imperative, then, that we make every effort to determine that the individual who best meets the requirements of the job to be done is the one assigned to do the job. As nurses, it is our responsibility to the patients we care for to ensure that they receive the best that we can offer by delegating wisely.

Effectiveness, or doing the right things, will be apparent when outcomes are what we desired them to be. Reducing the number of visits required for an outcome, healing a wound faster without infection complications, and restoring autonomy to patients who have been dependent on others to meet their basic needs are all outcomes we can plan for and achieve.

If periodic evaluation (we recommend daily) does not reveal the desired results, review each step of the process that you used to determine what needed to be done and by whom. In your analysis, be sure to consider input from other members of the team, as well as the patients.

CHECKPOINT 6-8

Review how you currently start your day. Do you set aside time for planning? Who do you include in this time? Are there ways that this could be improved, or do you feel satisfied with the information received, and are you able to plan effectively and be organized regarding what needs to be done?

CASELOAD/WORKLOAD ANALYSIS

Often it is necessary to take the time to review and practice the process of delegating and planning care. As noted previously, this is not usually a skill that is taught, other than sharing some time-honored principles regarding equality ("give everybody the same number of visits" and "don't assign cases all over the territory to one person"). Yet this initial act of planning will have a significant impact on work flow and patient and employee satisfaction.

We have included here a tool called the "Easley-Storfjell Instruments for Caseload/Workload Analysis which was designed to give home care case managers a tool to plan, monitor and evaluate nursing activities simply and effectively" (Storfjell et al., 1997). (For the full details in how to use this tool, refer to *Journal of Nursing Administration*, September 1997). The tool is designed to facilitate the supervisory process; is simple and flexible to use; includes complexity, time, and intervention measure; is compatible with other tools presently in use; and provides needed management information. The two major components of this tool are caseload analysis and workload analysis. This tool can be used for determining what needs to be done and consequently, based on what you have learned so far about delegation, who should do the particular intervention (see Exhibits 6–7 through 6–11 in Appendix 6–A).

Planning care and assigning the most appropriate person to accomplish the task may mean the difference in whether your agency remains financially viable. You as the nursing case manager hold the key. This is a significant cultural and procedural change for most RNs practicing today and will require continued support if we are to move from being slaves to a task list toward full realization of the role of the professional nurse.

> Plan your assignment, identifying your patient outcomes first! Determine which tasks you would delegate based on your team members and the planned outcomes.

> By realizing your part in determining what needs to be done, you are allowing yourself the time to practice the professional component of nursing—the implementation of the nursing process.

Plan your assignment, identifying your patient outcomes first! Determine which tasks you would delegate based on your team members and the planned outcomes.

CONCLUSION

There is so much to be done, and there are a limited number of people to do the job. How do you best plan to delegate appropriately while ensuring efficiency and effectiveness? Remember to use the nursing process: assessing, planning, implementing, and evaluating your practice. Focus on outcomes and an awareness that evaluating the achievement of those outcomes will increase nursing's visibility in all areas. Prioritize care, using the parameters of "life-threatening," "safety," and "essential to the medical/nursing plan of care," and delegate by matching the correct individual to the job based on a simple job analysis.

By realizing your part in determining what needs to be done, you are allowing yourself the time to practice the professional component of nursing—the implementation of the nursing process. Your extensive knowledge and sound judgment are the key ingredients to planning and delivering quality patient care.

ANSWERS TO CHECKPOINTS

6–1. a

6–2.

The PTA Model	Professional "The Whole Picture"	Technical "Expert Skill Level"	Amenity "The Extra Touch"
Example 1	discharge planning	passing medications	changing linen
Visible to	colleagues	physicians/patient	patient/family
How measured	length of stay	medication errors	patient surveys/ letters
Example 2	diabetic teaching in the home setting	giving insulin injection	fixing a snack for the patient's family
Visible to	patient, family, physician	patient, colleagues	family

How measured	patient behavior, follows rx	number of attempts	patient survey, response
Example 3	medication instructions	changing a dressing	changing ice water
Visible to	patient, family, physician	physician, patient, colleagues	patient, family
How measured	patient behavior	healing status	patient/family comments
Example 4	your choice		
Visible to			
How measured			

6–4.
1. Life threatening
2. Essential to care plan
3. Essential to care plan
4. Nice
5. Safety
6. Safety

6–5.
1. Assessment of AM vital signs:
   a) knowledge—how to take pulse, temperature, respirations, and blood pressures
   b) skills—math, ability to work electronic or mercury thermometer, electronic or manual sphygmomanometer
   c) traits—conscientious, friendly, organized
   d) who—NA or any trained unlicensed assistive personnel would be best choice
2. Teaching insulin administration:
   a) knowledge—process of administration, side effects and desirable effects of insulin, and the various types, sites for injection
   b) skills—ability to give a subcutaneous injection, psychomotor skill
   c) traits—calm, confident, reassuring
   d) who—LPN or RN

6–6.
1. yes
2. no, maybe to an LPN
3. yes

4. no
5. yes
6. yes

REFERENCES

American Nurses Association. 1993. Press release, October 13.

Conger, M. 1997. Delegation decision making. *The intersystem model: Integrating theory and practice.* Newbury Park, CA: Sage Publications.

Donahue, M.P. 1985. *Nursing: The finest art.* St. Louis: CV Mosby.

Evans, S.A. 1991. Delegation: What do we fear? *Heart & Lung* 20, no. 1: 17A–20A.

Hanrahan, T. 1991. New approach to caregiving. *Healthcare Forum Journal* 34: 33–37.

Health Care Financing Administration (HCFA), revised 2/21/95.

Lindeman, C. 1996. A vision for nursing education. *Creative Nursing* 2, no. 1: 5–8.

Manthey, M. 1991. A pragmatic concern. *Nursing Management* 22: 27–28.

McCloskey, J.C., and G. Bulechek. 1992. *Nursing interventions classification.* St. Louis: Mosby-Year Book.

Miller, K. 1995. Keeping the care in nursing care. *Journal of Nursing Administration* 25, no. 11: 29–32.

National Council of State Boards of Nursing. 1995. Delegation: Concepts and decision-making. *Issues.* Chicago: NCSBN, 2.

Storfjell, J., et al. 1997. Analysis and management of home health nursing caseloads and workloads. *Journal of Nursing Administration* 27, no. 9.

Urden, L., and J. Roode. 1997. Work sampling: A decision making tool for determining resources and work redesign. *Journal of Nursing Administration* 27, no. 9: 34–41.

Washburn, M. 1991. Delegation: The art of getting things done through others. *AZ Nurse Times* (January): 1.

Appendix 6–A

Caseload/Workload Analysis

Exhibit 6–7 Caseload Analysis Roster

Caseload Analysis Roster

J. LLOYD	RN	10-5-97
Name	Position	Date

Case Number/Name	Days/ Weeks Open	Priority/ Program/ Diagnosis	Complexity Rating	Time Rating	Total Visits Required This Month
1. J.C.	12	MED SURG	2	1	1
2. K.K.	2	IV	4	4	16
3. B.D.	1	MED SURG	3	2	6
4. T.D.	1	MED SURG	3	3	6
5. D.C.	8	MED SURG	4	3	6
6. B.S.	1	PSYCH	3	3	6
7. P.E.	12	PSYCH	2	2	4
8. J.S.	2	MED SURG	3	3	6
9. E.P.	1	HHA	3	1	2
10. T.S.	2	MED SURG	3	3	6
11. C.B.	1	IV	4	3	6
12. J.H.	2	PSYCH	3	2	4
13. M.G.	3	PSYCH	3	2	4
14. P.B.	8	HHA	2	1	2
15. A.D.	4	MED SURG	2	2	4
16. L.J.	7	MED SURG	3	1	1
17. F.G.	4	MED SURG	3	2	4
18. F.G.	4	PSYCH	4	3	6
19. J.I.	6	MED SURG	4	3	6
20. J.P.	2	HHA	2	1	2
Totals	83		60	45	98
Averages	4.15		3.0	2.25	

Source: Courtesy of C. Allen, Huntsville, Alabama, C. Easley, University Center, Michigan, and J. Storfjell, Berrien Springs, Michigan.

Exhibit 6–8 Complexity Classification System

COMPLEXITY CLASSIFICATION SYSTEM

Directions: Assign the highest numerical categorical rating (most difficult or complex) in which the case meets two or more of the criteria. Ratings are based on the following areas:

A. Clinical judgment/assessment   D. Psychosocial needs
B. Teaching/education needs   E. Coordination/case management
C. Physical care   F. Number and severity of problems

1. **Minimal**
    A. Requires limited judgment, use of common sense, observation of fairly predictable change in patient status
    B. Requires basic health teaching
    C. Requires simple maintenance care or no physical care
    D. Requires ability to relate to patients and families
    E. Limited involvement of only one other provider/agency
    F. Few or uncomplicated problems

2. **Moderate**
    A. Requires use of basic problem-solving techniques, ability to make limited patient assessments
    B. Requires teaching related to common health problems
    C. Requires basic rehabilitation or use of uncomplicated technical skills
    D. Requires use of basic interpersonal relationship skills
    E. Limited involvement of two other providers/agencies

3. **Great**
    A. Requires use of well-developed problem-solving skills enhanced by comprehensive knowledge of physical and social sciences, ability to make patient and family assessments
    B. Requires teaching related to illness, complications, and/or comprehensive health supervision
    C. Requires use of complicated technical skills
    D. Requires professional insight and intervention skills in coping with psychosocial needs
    E. Extensive involvement of at least one other provider/agency or coordination of several providers/agencies
    F. Several complicated problems

continues

Exhibit 6–7 continued

4. **Very great**
    A. Requires use of creativity, ability to initiate and coordinate plan for patient or family care, use of additional resources and increased supervisory support, ability to make comprehensive patient and family assessment
    B. Requires teaching related to unusual health problems or teaching/learning difficulties
    C. Requires knowledge of scientific rationale that underlines techniques and ability to modify care in response to patient/family need
    D. Requires ability to intervene in severe psychosocial problems
    E. Numerous or complicated problems requiring augmentation of the knowledge base

Source: Courtesy of C. Allen, Huntsville, Alabama, C. Easley, University Center, Michigan, and J. Storfjell, Berrien Springs, Michigan.

Exhibit 6–9 Caseload Analysis Graph

Caseload Analysis Graph

J. LLOYD	RN	10–5–97
Name	Position	Date

Complexity

Time ↓	1	2	3	4	Total Cases
4				1	1
3			1 1 1 1	1 1 1 1	8
2		1 1	1 1 1 1		6
1		1 1	1 1 1		5
Total Cases	0	4	1 1	5	2 0

	Codes		
Time	**Complexity**		**Based On**
1. Monthly, One Visit	1. Minimal	A.	Clinical judgment (assessment)
2. Biweekly	2. Moderate	B.	Teaching needs (education)
3. One–Two Times Per Week	3. Great	C.	Physical Care
4. Three–Five Times Per Week	4. Very great	D.	Psychosocial Needs
		E.	Coordination
		F.	Number & Severity of Problems

Source: Courtesy of C. Allen, Huntsville, Alabama, C. Easley, University Center, Michigan, and J. Storfjell, Berrien Springs, Michigan.

Exhibit 6–10 Time Allocation Worksheet

Time Allocation Worksheet

J. LLOYD   RN   10-5-97
Name   Position   Date

Time Available (Monthly, Yearly)	2080

Time Utilization

1. Personal Adjustments:	Hours	Totals
a. Annual Leave/Holiday	144	
b. Other SICK TIME	24	168

2. Supportive Activities:		
a. Supervisor/Nurse Conference	12	
b. Staff Meetings	24	
c. Continuing Education/Workshop	40	
d. Committees	24	
e. Other		100

3. Special Assignments:		
a. Classes		
b. Hospital Liaison	48	
c. Field Advisor		
d. Other		48

4. Field Activities (Community Service):		
a. Committees/Meetings	12	
b. Clinics		
c. Other		12

Total Scheduled Time	328
Time Available for Home Visits, Consultation, Documentation & Follow-Up	1752

Source: Courtesy of C. Allen, Huntsville, Alabama, C. Easley, University Center, Michigan, and J. Storfjell, Berrien Springs, Michigan.

Exhibit 6–11 Caseload/Workload Summary

Caseload/Workload Summary

J. LLOYD	RN	10-5-97
Name	Position	Date

A. Caseload	Total	Average
1. Total cases	20	
2. Time factor	45	2.25
3. Complexity factor	60	3.0
4. Total required home visits	95	
5. Average weeks open	83	4.15
6. Program categorical analysis *(priority/program/diagnosis)*	CASES	MONTHLY VISITS
MEDICAL/SURGICAL	10	46
INFUSION	2	22
HHA SUPERVISION	3	6
PSYCH NURSING	5	24

B. Time (monthly, yearly)	Monthly	Yearly
1. Total time available	173	2080
2. Scheduled time	27	328
3. Time available for home visit	146	1752
4. Time per home visit	1.3	1.3
5. Number of home visits possible *(divide 3 by 4)*	112	1348
6. Number of home visits required by caseload	98	1176
7. Number of home visits to new referrals	6	72
8. TOTAL required home visits	104	1248
9. Excess home visits required *(8 larger than 5)*		
10. Additional home visits possible *(5 larger than 6)*	8	100
11. Average mileage *(optional)*		

Source: Courtesy of C. Allen, Huntsville, Alabama, C. Easley, University Center, Michigan, and J. Storfjell, Berrien Springs, Michigan.

CHAPTER 7

Know Your Delegate: How Can I Determine the Right Delegate for the Job?

Ruth I. Hansten and Marilynn J. Washburn

"Sometimes we use personnel from a temporary staffing agency. Some do okay, others are frightening to work with because they just don't know what they don't know! How can I feel comfortable working with these people? The way I understand the supervision clause in the state nurse practice act, I need to know the competencies of those to whom I delegate."

So far, we've looked at what needs to be done and how the registered nurse (RN) is accountable for leading the team to achieving outcomes. Now it's time to examine the other most pivotal person in the delegation process: the delegate. For those nurses who have been used to doing all their patient care without help, trusting some of the tasks to another person is difficult at best. But it is possible to know that delegate, just as we get to know those we serve.

As an example of how we get to know those to whom we delegate, think of the family. Whether you must hearken back to your family of origin or have a family now, think about how you've found out about the strengths, weaknesses, motivation, and preferences of those in your family. If you tell a 10-year-old to clean out the kitty litter box or fix dinner while you are at work, chances are the assignment will be incomplete or, worse yet, forgotten unless you supervise on a one-to-one basis. If you go to work, and a parent or a responsible young adult son or daughter is at home during the day, chances are they won't even have to be told to do the breakfast dishes or get dinner in the oven. Within your work group, you may see variations in the need for supervision and also many different manifestations of strengths and weaknesses (more politically correct, "areas for improvement") in your staff, as well as how they fulfill the requirements of their job descriptions.

In this chapter, we'll briefly revisit the fundamental importance of state practice acts, explore job descriptions and competencies, and then identify strategies to clarify the personal expectations you may hold for your coworkers. Then we'll examine how we can best assess each delegate's strengths, weaknesses, motivation, and preferences, and how these combine to give you the information you need to match the best delegate to the work at hand.

WHO ARE THE DELEGATES?

To whom do you delegate on a daily basis?

_____

_____

_____

Here are some of the answers we've heard from nurses throughout the country:

- Student nurses
- New personnel (RNs)
- LPNs, LVNs
- Home health aides
- Respiratory therapists (or speech, occupational, or physical therapists and aides)
- Multiskilled workers (combination of roles such as therapists, nursing assistants, phlebotomists)
- Pharmacy people
- Secretaries
- Volunteers
- Social workers
- Psychologists
- Medical technologists
- Phlebotomists

Whether we are delegating to all of these people in the strict sense of the nurse practice act or asking them to do things for our clients as we coordinate the care, the same principles apply.

Those nurses who are attempting to find a workplace in which there is no delegation may need to think twice. How frequently do you find yourself in a supervisory role as a delegator?

ASSESSING THE ROLE PLAYED BY EACH DELEGATE

What was it like in your family? Did your mom do the cleaning and the cooking and the yardwork? Did Dad or Grandpa or Uncle fix the car? Roles that were standard in the "Leave It to Beaver" era are no longer useful in the present family configurations. But no matter how your family or significant-other group is formulated, each person has certain roles. The analogy of the family situation may not fit for all of us as we compare it to work life, but the new flexibility and resiliency we find in the 1990s and the next century in family or social roles are characteristics that are also required of us in our organizations as we explore new methods and caregiver job descriptions.

What was your job description in your family? It may not have been written, but it was certainly present. In our health care organizations, we must pay close attention to the written as well as the unwritten roles given to each worker.

OFFICIAL EXPECTATIONS OF EACH ROLE

Before we explore the underlying issues of what people really are expecting of each other in your workplace, let's take a closer look at the official documents. In Chapter 3, we asked you to examine the practice act for those with whom you work each day.

With the practice statutes, your organization's mission and/or values statement, and your job descriptions by your side, let's examine how these documents determine the official expectations of each role.

PRACTICE ACTS AND REGULATIONS

As we discussed in Chapter 3, the fundamental expectations of each health care worker's job are based on state regulations and rules. In assessing your delegate, these statutes are the necessary framework on which you base your supervision and assignment of the delegate. For example, New Hampshire has decided to license nursing assistants. Other states (Ohio, for example) have developed specific rules for delegation to assistive personnel. These provide a basis for the tasks that are delegated.

One concern that we have voiced as we travel across the country has been the decision of some state boards of nursing to issue a task list for assistive personnel. Although these lists are often requested by the nurses within the state, and seem to be helpful to organizations as they draw up job descriptions, we question any list that would seem to eliminate the licensed nurse's responsibility and accountability for delegating based on his or her assessment of the individual delegate's competency and of the situation and the patient at that specific time. This warning has been seconded by the National Council of State Boards of Nursing (NCSBN) (Simpkins, 1997, p. 1).

> "By creating task lists for UAPs (unlicensed assistive personnel), an unofficial scope of practice is created. . . . Training of UAPs is not based upon the notion that such individuals will be performing activities independently. . . . Task lists . . . suggest no need for delegation, as the UAP already has a list of nursing activities he or she may perform without waiting for the delegation process. But what happens when the condition of a client changes? Is the UAP with 75 hours or more of training astute enough to recognize there has been a change in the client's condition and alert the licensed nurse?"

We agree that list making can take some of the judgment away from the process, if the RN relies solely on the list as approval for any delegate to perform the task. The concerns expressed by many nurses have been twofold: can home health aides and unlicensed staff really complete these tasks safely, and where is my role as the RN if all this direct care is provided by someone else? The expansion of the home health aide's role to include medication administration, insulin injections, gastrostomy feedings, catheterizations, and dressing changes strikes a loud note of concern for many home health nurses across the country.

> The expansion of the home health aide's role to include medication administration, insulin injections, gastrostomy feedings, catheterizations, and dressing changes strikes a loud note of concern for many home health nurses across the country.

It's really not legal (or common!) for an agency to assign duties in job descriptions that are beyond the scope of legal practice as determined by the practice acts of the state. More frequently, however, agencies may interpret regulations differently or limit the scope of legal practice within their organization, or individuals may attempt to practice beyond the legal and official boundaries.

In home care, it's so tempting to stretch beyond the boundaries when there is a staffing/economic shortage and "no one is looking." The home health aide may be called on by the family member to do a task for which she is not legally prepared, but because she's the only one in the home with the family at the moment, why not reset the IV pump? Or "just get the nitro out of the bottle for George—the third bottle from the left on the shelf. . ."

The NCSBN has responded to questions of competence due to the work of the Pew Commission (see Chapter 2, "Know Your World") and public concerns regarding continued competence of the nurse and other health care workers. Their interdisciplinary and multistate work on determining competency (in conjunction with other professional boards) has been pivotal in determining the future direction of health care worker competency evaluation and will be covered in detail later in this chapter. (Don't miss it; these emerging trends will surely affect your practice!)

As you examined your state practice acts and your agency job descriptions, did you find any questions or inconsistencies? (If you are a student, ask your clinical experience agency for examples of their job descriptions.) If you found some discrepancies, take time now to answer your questions by initiating a phone call to your state regulatory board or discuss the issue with administrative personnel.

THE QUESTION OF COMPETENCY: EVALUATING AND MAINTAINING FROM A REGULATORY PERSPECTIVE

As referred to earlier in this chapter, the rapid changes in health care roles in the past decade have provided impetus for challenging the old methods used initially to assess competency of a new worker from a state licensing perspective. Technology has moved forward very quickly, new roles have developed, and delivery systems have left both regulatory agencies and the public concerned about the accountability of the individual practitioner, the employer, and regulatory boards in protecting the public. In 1994, the Nursing Practice and Education Committee of the NCSBN published the Model Nursing Practice Act and Model Nursing Administrative Rules to act as a guide to some standardization for national competency of licensed nurses (RNs, LPNs). The Pew Health Professions Commission (1995) Taskforce on Health Care Workforce Regulation recommended that states should standardize practice entry requirements and that state regulatory boards should evaluate continuing competency requirements as well as continuing or improving their disciplinary processes. The public voiced its concern in a report published by the Citizen Advocacy Center, which stated that the public cannot be confident that health care professionals remain competent as they deliver care (NCSBN, 1997a).

CHECKPOINT 7-1

❑ I have located the mission and/or values statement for my organization.
❑ I have also located the latest revised job descriptions for those I work with, as well as my job description.
❑ I have called the state board of nursing and have obtained current copies of the regulations, rules, and administrative code for RNs, LPNs (LVNs), and other health care workers on my team.

Reviewing these documents now, I can answer the following questions:

1. I know what type of health care provider is allowed to:
   a) pierce the skin to perform procedures
   b) start IVs
   c) perform the nursing process
   d) gather data for the nurse as he or she performs the assessment, nursing diagnosis, planning, and evaluation
   e) perform personal care
   f) educate the patient and family
2. I can locate several competencies in our job descriptions that reflect our mission and the values of the agency.

Regulatory boards for all professions are required to provide assurance to the public that the practitioner (whether a physician, physical therapy aide, or speech therapist) has met entry-level competency standards, that those who do not will be disciplined in a timely manner, and that this information is available to the public. To approach these responsibilities in a systematic manner, the regulatory boards must take the following steps:

1. Define competence.
2. Set standards of competence.
3. Evaluate the practitioners.
4. Identify measurable behaviors that demonstrate competence.
5. Implement a system to discipline those who fail to meet those standards (NCSBN, 1997a).

Defining Competence

> Competence is defined as "the application of knowledge and the interpersonal, decision-making, and psychomotor skills expected for the practice role, within the context of public health, safety, and welfare" (NCSBN, 1997a, p. 5).

The NCSBN further clarifies the process of demonstrating competence by establishing requirements for licensure at certain stages (see Exhibit 7–1): at entry level into practice, at renewal of licensure, when reentering practice after extended time out of practice, and after disciplinary action (NCSBN, 1997a, p. 7). Three processes, including competence development, competence assessment, and competence conduct are defined.

Exhibit 7–1 Licensure Competence Requirements

	Competence Development	Competence Assessment	Competence Conduct
Initial Entry	Graduation from an approved program	NCLEX	Board review upon application; discipline check
Continuing authority to practice at renewal	Verified practice during authorization period	Subject to random/targeted group assessment; board-identified mechanism, e.g., peer review, professional certification, professional portfolio, testing, retesting	Board review upon application; discipline check
Reentry to practice after absence	Refresher education	Retest, e.g., NCLEX	Board review upon application; discipline check
After discipline	Board-identified mechanism, e.g., continuing education	Board-identified mechanism	Board review upon application; discipline check

Source: Courtesy of the National Council of State Boards of Nursing, Inc., Chicago, Illinois.

> **"Competence Development:** the method by which a practitioner gains, maintains, or refines practice knowledge, skills, and abilities . . . through formal education program, continuing education, clinical practice, and is expected to continue throughout the practitioner's career . . .
>
> **"Competence Assessment** can be accomplished through peer review, professional portfolio, professional certification, testing, re-testing. . . . Identified triggers could be used . . . a practitioner in independent or isolated practice, multiple jobs in a short period of time, prior discipline . . .
>
> **"Competence Conduct** refers to health and conduct expectations which may be evaluated through reports from the individual practitioner, employer reports, and discipline checks" (NCSBN, 1997a, p. 7).

The Interprofessional Workgroup on Health Professions Regulation (IWHPR) *Views on the Licensure and Regulation of Health Care Professionals* (November 1996) defines competence similarly:

> Professional competence is "the application of knowledge and skills in interpersonal relations, decision-making and physical performance consistent with the professional's practice role and public health, welfare and safety considerations" (IWHPR, 1996, p. 2).

This workgroup recognizes that the standards or requirements for competence are changing over time as the practitioner specializes or as other factors (technology, overlap of scopes of practice) influence the roles. It has also discussed that uniformity throughout the states should be encouraged but not mandated, and that a distinction must be made between initial, minimum practice standards and those of ongoing competence, and that each should be measured (IWHPR, 1996, p. 6). This group includes audiology, chiropractic, medical lab technology, dentistry, dietetics, medicine, nursing, nursing home administration, occupational therapy, optometry, pharmacy, physical therapy, physician assistants, respiratory care, social work, and speech-language pathology, adding up to more than four million health care practitioners (p. 1).

Both the NCSBN and the IWHPR agree that the primary responsibility to remain current and competent lies with the individual professional and that each person must ensure his or her own competence through choosing education or other means for maintenance and improvement, as well as participating in peer review, and by acting on any conduct by other practitioners that would indicate incompetent performance.

Setting Standards: The Home Care Aide

The NCSBN has led the way in setting standards and in testing nurses by formulating and administering the NCLEX RN and NCLEX PN (LPN or LVN) examinations for entry into practice. It has based its work on research into job analysis of newly licensed nurses, both registered and licensed practical, and the input of educators and expert clinical practitioners across the United States.

As a result of OBRA 1987 (the Omnibus Budget Reconciliation Act), real strides were made in beginning to develop and track basic competencies for nursing assistants in long-term and home health care. The basic requirement of the completion of 75 hours of training and the certification of nursing assistants has established a baseline of competency that had not previously existed. This training is mandatory for all Medicare-funded agencies (long-term care and home health), and the majority of acute care facilities have adopted the requirement for all nursing assistants to be certified as well. Model nurse aide administrative rules were published by the National League for Nursing in 1990, and a Nurse Aide Competency Evaluation Program (NACEP) was established in 1991. In 1997, development began for a National Nurse Aide Assessment program, including the strengths of the Assessment Systems, Inc., National Nurse Aide Examination and the NACEP, based on 1995 research into job analysis of the reality of nurse aide roles in the United States. In the year 2000, national testing for nursing assistants should be standardized for use by all states (Wiesmiller, 1997, pp. 1–2).

The Home Care Aide Association of America proposes standards for paraprofessional titles, qualifications, and supervision in its position paper (HCA Paper, 1998). In addition to the uniform title of home care aide (HCA), the paper proposes three classifications of provider to meet the range of

> The basic requirement of the completion of 75 hours of training and the certification of nursing assistants has established a baseline of competency that had not previously existed.

In the year 2000, national testing for nursing assistants should be standardized for use by all states (Wiesmiller, 1997, pp. 1–2).

client needs in the home. Each level is accompanied by recommended training and supervision requirements.

Home Care Aide I

This position assists with environmental services such as housekeeping and homemaking services and does not provide any personal care. Training would include 16 hours of a defined curriculum with an additional 24 hours within 6 months and a recommended 6 hours of inservice per year. Supervision should occur as required by HCFA guidelines, that is, every 62 days during the provision of service to a client.

Home Care Aide II

This attendant assists the client/family with home management activities and nonmedically directed personal care (ambulation, grooming, bathing, dressing, toileting, transfer activities, activities of daily living, and special diets.) Sixty hours of educational preparation is required, with a recommended 10 hours of inservice per year. Supervision is the same as the HCA I, every 62 days.

Home Care Aide III

This assistant works under a medically supervised plan of care to assist the client/family with household management and personal care. All duties of an HCA I and II can be performed plus nonsterile wound care, assistance with medications, assistance with exercises and rehab activities, simple procedures, help with assistive devices, and appropriate client instruction. Training would require 75 hours of instruction and completion of a competency evaluation. Inservices must meet the requirements of the Health Care Financing Administration (HCFA) for home health aides in a Medicare environment. Supervision shall occur at least every 62 days (HCA Position Paper, 1998).

For RNs, three standards for competence have been developed:

- Apply knowledge and skills at the level required for a particular situation.
- Demonstrate responsibility and accountability for practice and decisions.
- Restrict and/or accommodate practice if cannot safely perform essential functions of the nursing practice role (NCSBN, 1997b).

The NCSBN's expected behaviors for individual nurses include the caveats that nurses must attain competence and must be responsible for evaluating and maintaining competence according to the current job requirements and any change in practice setting (NCSBN, 1997c). The expected behaviors for individual practitioners amplify the three general standards with specific and measurable performance; the methods or sources for maintaining that competency are included after each standard (see Exhibit 7–2).

Exhibit 7–2 Individual Competence Evaluation

---

1. Apply knowledge and skills at the level required for a particular practice situation.
   a. Identify role expectations through
      - position descriptions
      - review of literature
      - networking
      - observe, shadow another nurse
   b. Determine individual level of knowledge and skills needed for the role.
      - skills inventory
      - assessment test
      - cognitive appraisal
      - peer review
   c. Identify strengths and learning needed.
      - cognitive comparison of role expectations and individual abilities
   d. Develop and implement a learning plan.
      - job or role orientation
      - formal or continuing education
      - independent study
      - refresher course
      - precepted learning experience
      - simulated learning experience
      - other experiential learning
   e. Evaluate the effectiveness of learning and its impact on the practice role.
      - reassessment (formal or informal)
      - testing
      - peer review
      - performance evaluation
2. Exercise sound nursing judgment.
   a. Synthesize knowledge and skills relevant to client needs in carrying out the nursing role.
   b. Delegate nursing activities appropriately.
   c. Identify cause-and-effect relationships.
   d. Recognize limits of knowledge and skill.
   e. Use resources appropriately.
   f. Monitor outcomes.

---

continues

Exhibit 7–2 continued

3. Employ personal principles reflective of professional, ethical, and legal standards of practice.
   a. Articulate an awareness of regulatory, professional, and ethical standards.
      • Nursing Practice Act
      • American Nurses Association Code of Ethics
4. Ensure that client welfare prevails.
   a. Articulate respect for the social, cultural, and spiritual diversity of clients.
   b. Maintain therapeutic boundaries.
   c. Ensure that clients' needs are articulated.
5. Enable client participation in health care decisions and outcomes.
   a. Facilitate client decision making by providing information.
   b. Facilitate the identification of choices and possible outcomes.
   c. Support client decisions.
6. Participate in professional activities that support the nursing knowledge and skills needed for safe and effective practice.
   a. Develop professional growth and development criteria recognizing individual level of experience.
   b. Conduct regular evaluation of professional development needs. (See standard 1.)
   c. Select professional development activities based upon identified needs.
   d. Review own professional development portfolio.
7. Collaborate with appropriate professionals to attain desired client health care outcomes.
   a. Differentiate nursing functions from functions of other providers.
   b. Communicate with the health care team.
   c. Assess the effectiveness of referrals.
   d. Monitor outcomes by assessment of the impact of collaboration on health promotion, maintenance, and illness prevention for the client.
8. Recognize the relationship of personal cognitive and functional abilities to safe and effective practice.
   a. Identify abilities necessary for the essential functions of a nursing practice role.
   b. Identify accommodations needed to ensure safe and effective practice.
   c. Limit practice based on abilities and accommodations.
9. Demonstrate responsibility and accountability for nursing practice decisions and actions.
   a. Identify the legal and ethical obligations of the profession.
   b. Answer for one's own actions and decisions.

Source: Reprinted from "Individual Competence Evaluation," *Assuring Competence: Attachment One,* pp. 1–6, © 1997, National Council State Boards of Nursing, Chicago, Illinois.

ACCOUNTABILITY FOR COMPETENCE

Although we have already established that each practitioner, no matter what role, is accountable for maintaining his or her own competence, the NCSBN has offered some guidelines regarding the accountability of the regulatory boards, the employer, the individual, and the educator. Figure 7–1 demonstrates the complexity of maintaining safe practice of a myriad of practitioners from entry into practice through the rapid changes in practice inherent in health care today. The model places the consumer of care in the center, emphasizing the real reason behind this focus on competence.

Nurse Aide Registries

Prior to the implementation of OBRA 1987, there was no means of "tracking" unlicensed assistive personnel in terms of disciplinary action. Many home health agencies fell prey to the traveling nursing assistant who would abuse the system, then move on to the next agency. Home care clients, particularly the elderly and infirm, were vulnerable to care by a home health aide hired with a criminal history unknown to the employing agency. Theft and abuse became real concerns, with no mechanism in place to alert hiring agencies to the background of the potential employee. In recent years, due to the requirement of certification for nursing assistants, many states have developed "registries" that provide a tracking mechanism for the assistant's work history, criminal record, if any, and complaints resulting in disciplinary action. The state of Indiana added home health aides to its registry in 1997, as many other states had already done. Boards of nursing or departments of health have become the disciplinary body for these personnel, helping to assure the nurse and the client that the assistant is competent and reliable.

JOB DESCRIPTIONS

As described in the previous discussion about accountabilities for the employer, organizations must incorporate state standards into institutional policies. These policies, coming in the form of job descriptions, have many structures and may be based on competencies or standards, performance criteria, the nursing process, or specific required behaviors or responsibilities. These documents may double as competency checklists or as performance review tools. Job descriptions may be considered a type of contract between the employee and the management team to perform a given role as specified in the written information, which will include such topics as the necessary qualifications, reporting relationships, scope of responsibilities, and a position summary discussing the overall role. In unionized environments, the union contract for each type of worker will also influence

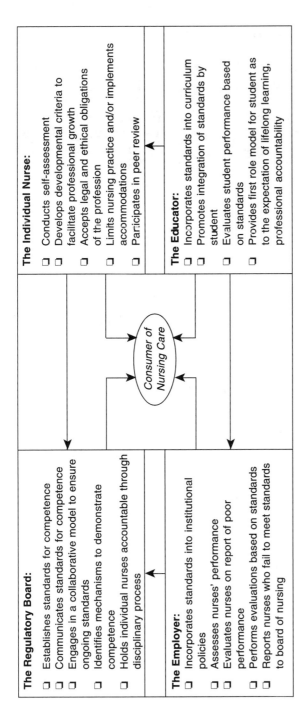

The Regulatory Board:

☐ Establishes standards for competence
☐ Communicates standards for competence
☐ Engages in a collaborative model to ensure ongoing standards
☐ Identifies mechanisms to demonstrate competence
☐ Holds individual nurses accountable through disciplinary process

The Employer:

☐ Incorporates standards into institutional policies
☐ Assesses nurses' performance
☐ Evaluates nurses on report of poor performance
☐ Performs evaluations based on standards
☐ Reports nurses who fail to meet standards to board of nursing

Consumer of Nursing Care

The Individual Nurse:

☐ Conducts self-assessment
☐ Develops developmental criteria to facilitate professional growth
☐ Accepts legal and ethical obligations of the profession
☐ Limits nursing practice and/or implements accommodations
☐ Participates in peer review

The Educator:

☐ Incorporates standards into curriculum
☐ Promotes integration of standards by student
☐ Evaluates student performance based on standards
☐ Provides first role model for student as to the expectation of lifelong learning, professional accountability

Figure 7–1 Competence Accountability. *Source:* Courtesy of the National Council of State Boards of Nursing, Inc., Chicago, Illinois.

CHECKPOINT 7-2

Pat reviewed his state practice act for LPNs and found that nothing was specified about ventilator management. It also stated that the LPN acts as an assistant to the RN in completing the nursing process. However, he noted that the new LPN was assigned to care for a ventilator-dependent six-month-old, providing night relief for the mom. He wondered if this was legal.

See the end of the chapter for the answers.

---

the roles played by each union employee, and should be in agreement with the job description.

For our purposes here, turn now to the job summaries and lists of duties or responsibilities you've assembled from your clinical areas. Generally, RN job descriptions will contain such descriptors as:

- provides patient care using the nursing process
- assists in coordinating patient care activities
- acts as a communication liaison among community resources and with physicians
- functions in a leadership role
- is accountable for the standards of nursing care
- assesses, plans, implements, evaluates, teaches

As organizations revise care delivery systems, job descriptions for the RN are beginning to include such statements as:

- delegates appropriately and directs the activities of other team members
- effectively supervises team members
- evaluates care given by team members and gives feedback
- actively engages in solving problems in the organization

Job descriptions of assistive personnel reflect their dependence on the leadership of the RN:

- works under the supervision of the RN and receives written and/or oral assignments and direction
- gathers data for planning the care of the team's patients
- reports appropriately and in a timely manner to the RN who is accountable for the care of those patients
- performs various patient care and attendant activities under the direction of the RN
- participates in planning, implementing, evaluating, and modifying the plan of care by sharing information and reviewing care administered.

Duties or specific responsibilities are often outlined. These lists will help you determine what tasks can be assigned to a specific delegate once competency and understanding of the assignment are ascertained.

Examples of some of the duties listed for assistive personnel may be:

- performs oral/nasal suctioning
- measures and records intake, output, and vital signs
- performs tasks such as bathing, feeding, and hygienic care
- observes patient carefully for significant changes
- assists with bowel and bladder retraining

If the job descriptions in your agency do not reflect what is actually happening in your department or facility with your patients, ask some questions!

VALIDATED COMPETENCIES: THE ORGANIZATIONAL PERSPECTIVE

Many of you may have enjoyed the opportunity to supervise the completion of a competency checklist for a peer, an orienting employee, or assistive personnel. Often attached to the job description or as a part of the orientation packet, these checklists are based on what the state law says about scope of practice, how the organization interprets those rules within its system in the form of job descriptions, and the education or orientation attended by the employee. The portion of the state regulatory information that describes the subject matter for the educational program, as well as standards and competencies expected for the beginning graduate of an educational program, may provide a starting point for competency checklists for new employees.

For an example of what is commonly required in some assistive roles, let's review the state of Arizona's project in which the Arizona Department of

Education (1985) published a validated competency list for nursing assistants, LPNs, and associate degree RNs. Fifty competencies were expected for the beginning nursing assistant, each divided into more specific behaviors. In this document, nursing assistants were expected to be competent in such skills as:

- collecting sputum and stool specimens
- testing urine using routine methods
- applying protective restraints, Ace bandages, flexible abdominal binders
- applying ostomy appliances and irrigating established colostomies
- taking vital signs
- giving a cleansing enema

These competencies are consistent with the Standards of Function for the Nurse Aide published by the NCSBN in 1990. The NCSBN warns that enemas may be delegated to nursing assistants but that sterile procedures should not be delegated (NCSBN, 1990). These guidelines have been a basis for the adoption of rules by states. Although multistate licensure is being discussed (see Chapter 3, "Know Your Practice"), it appears at the writing of this book that each state will likely continue to maintain overall responsibility for interpreting the statute; issuing rules that explain the statute; and being accountable for granting licenses, dealing with complaints, and performing disciplinary acts.

Validated competencies (Arizona Department of Education, 1985) for LPNs numbered 72, and included such skills as:

- sterile technique
- administering medications and IVs, including calculating infusing rate, regulating gavages, and irrigating using previously inserted gastrointestinal tubes
- timing contractions and measuring and recording fetal heart tones
- performing normal newborn care
- recognizing substance abuse in the child and adolescent

Documenting Competencies

Seminar participants often ask us clarifying questions such as, "Mrs. Fujini's bowel was perforated when Sally gave her that enema, so how can I support or document that I was correct in asking Sally to perform that procedure?" When you are familiar with the job descriptions of a home health aide in your agency, and when you also know that Sally was "checked off" on giving a cleansing enema, the job descriptions and competency checklist are your documentation. If Sally had also been performing enemas without problems, and if in fact you recently observed Sally's technique when you happened to make a home visit while Sally was performing this skill, even better! Because you had not assessed any potential problem with the patient, your decision to ask Sally to give Mrs. Fujini the enema followed the delegation process to the letter.

Following the nurse practice act requirements in many states, agencies provide documentation of competencies specific to each client. Training and task performance is often client specific in home care and must be documented for each case. JoAnn may be able to administer insulin every morning to 85-year-old Mrs. Hughes, but may not be able to mix the two types of insulin required for Mr. Smith when he is admitted to your care on Friday.

THE IMPACT OF THE MISSION ON JOB ROLES

We've spent a fair amount of time focusing on job responsibilities and the details of roles within your team. Earlier in the chapter, we asked you to determine how the mission was reflected in your job descriptions.

As discussed in Chapter 4, a mission statement may include such phrases as the following:

- providing high-quality, cost-effective, integrated health services that support independence and respond to the needs of individuals, families, and the community
- promoting wellness, absence of disease, comfort, education, and independence by the collaborative health care team, in an environment that is responsive to the needs of the public, as well as being fiscally accountable and responsible

Values statements may include such concepts as:

- the respect and dignity afforded patients, the public, and employees, with an emphasis on communication skills
- a culture of professional growth
- proactive leadership in shaping change

Examine your facility's mission and/or values. Do you see an emphasis on collaboration, high quality, cost-effectiveness? Is the quality of personal relationships among the interdisciplinary team inferred, if not directly stated? If so, you'll recognize the related performance criteria in the job descriptions translated as:

- demonstrates positive interpersonal communication skills that enhance patient care and the functioning of the interdisciplinary team
- uses assertive language in interpersonal relationships
- participates actively in solving problems
- maintains confidentiality
- effectively uses human and material resources in planning and implementing care
- responds positively to guidance and feedback
- performs assigned work without discrimination on the basis of age, sexual preference, national origin, race, economic position, religion, disability, or disease

Why are we spending time detailing these parts of the official roles? Because you, as the supervisory RN, must understand fully the impact of the job descriptions and other organizational policies as you match jobs to delegates and evaluate their performance. This information is necessary not only for making assignments but for giving feedback to your team.

CHECKPOINT 7-3

You've been orienting a new RN on your team. He seems to be doing quite well clinically but has been avoiding performing the care of infants who are HIV-positive or are the babies of "crack" mothers (cocaine abusers). How does this employee's performance reflect that he is not fulfilling his job description?

See the end of the chapter for the answers.

UNOFFICIAL EXPECTATIONS OF EACH ROLE

In addition to the official expectations based on the state laws or regulations are the real expectations within your agency. If there is a discrepancy between what the state regulations say, what the job descriptions explain, and what really happens, there is a serious problem. Workers should not be performing beyond their roles in any case. Keep in mind the supervisory and evaluative responsibilities that are present in your state nurse practice act and that were discussed in Chapter 3.

> Often, the "unmet expectations" that cause anger and uncomfortable team relationships stem from silent "unofficial expectations."

However, often other "gray areas" concern what each individual may expect of his or her coworkers. For example, if you as an RN expect that the home health aide will telephone you immediately if the patient is complaining that the current pain control isn't effective, and if that doesn't happen, you will be justifiably angry. The operational definition of anger is "unmet expectations." If a home health aide expects you as an RN will be physically involved in helping him or her with hygienic care on a regular basis and you aren't doing that, he or she will be angry also. Although there tends to be more of a separation of duties in the home health arena, some common issues plague us in terms of working relationships:

- Whose patients are these, really?
- Who communicates what to whom, when?
- Who really has the authority to "make" you do what you are asked to do?
- Who should clean up the equipment and restock the supply closet in the office?

Understanding what each job entails, discussing your expectations within the group, and being realistic about what's reasonable to expect will go a long way toward promoting better teamwork.

There is a practical strategy for resolving these issues of "unofficial expectations." Each group must define its expectations of the other groups and discuss them in an open forum. We suggest that this be done in a staff meeting. If you are unable to do this in a more public and less threatening way (such as in a team meeting), then you must clarify expectations on a personal basis. For example, consider the past few times you've been angry or frustrated with a coworker. What expectation wasn't met by that coworker? It's time to clear the air and clarify what you expect.

For example, you've oriented an LPN to the client's plan of care and clarified your expectations. The client is an 80-year-old diabetic with an infected leg ulcer who likes to be seen by 8 AM as she is an early riser. You instruct the LPN that 8U of insulin is to be given, and tell her to change the dressing with algenate. When you check back with the client later in the day, you find that the LPN did not arrive until after 10 AM, delaying the client's breakfast beyond her usual time. She also changed the dressing with gauze, having forgotten the algenate. The client is upset, and requests that only you come from now on. What do you say when you follow up with the LPN? (See Chapter 8 on assertive communication.)

You may wish to use Checkpoint 7–4 in your staff meeting, sharing the responses. You'll find that some people focus on the very concrete tasks ("passes medications"), some will discuss issues that relate to organizational values ("shows respect to the public and coworkers; calls me by name"). You may wish to ask the questions in Checkpoint 7–4 of each other within your work group on a personal basis.

The following list shows some of the most common responses RNs and certified nurses' aides (CNAs) have given concerning their expectations of RNs:

• Competence
• Do your job
• Be a troubleshooter
• Be an advocate
• Call workers by name
• Respect team members
• Communicate progress and inform team
• Give clear and complete instructions
• Be courteous
• Teach other team members
• Assess
• Evaluate
• Plan
• Chart
• Trust others
• Organize care
• Give feedback
• Give clear, concise report

The following are some expectations of assistants reported by assistants and RNs:

• Respect each other
• Find out answers if you have questions
• Communicate progress, changes
• Take initiative, but ask questions

CHECKPOINT 7–4

(Fill in the blanks now for your own information, and plan to do this exercise as a group.)

I expect RNs to _____

I expect LPNs (LVNs) to _____

I expect home health aides to _____

I expect personal care attendants to _____

I expect the secretary to _____

I expect ___ (fill in the blank) to _____

I expect our boss to _____

On a person-to-person basis:

1. Have I been performing the way you expect me to?
2. Are there things I have or haven't been doing that some-times bother you?
3. In what ways am I doing a great job?
4. In what ways could I improve the way I do my job?
5. How could I help you perform your job better by the way I do mine?
6. Have you been disappointed about anything in your job?

- Be an extra pair of hands
- Be honest
- Trust
- Be motivated
- Follow RN orders
- Be positive and cooperative
- Work as team

- Be part of problem solving
- Organize work
- Beds
- Baths
- Vital signs
- Don't talk to patient about diagnosis or teach
- Don't eat the client's food

Talking about these personal expectation issues may seem like a risky process. However, not much is gained without risk. Throughout this process, you will find yourself understanding each other more fully. You'll clarify what each other's jobs should be, and you'll find many fewer conflicts getting in the way of excellent care of your patients or clients. Change frustration and anger to relief as you deal with those trying situations that make your job more difficult than it has to be!

ASSESSING THE DELEGATE'S STRENGTHS

Think back to your family. Do you know the strengths of your family members? Who was best at doing the vacuuming? Certainly you had years to get to know each other, and this lengthy process is not always available in health care. In each case, as we look at assessing the qualities of the delegate, we'll focus on how to determine the competencies of those you work with daily and those who are "short-term" help.

Before we consider methods of assessing strengths, it's important to remember why we are doing this. Think now of one reason you'd like to know your delegate's best qualities.

_____

_____

Perhaps asking this basic question seems too obvious. When we ask nurses around the country this question, it's common for participants to consider the good of the patients but rare for them to consider the positive effects for themselves or their delegates. You may have come up with other reasons, but we think several are compelling for all of us engaged in treating or caring for patients.

> First, the most obvious reason to consider your delegate's strengths is that when people are using their strengths to perform their care duties, the

> outcomes for the clients are the most effective.
> Second, people grow when their strengths are
> recognized and used for the good of patient care.
> And third, your ability to lead is enhanced be-
> cause there are fewer needless worries each day
> when people are working within their areas of
> competency.

Let's look at a couple of examples.

1. Do you remember the last time your supervisor gave you an evaluation or yearly performance review? What do you remember most about it? We are willing to bet you remember the competencies your supervisor checked as "needs improvement." Human beings tend to remember the critical before they remember the positive. Think back, though, about a well-earned compliment you were given. Perhaps your boss or colleague said, "I've noticed that in your caseload you are especially effective in working with families of those who are dying. All of us are impressed with your ability to communicate clearly with them and help them through the grief process." That feels pretty good, doesn't it? And the next time you take care of a similar case, you'll find that you redouble your efforts to do a fine job. You may even think more about the methods you use to be so effective and find that you are able to help others apply the same principles.

2. The Visiting Nurse Service employed a nurse who had been quite negative in her outlook for years. She had been married now for the third time to a person with a substance abuse problem. But she finally realized there was a pattern to her life and joined Al-Anon (a program for the families of alcohol-dependent persons). She learned about her codependent tendencies and further delved into all the literature about alcoholism and the community support available. Because of her specialized knowledge, she became the "group expert" on alcoholism, from treatment of the delirium tremens to the best programs for after-care in the area. As she found that her home life was improving and found herself to be a valued member of the team, her entire attitude changed. She was "making lemonade" out of the lemons she had collected during her life, and it helped her grow as she shared from her experience.

The Delegate's Strengths: Benefits and Warnings

We are clear on all the reasons why strengths are important. When you reflected on how you are using your own strengths and those of your delegates, you may have wondered how to discover the "gems" under the rough-hewn exteriors of those with whom you work. How do we determine those sterling qualities? As we discussed in our family example, we determine them from what we observe and hear. You see that Bob is a good cook and enjoys doing the cooking. Within your work group, if you have not been able to observe strengths in action, then ask. You may first ask someone, "What do you like to do best?" This is often a good indication of what that person believes he or she does best. If you haven't received enough information yet, ask the delegate, "What do you feel the most comfortable doing? What are you best at doing?"

For "short-term" workers such as temporary personnel, or others you may work with only for a short period of time, remember to just come out with it. Ask them what they are good at. Most people know.

A caveat is necessary, however. We have spent time focusing on the strengths, and we have established that they certainly are important. However, if people always do what they feel comfortable doing, they will not grow. Be careful not to get into a rut and allow people to become apathetic from a lack of challenge. (We realize that health care is not a boring, slow job and is full of challenges daily, but we felt it necessary to remind people of the potential hazards of becoming too comfortable in one way of doing things.)

Another warning: Some people perceive that they are skilled at tasks or processes, but you may observe that they aren't. The RN who is supervising the group cannot afford to take at face value a statement of "I'm good at doing brain surgery." You may also find yourself falling into the trap of the "halo or horn" effect. The person who seems to be an all-out super crackerjack cannot be perfect in all areas. The delegate whose personality rubs you the wrong way is not really the devil in disguise; he or she has at least one or two strengths. All of the assessment data regarding the delegate, the patient situation, and the work that needs to be completed are essential for your decision making.

ASSESSING THE DELEGATE'S WEAKNESSES

The potential weaknesses of the delegates are the most frightening aspect for the RNs we've talked with across the United States. They are afraid that "their license is on the line" and that they will be losing their licensure if a mistake is made by one of their delegates.

Remember that supervision means you will provide guidance for the accomplishment of a nursing task or activity, with initial direction and periodic inspection of the actual task or activity, and that the total nursing care of the individual remains the responsibility and accountability of the RN. The burden of determining the competency of the person who will perform the work and of evaluating the situation remains with the licensed nurse (NCSBN, 1990).

So it is very important to determine a delegate's competency, strengths, and weaknesses. We have already addressed the state regulations limiting practice, the

---

CHECKPOINT 7-5

How then, are you using your own and your coworkers' strengths in the way you divide and apportion your work? Think about your last week of work and a few examples of how your delegates' strengths were used effectively.

If you were unable to come up with situations, spend a few moments thinking about the strengths of each of your co-workers and how they could be used for positive future impact.

---

job descriptions of your agency, and the competency checklists that may be used by your organization. These are all excellent guides for your decision making.

At this point, however, the RN must determine the competency of that one individual for a specific set of circumstances for one day, one shift, one caseload. There is no exact scientific formula for this. Once again, your decision rests on your nursing judgment.

There is not a profession on this earth that allows its practitioners to avoid making these kinds of decisions. An attorney's decision to plea bargain or to try for acquittal for his client based on his knowledge of the situation affects all involved. An accountant's decision to try a new tactic to use impending tax laws to the client's best advantage, drawing up a limited partnership agreement, is based on her best judgment of the future and her past education and experience. As a professional RN, you are called on daily to make these types of decisions many times. You decide when to call the physician, when to approach the family for a code status, how to plan therapy for the newly diagnosed schizophrenic, how much pain medicine to administer to reduce the pain of the home-bound cancer patient.

For the short-term worker within your organization, the person you don't know well, you may ask the following ques-

> Remember that supervision means you will provide guidance for the accomplishment of a nursing task or activity, with initial direction and periodic inspection of the actual task or activity, and that the total nursing care of the individual remains the responsibility and accountability of the RN.

tions: "What do you feel you are best at doing? Have you completed these kinds of procedures before at our agency? There is a new procedure written up for this task. I'll get it for you and we'll go over it. Do you have any questions now? Let me tell you about our patients in more detail. I'm on this beeper if you have any questions later on."

For those colleagues who are within your work force on a general basis, how have you assessed their weaknesses in the past? You may be aware of their weaknesses from several sources:

- from personal observation as you have supervised them or followed them
- from the competency checklist
- from asking them for input as to what they feel uncomfortable doing or what they need to learn more about
- from the "grapevine"

Let's look first at the "grapevine." It can be valuable in making you aware of a potential need for increased supervision if you have heard that someone is "a quart low on energy." However, beware of the grapevine. Most nurses have heard of situations in which a new staff member was branded by a person who didn't like students or didn't approve of some aspect of the staff member's personality, and spread a negative image across the organization. Remember, an open but observant and listening attitude is the most useful.

This kind of communication will reap rewards in the future. For example, a new graduate may be frightened to death of patients with tracheotomies, but after being guided in caring for them, may be the most careful and the most well prepared to work with that type of client. Use your experience and judgment; ask people if they are uncomfortable with any aspects of their assignments. For example, if your caseload includes a paraplegic, what will you ask the personal care attendant on your team who is making the visit? "Have you ever worked with a paralyzed patient before? Let's review his needs and talk about what to look for when you do his bath."

Use your competency checklists and job descriptions! Find a place for team members to keep them so they can be responsible for having them available for your discussions.

What about the problems that you've seen with delegates because you've followed them, or observed or heard their actions? These shortcomings generally fall into the following categories:

> 1. They don't understand what is expected of them.
> 2. They don't understand that their perception of their activities does not fit within your acceptable parameters for behavior.
> 3. They may have unmet educational needs.
> 4. They may need more supervision and guidance.
> 5. They may not care.

Let's look at each of these underlying reasons for performance weaknesses, often aptly called "areas for improvement and growth," and determine your course of action with each.

1. They don't understand what is expected of them. Understanding expectations is essential. Although we have covered this in detail previously in this chapter, when someone doesn't know that it isn't okay to use the client's phone to make long distance calls, he or she needs to be told. Some people truly need to be told things that we may suspect "should be" common knowledge. Remember, don't "should" on each other. Clear communication about your expectations is essential. "I expect you to make phone calls on your own time, and to use a phone card for long distance in emergencies only."

2. They don't understand that their perception of their activity and your assessment do not directly coincide. As we discussed when we evaluated delegates' strengths, delegates may not recognize that they are not doing their job the way you believe it should be done. When you find this is the problem, remember to focus on outcomes. Does it make any difference to the patient outcome that John does the bath in a different order, or that Pat's charting on the intake and output chart is done after break? It may or may not be significant. Just realize that some of us tend to be a bit "set in our ways" and have difficulty seeing things done differently, even if it doesn't affect the outcome. Be clear about what you expect and why it makes a difference.

If patient welfare or safety is involved, immediate action must be taken. If you have reason to suspect the home health aide is abusing the client, you need to alert the manager of the agency immediately and take appropriate action.

3. They don't know, understand, or have sufficient information. Some weaknesses may be educational needs. Perhaps the delegate doesn't want to care for AIDS patients because he or she is afraid. If the staff member understands more about the transmission of the disease and attends the mandatory education about HIV, there will be a change in the delegate's behavior and acceptance of the assignment.

4. They need additional guidance and supervision. As we discussed in our example of family roles, some members of our family or social group need more supervision than others. The spouse who goes to the grocery store and picks up the children at the soccer game may need exact directions and a specific list of items to buy at the supermarket. The roommate who pays the electricity bill may need a reminder when it is due, whereas other roommates may clean out the tub without being reminded. Some of your delegates will take more energy than others in terms of your time and observation.

Remember that there is a bell curve of performance. The majority of people are on the competent level. Some are overachieving "stars" who go above and beyond the most highly competent and superior ratings in their job descriptions. But a few waver at the marginal performance line. These individuals cause us the most consternation, but we can't eliminate the possibility that we'll always have one or two (or more) within our staff, so we must address how to deal with these marginal performers.

Working effectively with marginal performers is one of the most challenging aspects of supervising others, but this offensive task is an essential accountability within the supervision process.

As we talk with nurses across this country, they often tell us that the most difficult part of their work life is dealing with this type of delegate. They often express anger at the managers: "Why doesn't the manager fire this person! She (he) should know that this person isn't performing well!" We then ask, "What have you done about the problem?" Part of your professional role is as patient advocate. You are required to report and to deal with any behavior that would adversely affect your charges: your patients. The nurse manager or other supervisory person must be given the exact data that will assist him or her in dealing effectively with the performance problem. As an RN who supervises others, you must confront any performance that does not fall within legal parameters or job descriptions, or could be detrimental to the patient. Changing the bed in a certain way may be just a personal preference issue, but leaving a confused patient on the bedside commode unattended while the aide makes a sandwich in the kitchen is unacceptable from a safety standpoint. Again focusing on potential outcomes, how will these behaviors affect the patient care or organizational goals?

> Working effectively with marginal performers is one of the most challenging aspects of supervising others, but this offensive task is an essential accountability within the supervision process.

As we'll discuss in more detail in Chapter 10, RNs must give their perceptions of the performance to the delegate and send on any information that will be necessary to the manager involved in formal performance counseling.

Let's discuss a difficult situation: that of the staff member who is wavering on the line of competent/incompetent while being assisted to either improve his or her performance or be counseled into another position (one perhaps that won't involve live human beings!). How does the RN supervise this delegate? Very carefully! This person will not be assigned tasks or processes that have been problematic in the past and may need to be partnered with a competent person who understands the limitations. The RN must then be very careful to check on the progress of this delegate, observing, assessing, asking questions, and obtaining report information from the delegate more frequently. This type of staff member poses special problems when the staffing is low. Although rare, this situation challenges RNs to use all their creative and innovative approaches to encourage the marginal delegate to use all of his or her strengths for the best possible patient care and safety.

5. They may not seem to care. This brings us to another parameter we need to be aware of as we assess the delegates: What makes them tick? What motivates them to do their job? We'll explore the delegate's motivation next.

ASSESSING THE DELEGATE'S MOTIVATION

How often have you traveled home from your workplace, wondering why Sue or John even showed up to work today? Why do some staff members bother to come to work when their apparent lack of commitment and energy forces us to push and pull them through the day?

Return to your past knowledge of Maslow's hierarchy of needs (Maslow, 1970). In clinical situations, we know that if a family needs food and shelter, these basic needs must be satisfied before we educate them about their child's diabetes, for example. In the work situation, we may all come to work for different reasons each day, and often these reasons are related to where we are currently functioning on the hierarchy of needs. Exhibit 7–3 shows these different levels of need and your possible response, as a supervisor, to employees functioning at these levels.

The first step of the hierarchy of needs is that of safety and security needs. Few of us are independently wealthy, and most of us certainly would notice if our paychecks were to disappear. But most of us have other reasons for working in the type of job we choose. Coworkers who are working only for their paycheck so that they can put food on the table and keep a roof over their heads will need to be supervised differently from those who chose health care because they feel an affinity for it. If the only thing that motivates people is getting that paycheck, they need to know that they must fulfill their job expectations for performance to remain employed. Although this may seem to be a "hard-nosed" point to empha-

Exhibit 7–3 Levels of Employee Needs and Supervisory Responses

Functioning Level	Your Response	Examples
Self-fulfillment	Encourage involvement in department functioning, variety, and new challenge Keep an eye on vision and purpose	Volunteering to head a new committee to discuss new care delivery design
Ego	Positive feedback (necessary for all motivation stages)	Saying thanks Detailed feedback
Social or belonging	Use social strengths for patients who need it, may need to observe progress closely	Potlucks, celebrations of the outcomes of a difficult case
Safety and security	Safe, secure climate; close supervision	Clear expectations Security guards in parking lot

Source: Reprinted from R. Hansten and M. Washburn, Know Your Delegate, *Clinical Delegation Skills*, p. 220, © 1998, Aspen Publishers, Inc.

size, as an RN supervising others, you must be prepared for such employees. They must know that if they do not fulfill the job requirements, they won't get their paycheck.

When there has been a recent reduction in force, or layoff of nursing personnel, many staff are concerned only about taking care of the safety and security needs. Few nurses will volunteer for a special committee or become excited about a quality management program when they are worried about having a job at all. Keep in mind each person's individual reason for being at work, and use this to your best advantage for the best patient care. As staff become more confident that their basic needs will be fulfilled, they may catch the excitement and climb to a higher level of motivation. We all waver in our motivational levels in a manner related to our personal life and how we perceive our impact on the world through work and other institutions.

The second level of motivation is that of social or affiliative needs. Many of us find fulfillment from the personal relationships we enjoy in health care, whether with each other or with those we serve. The staff who are significantly motivated at this level may be those who love to talk and to organize the baby showers or social events. They may hold very dear the time that they have to interact with their clients on a one-to-one basis. This staff member may be the perfect person to assign to the elderly client who requires more interpersonal time. He or she may also be buddied with a coworker who is very goal directed but gives the affiliative-need partner much positive feedback.

CHECKPOINT 7-6

1. You have noted that Joy, a new LPN (LVN), telephoned a physician for orders yesterday. This is not recognized as the LPN's role in this organization. You realize that Joy:
   a) may not know the role expectations in this agency.
   b) may have done this in past jobs and feels competent to do so, no matter what you say about this.
   c) probably won't do this again, and you decide not to mention it to her.
   d) will need to be told about the expectations and that you may also need to give feedback to the nurse manager, depending on her response.

2. Zachary, the secretary, has made several errors today as new referrals are being admitted to your agency. You, as supervisory nurse to Zachary, decide to:
   a) wait until the agency director of nurses hears about the problem.
   b) tell the director of nurses.
   c) find out if Zach's problem is an educational need.
   d) recommend action to the director after first discussing it with Zach.

3. Patty, an experienced personal care attendant, sighs loudly as she bends over to make the bed at one of the client's homes, disturbing the family. She also seems to need constant direction. You decide to:
   a) let it go. She's not your problem.
   b) ask her about her behavior. Find out if she's having back trouble, and if she knows her job description.
   c) determine why she is having trouble finding things to do when so much work needs to be done, without accusing her or putting her down.
   d) discuss your findings with her and ask her for some ideas for solutions. Share your conversations with the supervisor.

4. A temporary agency home health aide has just come to work with you on your team today. Your nurse manager

had given you the feedback that this person had made three errors during her last assignment here and is being observed by her agency. How will you assess what this person will be able to do today?

a) ask her for her competency checklist.

b) tell her you're working with her and that's that.

c) question her carefully on what she's done before, what she feels comfortable doing. Arrange to be available for specific checkup times for assessing and assisting.

d) call the supervisor and demand a competent person to care for your patients.

See the end of the chapter for the answers.

The third level of motivation is that of ego needs for self-respect or status leading to self-esteem. Staff who would like recognition and job growth may be motivated from this level. As RNs assign work or supervise staff at the ego level, the use of positive feedback, opportunities to be involved in task forces, recognition in the form of clinical ladders, and educational opportunities may be the most energizing. A CNA who is functioning primarily at this level may want to care for patients who have different diagnoses, which he or she can research and use in their care.

A note of caution here: When nurses or other health care professionals identify themselves too closely with their job description, so that they become interchangeable with what they do (i.e., what I do equals who I am and my value as a human being), and then their job roles change, they will be most disturbed. If asked who you are, how do you respond? Do you immediately think, "I'm John Jones, an oncology home health RN"? You as a human being have value beyond what you do for employment or as a profession. Be aware of this tendency when changes rock your workplace, and be especially good to yourself as you cope with the changes.

The fourth level of Maslow's hierarchy is that of self-fulfillment or self-actualization. We hope that, as professionals, many of you are doing your job because you are aware of how your role affects the lives of others and that you are aware of how you affect your own growth and the growth of those you serve by what you do. Staff who are motivated at this stage are a joy to work with because they often help you, as supervising RN, look beyond the daily frustrations to the real reasons that you do your job.

YOUR RESPONSIBILITY FOR THE "GENERAL CLIMATE" OF MOTIVATION

Whether you are currently working in the role of a student nurse, staff RN, charge nurse, or nurse manager in any portion of the health care system, you have an influence on the environment in which you work. It is true that you can't be in control of others' behavior, but you can behave in a way that will affect others positively.

Multiple studies have been done—within health care, with nurses, and in business—about what motivates workers.

Research has also proven a positive correlation between productivity, commitment to the organization, and job satisfaction. Specific leadership behaviors have been proven to directly influence productivity, commitment, and job satisfaction. The critical behaviors of "inspiring a shared vision, enabling others to act, modeling the way, challenging the process, and encouraging the heart are all positively related" (McNeese-Smith, 1992, p. 396) to the results you want to achieve in establishing a climate of motivation in your team.

Your communication with others is fundamental to building relationships in your facility. When you tackle problems with a proactive, positive outlook, others want to be around you. (How many people follow leaders, or want to be around colleagues, who consistently express feelings of defeat, discouragement, and gloom?)

> Specific leadership behaviors have been proven to directly influence productivity, commitment, and job satisfaction. The critical behaviors of "inspiring a shared vision, enabling others to act, modeling the way, challenging the process, and encouraging the heart are all positively related" (McNeese-Smith, 1992, p. 396) to the results you want to achieve in establishing a climate of motivation in your team.

A climate of achievement is promoted when everyone understands what he or she is expected to do and where he or she is going. Reinforcing expectations, making goals clear, and encouraging everyone to participate in decision making as much as possible will provide a basis for clear and open communication. With that open communication, trust will develop. Reminding people of why they are doing what they are doing (your mission) will energize them as they recognize how what they are doing contributes to the group's goals. Positive feedback (discussed in detail in Chapter 10) is one of the most powerful motivators in your formulary.

In assessing the quality of work life in home care, a study in 1994 (Hood and Smith, p. 45) concluded that home-makers (employed in a home health agency to provide house cleaning, personal care, and other relatively unskilled tasks) demonstrated an in-creased sense of involvement, increased job satisfaction, and a propensity to remain with the organization when

> The RN can do a great deal to establish a sense of "personal concern" for the members of the team that is highly motivating and sustaining.

the agency leaders showed personal concern. This concern included such con-cepts as trust, confidence, cooperation, personal interest, and personal recogni-tion. In brief, the RN can do a great deal to establish a sense of "personal concern" for the members of the team that is highly motivating and sustaining.

ASSESSING THE DELEGATE'S PREFERENCES

You may be surprised that it's taken us so long to get to the point of assessing the delegate's preferences. You will note that this is not the first of the criteria on the assessment list. This is because, all too often, the most aggressive delegate's preferences determine the assignments given to all the delegates. When it's possible, and reflects your best judgment clinically, delegates appreciate doing the tasks they like best. However, again there may be an issue of whether the comfort zone is the best choice, and if it seems unfair that "Railroad Rita" has an easier assignment and avoids caring for Mr. Difficult Patient once again, it's important to analyze the other criteria for matching the delegate to the assignment more carefully.

ASSESSING CULTURAL DIFFERENCES

As we work together to care for patients of diverse cultural backgrounds, we, the caregivers, are also influenced by our rainbow heritage of every hue of race, creed, color, gender, sexual preference, and age group. Even the community in which we grew up affects the way we communicate, prioritize and perform our work, and relate to each other.

A story illustrates the challenges we face as a multicultural team. A second-grade teacher announced to the class, "Boys and girls, four blackbirds were on the limb of a tree. One was hit with a rock from a slingshot. How many were left?" One little boy immediately waved his hand and breathlessly shouted, "I know, teacher,

I know! Three blackbirds were left!" A second boy interrupted. "No, there's not a chance any of those blackbirds would stick around! Zero blackbirds were left!" The first little boy placed a high priority on task, structure, and timely response to the teacher's question. The second little boy focused on reality and on relationships. Both were right.

This book is not a text on cultural diversity. However, we encourage readers to explore how their coworkers' backgrounds affect their understanding of the communications they give and receive each day. Even the body language and eye contact used by certain cultural groups can be misunderstood by coworkers. To you, is lack of eye contact a sign of respect or of dishonesty? It depends on your cultural heritage.

> The first step toward overcoming the possible hazards of miscommunication due to cultural differences comes from recognizing that these differences are a reality of who we are and, consequently, are not negotiable.

One could never find a totally homogeneous group with whom to work. Who would want to? Not only would it be boring, but few variations would enrich the service we provide to our clients!

> The second step is to embrace the differences.

Ask questions of each other about backgrounds, such as "How did you handle conflict in your family?" Enjoy the attending special strengths that can be enjoyed with cultural diversity. A potluck with ethnic foods can be a tasty way to celebrate differences.

> The most important step is to communicate, communicate, communicate. Clarify questions and perceptions.

For example, "When I told you that Mrs. Smith needed to be seen early in the morning, I didn't specify the time. Did you have another priority that came up?" (This situation may occur with a cultural background that looks at time in a different way.) "When you didn't look me in the eye when we were speaking together, I wondered if you were understanding me." (This type of clarification may assist you in learning that eye contact is not polite in the staff member's culture.)

Again, just as we must know our patients to care for them effectively, we must know our delegates.

CONCLUSION

Let's return to that pesky question nurses ask, "What about my license?"

When you as the RN are following the supervision clause in your nurse practice act, when you are delegating appropriately, you

- know the job descriptions and official rules and regulations for yourself and delegates
- understand the concept of competency and how it affects your own performance and that of coworkers, and your personal accountability for maintaining your competence
- know delegates' strengths, weaknesses, motivation, and preferences
- know the patients and clients based on your assessment, diagnosis, planning, intervention, and evaluation
- use your professional judgment to match delegates to the work that needs to be done
- continually supervise, evaluate, and give feedback to delegates

When you do these things, you are using your professional judgment and being responsible and accountable. The delegates themselves are accountable for their own actions as they perform their roles within their legal and organizational limitations. As much as you would like to control every one of their actions and protect patients from any mistakes, you cannot do that any more than you can prevent mistakes from happening within an all-RN staff. Delegates are accountable for their mistakes as they act within their job descriptions and practice limitations. You as an RN are accountable for the total care of the patient and for correcting the effects of an error. You must also address the cause of the delegate's error, be certain that charting and other paperwork (such as the Unusual Occurrence Report) is completed, and pass on the information to those who need to know (possibly the manager, and the next shift). You have acted with excellent nursing judgment. Although you could not control every action of those you supervised, you followed professional standards to be accountable for your supervisory duties.

Getting to know delegates' qualities, just as you get to know qualities of family members, allows you to match delegates to the work that needs to be done for more effective patient care. In the next chapter, we'll discuss how to communicate your delegation decisions to the members of your team and how to keep the group from becoming a dysfunctional family!

CHECKPOINT 7–7

1. Knowing a delegate's motivation is important because:
   a) It is one of the assessment parameters that will allow me to make the correct decision about matching the delegate with the correct assignment.
   b) It will help me understand how to help him or her grow as we provide safe, effective patient care.
   c) I need to know how closely I will need to supervise this person.
   d) It's not important because no one could possibly take the time to know all this stuff about the people they work with.
   e) Understanding my coworkers better decreases the frustrations I may have to face each day.
2. I keep asking for feedback from Lew, but I can't seem to get an answer. She also asks someone else to do any personal care to any males. I can't decide if she's lazy or what!
   a) Both of these issues could be a cultural barrier we need to discuss.
   b) She may not be motivated to do the job.
   c) I will speak about this to her.
   d) I will just understand that this is who she is and forget about straightening it out.
3. A student nurse will be caring for my patient who has a tracheotomy and a feeding tube. I will ask the following questions:
   a) Nothing. The instructor should be there for all of the care. It's his problem.

b) I'll ask the student what parts of the care she is planning to do.
c) I'll ask about whether she's done any of this care before.
d) I'll ask her detailed questions about positioning, suctioning, tube feedings, and trach cuffs, and will be involved in the care of this patient all day.
4. Return to the questions we asked at the beginning of the chapter. Which type of health care professional in your organization can perform the following procedures?
a) Pierce the skin to perform procedures.
b) Start IVs.
c) Monitor IVs.
d) Perform the nursing process.
e) Gather data for the RN as she or he performs the assessment, nursing diagnosis, planning, intervention, and evaluation.
f) Perform hygienic care.
g) Deliver medications.
h) Be in charge of coordinating care in your health care setting.

See the end of the chapter for the answers.

ANSWERS TO CHECKPOINTS

7–2. Pat needs to consult with an administrative person in the agency to determine what steps were taken to support the provision of ventilator management at the LPN level. (Hopefully, they contacted the state board for an advisory opinion, which determined that LPNs could participate in ventilator management if educated in this area. Competency would have to be determined and "checked off" after the education program was completed.) As for LPNs as "primary nurses," the LPNs may be functioning nearly independently because RNs do not understand their own accountability by law. Pat needs to discuss his concerns about LPN supervision with his manager and help solve this problem. RNs' assessments and/or care planning involvement should be documented on the patient record as well.

7–3. This new RN may be discriminating based on disease. Or he may need some more education about HIV and how to treat crack babies. He may not be aware of the pattern of his behavior. (Read more about performance problems and giving feedback in Chapter 10.)

7–6.
  1. a, b, d
  2. c, d
  3. b, c, d
  4. a, c

7–7.
  1. a, b, c, e
  2. a, b (but probably not), c
  3. b, c, d
  4. We suspect that only RNs can perform d and h! Refer to your state practice act and organizational job descriptions to determine your answers.

REFERENCES

Arizona Department of Education. 1985. *Inventory of validated competencies and skills for nursing assistant, practical nurse, and associate degree nurse graduates.* Phoenix: Arizona Department of Education.

Hood, J., and H.L. Smith. 1994. Quality of work life in home care. *Journal of Nursing Administration* 24, no. 1: 40–47.

Interprofessional Workgroup on Health Professions Regulation. November 1996. *Views on the licensure and regulation of health care professionals.*

Maslow, A.H. 1970. *Motivation and personality.* 2d ed. New York: Harper & Row.

McNeese-Smith, D. 1992. The impact of leadership on productivity. *Nursing Economics* 10, no. 6: 396.

National Council of State Boards of Nursing. 1986. *National Council position paper (1986): Statement on the nursing activities of unlicensed persons.* Chicago: NCSBN. http://www.ncsbn.org/iwhpr/ipw/1196.html.

National Council of State Boards of Nursing. 1990. *Model nurse aide administrative rules by the Subcommittee for Model Nurse Aide Language and the Nursing Practice and Education Committee.* Chicago: NCSBN.

National Council of State Boards of Nursing. 1997a. *Assuring competence: A regulatory responsibility.* Chicago: NCSBN. http://www.ncsbn.org/iwhpr/ipw/1196.html.

National Council of State Boards of Nursing. 1997b. *Definition of competence and standards for competence. Assuring competence: Attachment two.* Chicago: NCSBN, 1–2.

National Council of State Boards of Nursing. 1997c. *Individual Competence Evaluation. Assuring Competence: Attachment two.* Chicago: NCSBN, 1–6.

Pew Health Professions Commission. 1995. *Reforming health care workforce regulation: Policy considerations for the 21st century.* San Francisco: UCSF Center for the Health Professions.

Simpkins, R.W. 1997. Using task lists with unlicensed assistive personnel. *Insight* 6, no. 2: 1.

Wiesmiller, W. 1997. Explaining the national nurse aide assessment program test development process. *Insight* 6, no. 2: 1–5.

CHAPTER 8

How Can I Communicate So That the Work Gets Done Right?

Loretta O'Neill

"Believe me, I'd love to delegate more comfortably, but I get anxious about asking anyone else for help because I'm concerned that they will think I can't handle my caseload. I worry about what happens when I'm not right there in the home to watch the home health aide work. Then, when I'm really bogged down and do delegate or assign something, I spend time worrying if it is getting done right or done at all, following up, finding out that it wasn't even done correctly, and finally doing it myself. It seems I save a lot of energy by just doing it myself in the first place! That doesn't even begin to figure in the extra paperwork to do!"

Sound familiar? You can probably see the necessity for delegating in your workplace. You think it is important, and know that your role is that of a leader, but somehow in the thousands of details that make up your busy work assignments, learning the skill of delegation isn't at the top of your "to do" list. When you delegate, you entrust another to act in your place for that particular task or cluster of tasks. You are still responsible for the delivery of the task. How can you be sure it will be done satisfactorily and on time? Notice that the criteria for successful delegation is satisfactory accomplishment of the task (which includes important safety and patient interaction components) resulting in the planned patient outcomes. Because the delegate is not you, he or she may not perform the task the exact way you would.

A key to successful delegation is in understanding, first, that delegation is an investment of time and energy that doesn't always have immediate returns, and second, that delegation is a skill, which implies that it has discrete steps or components, that it requires practice to improve, and that repeated practice of it will facilitate improvement.

DELEGATE RESPONSES

Assuming that the task(s) delegated and the delegate selected were appropriate, your request may receive a number of responses, all of which are probably familiar to you. We are assuming that your instructions were clear and complete.

> The delegate's responses may fall into one of three categories: agreement, refusal, and absence.

Agreement Response

This represents the happy scenario of a delegated task willingly accepted. You delegate a task, and the delegate agrees to perform it. The response is basically, "Yes, I'll do it." You have delegated the authority to the delegate to complete the task. You have also indicated time frames for completion and situational boundaries for which you need to be notified. In many cases, you'll have completed training of the delegate as well as documenting his or her competency to perform the work.

Possible results of agreement response are:

1. You monitor the delegate's progress and find out that the task(s) has been accomplished satisfactorily and on time.
2. The initial willingness of the delegate to perform the task leads to partially satisfactory results. The task may actually be completed but not satisfactorily, or it may be done correctly but not in the appropriate time frame. Many nurses habitually "fix it" when faced with this scenario. They complete the partially accomplished work or redo the incorrect work of their delegate. This has a number of negative effects. First, "plugging the gap" circumvents the accountability of the delegate to perform the agreed-upon task satisfactorily. The delegate needs feedback regarding what is and is not acceptable in the completion of the task. Without this feedback, the delegate is not likely to improve. Second, the delegating nurse becomes hypervigilant, checking, rechecking, and possibly redoing work that he or she thought was being done. This hypervigilance can lead to resentment toward the delegate, deterioration in the working relationship, and an unbearable workload for the nurse. Ineffective task completion also reflects on the patient and his family's level of trust in you and your agency.
3. A frustrating variation on this scenario of initial agreement to perform the delegated task is the delegate who willingly and cheerfully agrees to do the task but does not actually perform it. When you follow up on the delegate's

progress or lack thereof, you may hear, "I forgot," "I asked someone else to do that for me" (the delegate becomes a second delegator), "I got too busy with other patient requests," "I'm getting to it," or some other reason for nonperformance.

Once again, the delegating nurse will often reclaim the task and complete it him- or herself. Rationales given by the nurse for this action include urgent need for patient data to be collected; concern that the treatment or therapy needs to be done on schedule; and concern that the delegate will be angry or upset with the nurse if confronted and will make a scene, take his or her feelings out on the patient, or make an error.

In possible results 2 and 3, the delegating nurse shares responsibility for creating the delegation problem, usually by failing to monitor the delegate's progress until the deadline, then taking the task back. In doing so, the nurse participates in setting up a frustrating cycle: delegation; unsatisfactory accomplishment of the task by the delegate; reclaiming of the task by the delegating nurse; resentment and/or anger for both parties; recommitment to "doing it all myself"; work overload for nurse; attempted delegation; loss of trust by the patient. This cycle fails to motivate or develop the skill level of the delegate in doing the task or of the delegating nurse in holding the delegate accountable. It can also frustrate and stress the nurse, the delegate, and the patient unnecessarily.

If the nurse reclaims the task and does not offer corrective feedback, the nurse shares the responsibility for the delegation problem.

Refusal Response

This represents the unhappy scenario when the nurse attempts to delegate a task and the delegate indicates verbally or nonverbally, "No, I won't/can't do it." This may be accompanied by a number of reasons for the refusal. The reasons offered might be rational and based on stated but conflicting goals. For example, the nurses' aide can't seem to complete the personal care because the patient's daughter wants to discuss how sad she is about her mother's worsening condition, or the "patient said she doesn't feel like a bath." Or the refusal may be due to an inability or lack of knowledge about how to perform the requested task.

On the other hand, nonrational reasons based on hidden and unstated goals may be behind the refusal. The intended delegate's desire for personal

> If the nurse reclaims the task and does not offer corrective feedback, the nurse shares the responsibility for the delegation problem.

> As we discussed in "Know Your Practice," the delegate's accountability includes accepting the delegation, as well as his or her actual performance in carrying out the delegated task.

power, prestige, or revenge may be motivating the refusal response. A request for the home health aide to assist the patient in food preparation, for example, may be met with "I didn't go into this business to be a cook! If I'd wanted to do that, I'd be working at Burger Barn!" This refusal of a delegated task is based on a desire to equalize a power imbalance in the relationship between the delegating nurse and the delegate.

As we discussed in "Know Your Practice," the delegate's accountability includes accepting the delegation, as well as his or her actual performance in carrying out the delegated task.

Absence Response

In addition to the responses of "Yes, I'll do it," "No, I won't/can't do it," and a nonrational "attack," another scenario is that of the missing delegate.

As in a bad game of Tag, you are forever "it" because you can't find the delegate who did not show up for work at that patient's home today, and did not call to let someone know she or he wasn't able to be there. In this case, an absence response must be reported to the responsible managerial person in your agency.

COMMUNICATION STYLES: PASSIVE, AGGRESSIVE, ASSERTIVE

How do you, as the delegating nurse, deal appropriately with this wide scope of possible behaviors? How can you find the right words to communicate to the delegate, to keep communication channels open, and to resist the temptation to try to control the uncontrollable? The words you choose and the way in which they are delivered to the delegate make the difference between a successful and a frustrating episode in delegation. Your communication choices fall into one of three general categories: passive, aggressive, or assertive. Let's take a look at each of the three possible styles, taking passive first.

Passive or Nonassertive

As you review the new assignments from the weekend, you make out the home visit assignments based on the acuity of the patients and the skill level of the staff available. The LPN counts up each person's patient load and says, "I have all of the dressing changes, the others got all the morning diabetics! I think this should be divided up more evenly." You think the assignment is appropriate, based on the previous criteria, but this particular LPN can be quite difficult to work with and you don't want to start the week with a scene, so you say, "Oh, here. I'll redo the assignments so you have an easier week."

> The costs of habitually passive behavior include lowering of self-esteem and self-confidence, a negative self-image, avoidance of responsibility for the quality of one's relationships and life, and lost opportunities to develop skills in managing conflict and resolving issues.

This is a typically passive or nonassertive response, also termed avoidance. Although it is not advisable or even possible to deal with every conflict situation, a habitually passive response stems from a number of feelings, including fear, anxiety, timidity, inhibition, hurt, self-denial, helplessness, and physical and emotional stress. If words are spoken, they are often not reflective of the actual thoughts or feelings of the passive individual, adding an element of emotional dishonesty to the communication. Internally, an intense dialogue rages, with repeated replaying of the situation and various alternate responses that the passive person could have given.

The costs of habitually passive behavior include lowering of self-esteem and self-confidence, a negative self-image, avoidance of responsibility for the quality of one's relationships and life, and lost opportunities to develop skills in managing conflict and resolving issues. Problems are not faced or solved. Consequently, they multiply at the feet of the passive communicator. Effective delegation becomes impossible and the delegator ends up doing more and more work him- or herself. If the delegator's passivity is excessive, the delegates may become even less cooperative and control the amount and quality of work done.

Through constant acquiescence, the goals of others get accomplished, not the goals of the passive person. In addition, nonassertive behavior can engender feelings of pity, disgust, irritation, confusion, and anger in others. Why would anyone choose this communication style when the results seem so negative? A

> Effective delegation becomes impossible and the delegator ends up doing more and more work him- or herself.

passive response is based on the fear of rejection and retaliation caused by displeasing others. Conflict is avoided at the price of denying one's own feelings and needs. The reward is immediate avoidance of an unpleasant situation and the attendant feelings of tension.

> Eventually this strategy of avoidance backfires because feelings stay suppressed only for a time. Like a toxic chemical solution buried in a rusty drum, feelings of anger and resentment begin to leak out. These negative feelings show up in subtle, hostile behaviors and quiet ways of punishing or manipulating others such as forgetting, unconscious sabotage, withdrawal, sulking, or crying.

So the helpless, withdrawn, silent martyr actually has a method of communicating, though it is indirect and manipulative. You may have witnessed any of these behaviors among the personnel working at your home health agency.

Aggressive

Mrs. Smith is a new client with severe arthritis and needs moderate assistance with her personal care. In addition, she desperately needs her housekeeping, shopping, and meal preparation done. Gina, the home health aide, has been assigned to this case. You are reviewing the care plan with her. Gina states, "I really don't want to take this case. In fact, I won't. I am trained to be a home health aide and not a glorified housekeeper!"

You lose your cool. In no uncertain terms, you tell Gina, through clenched teeth, in a low and angry voice, "I don't really care what you were trained to do, you worthless, lazy woman. This patient needs help, and you are going to help her. If you refuse to do this case, you'll be without a paycheck at all and maybe you can get a job as a housekeeper!" In this scenario, neither the aide nor the nurse has problems expressing her thoughts, feelings, and wants. They are being expressive and their words honestly reflect the feelings they experience. You can see that both are annoyed, stressed, impatient, or angry.

However, the nurse's direct communication comes at the expense of the aide. Her words carry a tone of righteous superiority and "loaded" terms such as "worthless," "lazy," with references to job category. Such phrases have not been known to engender cheerful acceptance of delegated tasks! The communication she uses in this aggressive response is riddled with "you" messages of blame and labeling. How do you imagine the nurses' aide feels about herself? Probably hurt and humiliated, even though her response to the request for assistance was not effective. However, her feelings about the nurse are likely to be angry and vengeful. These characteristics of aggressive communication typify the verbal attack.

> Aggressive behavior is an encroachment or at-
> tack on another and is almost always hostile in
> intent. The communication flows from the aggres-
> sive person outward. Little listening takes place
> while he or she talks at, not with, others. This style,
> long on criticism and short on praise, successfully
> suppresses ideas and feedback from others. Such
> a tension-filled relationship evokes passive-aggres-
> sive behavior on the part of others, which perpetu-
> ates the cycle of overbearing authoritarianism and
> indirect aggression.

In another setting you may have witnessed aggressive behavior without actual speech. The pediatric clinical specialist who has just lost a child abuse case after a long fight may enter the agency with a flourish and then begin to throw charts or slam the telephone down on the hook when all does not flow in the intended sequence.

The will of the aggressive person often prevails in the conflict situation. The goal is to dominate and hurt the other. The price of winning is the animosity of the recipients. During the verbal storm the aggressive person speaks as if he or she has no "mental filter" but says whatever is on his or her mind. This brutal directness fosters fear and resistance, sabotage and resentment in the listener. Delegating with an aggressive manner of communication often has the same result as a passive style because real problems don't get solved and the delegator is avoided and ends up doing more work him- or herself. Coworkers do not easily forget these kinds of angry interchanges. In the home situation and in the community, we are role models for good interpersonal communication techniques. This kind of behavior will certainly damage the ability of the agency to do its work as a respected force for good health in the community.

Assertive

You assigned an LPN to do dressing changes on an abdominal wound in a rather challenging home situation. At your supervisory visit, you've noted that the wound is very crusty, with purulent drainage. These are signs you had asked to be reported to you, but the staff member did not report them. You've also noted a low-grade fever. When you approach the home health aide, you state, "I visited Ms. Brown today and saw quite a bit of pus and drainage on her wound, and a low-grade fever. What have you been noting there?" When you've heard the response, then ask the aide, "What did you understand about what kinds of things you were to report?" and verify the plan for the future. "How can you and I make certain that these sorts of things are reported quickly?" Clarify your expectations graciously, but without apology.

> No one approach will be best for handling every delegation situation, but knowing how to express yourself assertively can help you with the people-related problems of delegation.

Assertive communicators are confident and positive and lay claim to their own right to speak up for themselves. In the example above, the nurse is direct and expresses what she has observed, thinks, feels, and wants in this situation. The message is congruent with what she feels, so it is emotionally honest. She clearly addresses the problem without belittling herself or the other person. She knows what she wants and asks for it without apology. Assertive people feel good about themselves at the time they communicate and later. They are not ambushed by feelings of anger, resentment, or guilt. Because this style of communication addresses the problem in the situation, real problems get solved and stay solved.

Other people generally respect the assertive person because they themselves are treated with respect, not with deference, as in passivity, or with dominance, as in aggressiveness. And because the assertive person communicates directly when there is a problem, others can trust that problems will be shared with them and not inappropriately with others. This leads to the development of trust, an essential component of effective delegation.

At the heart of delegation is the skill of clear, effective, assertive communication. Improving your ability to express yourself can have a number of positive effects on your mental health and work life. Benefits for you include increased feelings of self-confidence, improved communication with coworkers, resolution of problems, nonmanipulative negotiation for behavior changes, and the ability to act as an advocate for patients. Again, role modeling good communication is a teaching tool for your patients as well as a positive commentary to engender the respect of patients and the community for your agency. A key strategy is to begin assertiveness practice in small nonemotional situations and build on your success. The most difficult, negative staff member on the unit is not the ideal recipient of your first efforts. Start out small and practice. Assertive communication will become easier and more natural to you. Please complete Checkpoint 8–1 before reading on.

CHECKPOINT 8-1

Determine what type of communication style the following personnel are using.

1. Rashad attended the team meeting with all the rest. When the topic of role clarification for assistive personnel came up, he stated that he thought part of his role was to anticipate the needs of the patients for toileting and personal hygienic care. Robin, one of the staff RNs in their psychiatric care group home, raised her voice as she firmly stated, "*You* are only an aide. *That* is in the RN role. We don't expect you to think, just to do what we tell you to when we tell you." Rashad sat quietly without responding because he needed to keep his job, but began to plan how he'd make Robin pay for her statement. Maybe he wouldn't do *anything* without being told.
2. Pamela, one of the school nurses in a rural county, was following up on some vision and hearing testing done by one of the volunteers, Brigite. In comparing Brigite's readings to previous readings, she was concerned about the accuracy of Brigite's work. Instead of discussing this with Brigite, Pamela decided to retest everyone herself.
3. Imelda and Maxine, both home health aides, have worked with Mrs. Rinaldi for several months. Imelda complains to the charge RN that Maxine is sloppy and doesn't complete Mrs. Rinaldi's bath appropriately, but doesn't mention this to Maxine. Maxine complains that the patient's son and daughter-in-law "would rather have me work every day of the week than have Imelda in their home!" Because of confusion in the schedule, both women ended up at the home at the same time, and the resulting discussion escalated to a loud exchange that brought calls to the agency from Mrs. Rinaldi's neighbors.

See the end of the chapter for the answers.

EFFECTIVE ASSIGNING

Many states and agencies have assisted nurses in learning to be specific by requiring forms for delegation, specifying why, who, what, when, where, and how in writing.

The first step in effective communication related to delegation is to be clear in your own mind about what you need to have done by the delegate, based on the outcomes you and the patient and family have determined are the priorities for this shift. A handy mental checklist can be borrowed from journalists, who routinely use the why, who, what, when, where, and how format in getting the details of their stories. By taking the time to share each of these aspects of the assignment with the delegate, you are communicating your specific expectations regarding the performance of the task.

> Sharing why, who, what, when, where, and how with the team member will help the communication be clear and complete.

Let's look at each of these in turn, starting with why.

Why

In giving feedback to others, you'll find that when goals and feedback are combined, performance effort is more than doubled (see Chapter 10). What would it be like to be a robot, each day going from home to home, doing the usual "personal care" without a clear understanding of *why* you are doing those tasks? In Chapter 6, "Know What Needs To Be Done," we emphasized the importance of first determining patient outcomes in partnership with the patient. Now you as the team leader must communicate the priority outcomes to the team members.

For example, if you've noted that a high priority for Ms. Jones for home visits is to maintain or improve her strength and to begin to build up her nutrition, then communicate that to others who will be assisting you. Imagine the difference in performance effort if you told Alicia (patient care assistant) to "be sure Ms. Jones is fed" versus saying "Alicia, for Ms. Jones to be able to stay off the ventilator and at home, we have to build up her nutrition quickly. Please be certain she eats at least 100 cc of the shake at 10 AM when you are there, and let me know how much she takes when her daughter feeds her today after you leave."

When people understand why they are doing their jobs, the difference may be critical, ranging from a useless "social call" type of home visit to the positive effects of celebrating Ms. Jones's ability to stay in her own home!

Who

Usually at least two people are involved in any patient care delegation situation: the intended delegate and the patient. Who is the delegate for this particular task? In Chapter 7, the process of identifying and assessing a delegate was discussed at length. The delegate may be a nurses' aide, patient care technician, LPN/LVN, another RN, a physical therapy aide, or someone outside the work group, such as a member of the patient's family. Be sure to specify the person who is your intended delegate.

The second "who" is the patient or receiver of the task. This seems incredibly simple and obvious, but avoidance of patient care errors begins with correct identification of the patient along with directions to that home!

What

What is the job/task to be done? Be clear and specific regarding the task or assignment that you are delegating. Unless you already know that the delegate understands the task, you need to take the time to explain the task thoroughly. Without adequate information, the chance that the task will be completed to your expectations is slim. What exactly do you want done?

Here are some examples of being specific about the delegated task:

- "Sandy, could you go (what) to the supply room and pick up (what) two boxes of irrigating syringes and 1,000 cc of sterile normal saline?"
- "James, I've noticed that your documentation (what) of patient teaching for cardiac and pulmonary rehab is excellent! Will you please review these practice guidelines to see if they are current (what)?"
- "Patricia, will you please go (what) to Mrs. Paulson's home today instead of tomorrow to do (what) her personal care?

"At this point, many nurses feel and respond to their own overcrowded schedules. "I don't have time to explain what he (she) needs to do. It's easier and quicker for me to do it myself." This is probably accurate. Unfortunately, it also ensures that you, and only you, are the one spending precious time on tasks that could be delegated. On the other hand, if you work with the same staff members often and begin to invest a little time in clearly delegating one new task at a time, you will develop delegates' repertoire of skills and expand the pool of competent persons. When nurses are not *complete* in their communication to others, the result is often incomplete work or unmet expectations. As we work with assistive personnel across the nation, they continually state, "Please tell the nurses to just

> *Clarity* also means not clouding the situation with too much information. Be *concise.* If you ask someone to measure a patient's output when draining the catheter bag, it's not necessary to discuss the details of how diuretics the patient is taking work on the pressure gradients in the kidney! Confusion will ensue as the delegate wonders what you really expect.

tell me what to do and what they expect, and I will do it. I can't read their minds!" As an attorney friend once told us, "The trouble starts when people stop talking."

A quick reminder as we discuss the "what" of communicating assignments to delegates: the task must fit within their scope of practice and job description and must be something they are competent at completing. Adding another "c" word to the list, the task you delegate must be *correct*, that is, legitimately within their capabilities and scope.

Another method to communicate the "what" of the task to delegates is to show (teach) them rather than tell. Take the delegate with you the next time you'd like to delegate a task. Use this opportunity to show him or her what is to be done the next time.

Clarity also means not clouding the situation with too much information. Be *concise.* If you ask someone to measure a patient's output when draining the catheter bag, it's not necessary to discuss the details of how diuretics the patient is taking work on the pressure gradients in the kidney! Confusion will ensue as the delegate wonders what you really expect.

Even experienced staff have gaps in their knowledge and appreciate being shown exactly what needs to be done, saving them from admitting they don't know how to perform a certain task.

When

When, meaning what time or by when, do you want the task completed? And when, or under what circumstances, should the delegate notify you? Your communication of the time frame for completion of a delegated task is crucial to on-time completion. Only when you specify the time parameters

> Even experienced staff have gaps in their knowledge and appreciate being shown exactly what needs to be done, saving them from admitting they don't know how to perform a certain task.

will the delegate share your prioritization of the task. Examples of communicating the "when" follow.

> - "Audrey, Mr. Pong needs to have his personal care done by 10:30 (when) because he has an appointment at noon."
> - "Angela, Mr. Phillips is back from the hospital. I'll do an evaluation visit and you can plan to begin seeing him again tomorrow (when)."
> - "If you receive a call on the answering machine about a poison control question, please notify me as soon as I walk in the door (when)."

Where

Communicating where you want a task done could mean either an anatomical location on the patient or a geographical location. *For example:*

> - "Susan, when you take the TED hose off Mr. Johnson, please clean the graft incision on the left calf (where—anatomical location) with Betadine."
> - "Mary Ellen, please ambulate Mrs. Darcy from her bedroom to her dining room and back (where—geographical location or distance) twice each visit."
> - "Liz, would you go to the medical supply room and pick up a replacement suture removal kit? They are on the bottom right shelf (where—location)."

How

How do you want the task done? There is a large range or scope of possibilities in answer to this question. Essentially, ask yourself if you have any assumptions about how the task will be completed. If you do, it is important to communicate these specifics to the delegate. Two examples of communicating "how" follow.

> - "Beth, Mr. Barnes has just had a double knee replacement and will be at home on Friday. The CPM machine will be placed on both knees (how)."
> - "Judy, please stay at the bedside with Mrs. Murphy and take her vital signs before and after dangling (how). She has a history of fainting and subsequent fractures."

Combining the Elements

It may seem that use of these components (why, who, what, when, where, and how) would be a lot to remember and take ages to communicate, but such is not the case. It is actually a quick, clear, and thorough method to delegate successfully. For example, "Martha (who—delegate), do you have time to add another visit today to ambulate (what) Mr. Parker (who—patient) before lunch (when) please? Good, thanks. He is slightly weak on his right side, so please walk on his left side (how) to give him support on his unaffected side (why). See if you can get him to walk down the hallway from his bedroom (where). Thanks."

When you are giving those instructions, ask yourself quickly, "Have I discussed the why, who, what, when, where, and how, and am I being clear, concise, correct, and complete in what I have said?" This is a good time to ask the delegate, "Have I given you enough (or too much?) information?"

In four short sentences, you have explained exactly the why, who, what, when, where, and how of a delegated task! And although it may seem obvi-

---

In communicating assignments to the delegate, remember the four C's:

Clear: Am I saying what I want to say and is the delegate hearing it?

Concise: Am I confusing him or her with too much information?

Correct: Is this a task I can comfortably delegate to a competent individual, within his or her scope of practice?

Complete: (This is where we most often err.) Am I stating the outcome we want to achieve (why this is being done)? Have I given times and parameters for reporting? Does the delegate have enough information to do the job accurately?

CHECKPOINT 8-2

Decide how you would clearly communicate the following tasks to be completed:

1. You want Geraldine, a medical assistant in your office, to check the temperatures rectally of all the babies under three years when they come in for a well-child checkup.
2. Linnea, your secretary, must complete the Medicare forms, or your agency will not receive reimbursement.
3. You'd like Antonia to pick up the psychiatrist's evaluation and referral from the homeless shelter on her way back from home visits.

See the end of the chapter for the answers.

---

ous, a liberal sprinkling of "pleases" and "thank-yous" really makes a difference to your coworkers!

ASSERTIVE FOLLOW-UP

So you have now clearly delegated a task. On the follow-up, you find that it has been done satisfactorily and on time, that it has been done partially satisfactorily, or that it has not been done. How can you respond in an assertive way, mindful of your needs and those of the delegate? How can you communicate assertively in all these situations? How can you think of the appropriate words when you are pressured for time and have strong feelings about the situation?

Step 1. Determine an Outcome

Before you begin, think about what outcome you'd like to achieve from your talk with this individual. Determining the outcome (what you want to have happen in the future) will create time to allow you to decompress, think clearly, and plan what you will say. This first step is the most essential!

Step 2. "I Noticed That . . ." or "When You . . ."

Here you describe the actual verifiable behaviors that you have seen or heard. Be specific and give as many concrete details as you can recall, such as time, place, and frequency of action.

For example, "Melissa, I asked you to call for additional nurses for tomorrow about 15 minutes ago. Since then I noticed that you have been on the phone discussing your plans for the evening. I am anxious to fill the need for help as soon as we can. Please begin calling now." Notice that this is a description of the events, not an assumption about Melissa's motivation or character flaws.

> "I noticed that. . ." or
> "when you . . . ,"
> "I feel . . . ,"
> "I want . . . ," (the desired outcome) is the recipe for assertive communication.

If you give others feedback about their behavior, take note of your language choices. Do you use "you" messages, such as "You are late!" or "You forgot to change the dressing at Mr. Smith's"? A "you" message sounds like an accusation, and others may feel defensive and resist hearing your message. An important principle of assertive communication is the use of "I" messages, such as "I've noticed that . . ." or "I would like you to bathe Mrs. Dove."

Step 3. "I Feel . . ."

Here you describe an emotion. You communicate a great deal to others when you share the impact of their behavior on you. They can get a clearer picture of the effect on others. An example is, "When I asked you to help me with that mess and you said you weren't being paid the big bucks like RNs, I felt overwhelmed. If you have a reason you can't help me when I'm in a jam, let me know, but please understand my request was reasonable. Next time I want you to either come and help, or let me know why you can't."

Use this step judiciously. If you are confronted with an angry physician who is screaming over the phone "I'll never use this agency again!" you may not wish to share that "I feel intimidated by your behavior." That physician may be so angry as to state, "Well, I hope you are intimidated! That was my intent, to get someone to react to get your agency to improve its care!" You may, however, want to share your feeling that "I am concerned that I can't help with your current problem if you continue to raise your voice. Please be more specific and I'll deal with the problem."

Step 4. "I Want . . ."

Here you are able to use that outcome that you determined in the first step: Specify what action you want the person to take or what behavior you want him or her to change. Your best bet is to start by requesting small changes of behavior, and only one or two changes at a time. But let's face it, by the time you have noticed a behavior significant enough for you to spend time, effort, and adrenaline to ask for a behavior change, you really want more than a small change. In your heart of hearts, you secretly wish for a complete conversion experience that totally reforms both the offending behavior and the accompanying attitude! And when you point out the problem, you want the person to say, "You are absolutely right! I am so grateful to you for showing me the light. I can't believe I didn't see this about myself. Believe me, from now on I'm going to be different. Thank you again." This fantasy is entertaining but unlikely.

Remember, it can take years to change an attitude. Focus on a small change in behavior related to your goal. And remember that you cannot control another person's behavior but can best influence him or her by your good communication and example!

An illustration is, "Jeff, you are late getting back to the office. I expected you about an hour ago. The next time you get tied up, I would appreciate it if you

---

CHECKPOINT 8-3

"When you . . ." or "I notice that . . . ,"
"I feel . . . ," and
"I want . . . ,"
Use the phrases above to respond to the following situations:

1. The jail chaplain, who is on contract with your home health agency, has once again intruded into a counseling session when you are discussing problems with one of the physical therapy aides.
2. When the roster for your family planning class was finally located, it had been placed in the wrong public health nurse's mailbox by the agency secretary.
3. The rehabilitation aide has not charted the range of motion exercises for the past two days.
4. All the RNs and secretaries are busy on phone calls, except Alice. She is standing at the box of chocolates sent by an appreciative family, chewing away as the phones continue ringing.

See the end of the chapter for the answers.

> Research on human communication has shown repeatedly that the majority of the message we communicate comes from the nonverbal components.

would call me [small behavior change] and let me know you are going to be late so I can plan for it. We have been worried about your safety."

NONVERBAL BEHAVIORS

What you say is very important, but how you say it carries even more weight. Nonverbal behaviors can either enhance or conflict with the verbal message. And when confronted with such a mixed message, most listeners choose to believe the nonverbal message is the "real" one. So paying attention to your nonverbal behaviors can strengthen your verbal message.

The assertive delegator uses a level, conversational tone of voice and audible volume appropriate to the situation. Words are enunciated firmly and confidently. The assertive delegator is also comfortable with silence and pauses after key points to allow others to process the information. These behaviors communicate that the speaker has the legitimate authority to delegate and that the delegator is respectful of the delegate.

Eye Contact

An assertive delegator has a relaxed, steady gaze into another person's eyes. Looking away or down while speaking is usually suggestive of lack of self-esteem or confidence, although there are cultural variations on this interpretation. Avoid staring, blinking, squinting, or excessive eye movements.

Body Posture

How you hold your body while speaking says a great deal about you and your message. Face the person you are speaking with and place yourself at the same level, sitting or standing appropriately close. Hold your head erect and avoid slumping. Lean forward slightly. If you are standing, avoid shifting your weight from one foot to another. These attending behaviors say you are paying attention to what is being said.

Gestures

While speaking assertively, maintain a relaxed use of hands and arms. Use gestures for emphasis but avoid gestures such as arms folded across the chest (defensive), making a clenched fist (threatening), or finger shaking (aggressive/

shaming). Also avoid the myriad of other nonassertive behaviors such as excessive head movement; covering your mouth with your hand while speaking; and playing with jewelry, coins, keys, hair, beard, or clothing. This fidgeting distracts from your message.

Facial Expression

Your facial expression should be relaxed with a pleasant to neutral expression. Most important, be consistent with the verbal message. If you are angry or upset, do not smile because this nullifies your words. Relax the muscles in your face and maintain a neutral expression. Avoid a drawn, tight-lipped mouth, wrinkled forehead, repeated swallowing, or nervous habits such as excessive throat clearing or lip licking.

Personal Space

Maintain an appropriate distance, not crowding or invading the personal space "bubble" of the other. Avoid wandering and pacing.

Voice Qualities

Although this topic can't be considered "nonverbal behaviors," voice qualities are paramount in effective communication. We all know individuals who are considered "difficult people," many of whom would be considered perfect communicators if we could somehow delete the sound of their voice or view of their body language, and merely read a written dialogue. The rate of speech, tone, accent, pitch, and volume all lead the person receiving the communication to presume an intent by the speaker. Think of the many ways in which the following statement could be altered based on body language and voice qualities:

"You missed the meeting." If *you* is emphasized, the tone could be derisive or judgmental. The meaning changes again if the statement is coupled with laughter or smiles, or a pointed index finger; the content switches from perhaps being "fortunate to miss" the meeting to anger for unmet expectations. If *missed* is emphasized, the speaker may be relaying to the hearer that he or she was not participative. If *meeting* is emphasized, one could assume that the person is being reminded of how forgetful he or she is! Think of how a close, aggressive stance hovering over a person seated, with a loud volume, would differ from a smiling approach as a person walks down the hall and asks, "You missed the meeting?"

Ask a good friend (who will be honest!) to give you some insight into how your body language, tone of voice, and other nonverbal and verbal behaviors affect your ability to communicate. Glance at a mirror as you pass one while thinking or at rest. What kind of impression is left by the expression you see? Understanding oneself and knowing how to use the personal skills we possess effectively is a cardinal quality of good leaders.

CONCLUSION

Nurses have tremendous responsibilities and need to be able to delegate effectively through clear, assertive communication. Assertiveness is a learnable skill that improves with successful practice. Start out in small, low-emotion situations to gain skill and confidence.

Whether the response to your delegation is agreement, refusal, or absence, you can develop an assertive dialogue with your delegate that addresses the real problem and begins the process of resolution. And what is in it for you? Just increased feelings of self-confidence and self-respect, improved communication with coworkers, resolution of actual problems, above-board negotiation for behavior changes, and the ability to act as an advocate for yourself and patients.

ANSWERS TO CHECKPOINTS

8–1.
1. The psychiatric nurse was being aggressive. Rashad responded by being passive but planned to be passive-aggressive in the future.
2. This school nurse was being nonassertive.
3. Imelda was being passive-aggressive by talking behind someone's back. Maxine's behavior followed similar paths. However, due to their avoidance of positive action, possible accommodation of improper care, and passive-aggressive behavior, more aggression and conflict ensued. What could the supervising RN have done to improve the situation? Supervision of the home care (are Imelda's concerns about Maxine's care factual or is this a personality conflict?) and mediation for both women to discuss their differences calmly may have avoided the negative impacts. More on this in the chapter on conflict!

8–2.
1. Geraldine, will you please take rectal temperatures on all patients who are under three years of age when you do their admission work for the next two weeks? Please let me know verbally before I go into their physical assessment if any are over 100°F. I think we've had some problems recently with

the accuracy of the tympanic electronic thermometer, and I'm sending it off to be fixed. Any questions? Great! Thanks. I think we'll avoid giving sick kids their immunizations this way!

2. Linnea, I am concerned about this new Medicare paperwork. If we don't get it right and send it in before two days have elapsed postdischarge from acute care, we won't be paid the full amount we have coming. Let's go over how to fill it out. Is there any reason you can't get these sent off the day the RN completes the paperwork, or at least the day after? Great! I appreciate your help in keeping this agency running!

3. Will you possibly have time to go by the Midtown Homeless Center before you come back to the office today after visits? Good! Mrs. Burn's psychiatric evaluation is waiting there at the front desk to be picked up. I'll call Sammy, the secretary there, and let her know you'll come about 3:30 to pick it up. Thanks! We need this evaluation to do her team planning tomorrow morning.

8–3.

1. When you come into my office while I'm involved in a private conversation, I feel concerned about maintaining confidentiality, and I'd appreciate it if you'd knock before you come in.

2. I noticed that the class roster was in the wrong mailbox today. I felt panicked when I couldn't find it. Would you please put it in my in-box the next time? Thanks!

3. I noted that the charting on range of motion has not been completed the past few days, and I feel particularly frustrated by this because the accreditors are visiting tomorrow. Please chart them now and plan to get them in the charts as soon as you can after completion. I appreciate it!

4. Alice, when everyone else is busy, and the phones continue to ring and I see you are standing at the desk eating chocolates, I feel frustrated and disappointed because I think it's up to all of us to be sure we respond to the calls of the public. Please answer the phones when you aren't busy. (Please note: This is not all you might say in these circumstances. We will be adding to this kind of communication when we discuss conflict resolution and giving feedback in the next chapters.)

RECOMMENDED READING

Anderson, K. 1993. *Getting what you want.* New York: Dutton Publishing.

Burley-Allen, M. 1983. *Managing assertively: How to improve your people skills.* New York: John Wiley & Sons.

Genua, R. 1992. *Managing your mouth.* New York: American Management Association.

Ober, S. 1998. *Contemporary business communication.* New York: Houghton Mifflin Co.

CHAPTER 9

How Do I Manage My Team and Resolve Conflict?

Ruth I. Hansten and Marilynn J. Washburn

CONFLICT AS A CONCEPT

> *"You may* tell *me to take this case out of my area, but that doesn't mean I'm going to do it. In fact, there's no way that I am going to care for that Mrs. Smith, or work with Jerry in that home!"*

In the last chapter, we discussed how to communicate clearly and assertively and began to look at situations in which delegation may precipitate some uncomfortable interpersonal situations.

Conflict! It is definitely something most of us fear or avoid. However, when working with people, conflict of some kind is inevitable. Our attitude toward the possibility of conflict often influences the manner in which we delegate. "But if I ask someone to do something, or give them feedback, there's a chance they will disagree, and then there will be conflict!"

Conflict, although uncomfortable, must be accepted as a part of living and working together. Consider the whole concept for a few moments, and think about what life would be like without any conflict. (Those of you who are breathing a sigh of relief and envisioning a world with prancing Bambis and fluttering butterflies, read on!)

There would be no new ideas or inventions. Most of these arise from conflicts over which idea is better.

Some of us would not put in the required effort to improve our performance. If negative feedback is given to us, even though we may disagree and begin a discussion about our own perceptions, we will be more aware of our supervisor's perceptions and focus on those problem areas.

More open relationships and better communication occur when colleagues are not afraid to disagree. Each person's point of view can be considered, and patient care improves from sharing varying perspectives.

Procedures and systems can improve through conflict. When a member of the team argues that things need improvement and that his or her way is better, a window is opened for changing things that need to be changed.

Conflict can be constructive, depending on the way it is handled. As the energy from the conflict is channeled to making things better for all, staff performance and better patient care can result.

Unless you work totally alone, we know you probably have ample opportunity to experience conflict. You may have developed your own philosophy of the origins of conflict. To make certain that you've covered all the bases when you steam away in frustration at those difficult situations in your work setting, let's take a look at the more common sources of conflict.

SOURCES OF CONFLICT

Why bother to look at sources of conflict? As nurses, you know that at least 100 horrible physiological events begin to take place in the human body when a patient is immobile, and you've learned to expect them and take measures to avoid the negative sequelae of such conditions as constipation, pneumonia, or deep vein thrombosis. Similarly, if you understand the usual sources of conflict, you'll be able to anticipate them as normal, even healthy, phenomena. This mind-set will make dealing with those issues much less stressful, and you may even be able to take steps to plan for them.

Ambiguous Jurisdiction

Not knowing who should be doing what and how roles and duties overlap is a common cause of conflict. This is a common problem when new roles are undertaken and systems change. Often, in home health, many different agencies may be working with a family, and each may assume that another agency "should" be doing something that it isn't. Inherent in these conflicts are questions of responsibility and authority, or such issues as which agency is being reimbursed for what. Instead of wasting energy on unnecessary disagreement, clarify job descriptions, state practice acts, and role expectations to reduce this source of conflict.

Conflicts of Interest

Where do you see these types of conflicts occurring in your health care setting? Everywhere! Whether a home health agency is perceived by staff to be solely interested in the bottom line or whether staff seem to define quality of patient care by the numbers of visits they make, we see conflict of interest each day. Certainly, survival of an organization

> "He who understands all, forgives all."

in these times of unsettled reimbursement can generate a fair amount of focus on finance, which may seem "uncaring" to one group and "responsible and prudent" to another. In your specific setting, you'll see delegates having a conflict about care methods or about priorities based on their own personal values. Recognizing conflicts of interest will help you begin the conflict resolution process by identifying what each party really wants. (This will be covered later in the chapter.)

Communication Barriers

Physical and time barriers abound in health care. The very nature of our work in community care requires interaction with many agencies and personnel you've never seen. The pharmacist who works in the third-level underground in the medical center may not have as clear a concept of the needs of an oncology patient in the home as the family who cares for that patient. The inpatient home care coordinator may find that conflicts occur regularly with the outlying ambulatory care clinics or home health referral agencies. The French have a wonderful saying that translates as "He who understands all, forgives all." Our communication barriers prevent us from understanding each other, and conflict results.

Dependence of One Party on the Other Party

Delegation, from the physician to the nurse, the nurse to the assistive personnel, or the nursing care team to other professionals, creates potential for disagreement and anger. When one party doesn't complete the job on time or correctly, righteous indignation blooms as the delegator sputters, "But I was counting on you! The patient and his family were counting on you!" When one party is dependent on another and the process doesn't progress well, expect this kind of reaction. Anticipating it allows you to take steps to rectify the problem, and will encourage the necessary communication and supervision to be certain the work is completed as planned.

Association of the Parties

The dictator type of management, in which the supervisor does not request participation and input, is uncomfortable for staff and stifles creativity and job growth. However, as interaction increases among workers, the potential for disagreement also grows. We've stated previously that disagreement can be positive, and a climate that encourages participation is excellent for improving staff motivation and the overall products we produce. Increased association of the parties becomes a source of conflict when the parties are unable to tolerate disagreement, do not have the communication skills to deal with the disagreement positively, and are working in a pressure-cooker environment. Expect that you'll need to help resolve conflicts when all have been under particular stress and when some members of the team are not employing assertive communication skills.

Behavior Regulations

Standardized policies, procedures, and rules seem to do two things at once. These regulating mechanisms are intended to reduce conflict by providing guidelines for performance. In some circumstances, however, the individual who wants more autonomy and less structure will chafe under the organization's regulations. For example, if your state's nurse practice act allows an LPN (LVN) to perform many procedures that are prohibited by your agency's job description for LPNs, expect some annoyance from some of the LPN staff. This discomfort will certainly surface as conflict.

Unresolved Prior Conflicts

The most common cause of conflict is unresolved prior conflicts. Consider those people of whom you aren't extremely fond, and time how quickly a list of past insults or negative incidents arises in your memory. Human beings often store up data that reinforce their viewpoint of a given individual. This data storage has been called "gunny sacking," a process that promotes an aching back and head. When the offending person once again commits his or her crime, the gunny sacker finally dumps the overflowing bag onto the unprepared recipient. "You never listen to my instructions! You always act like a lazy bum!" The ability to deal with conflicts effectively as they arise allows both parties to feel better about themselves and their work, unencumbered by the weight of past, unresolved problems.

Conflicts Unique to Health Care

Whereas these are broad, somewhat generic categories of sources of conflict, it's important to note some very specific areas of conflict unique to health care. Consider the following:

- *Physicians versus nurses:* An age-old battle still goes on in some settings, due to many factors, including a gender bias, "curing versus caring," the interdependence of the roles, and the impact of health care revisions on both professions.

- *Home care nurses versus the rest of the world:* Acute care nurses, those in ambulatory care, never really understand the needs of the patient in his home until they have been there. Social workers and others who work in acute care facilities who make referrals to home care agencies may not understand the medical situations that will inhibit the patient care situation in the home.

- *Nurses versus assistive personnel:* If the change in care delivery from an all-RN staff to one of a team model using assistants is imposed on nursing, rather than of their own design, conflict often results. Although most home care agencies have used assistive personnel for years, some states have added many new skills to the roles of assistive personnel in the home. A difference in values and accountability may be perceived, as well as a fear of loss of control of the home environment when fewer RN visits are being made. Nurses have been heard to say, "Assistants don't care about the patients as much as I do!" and "I'm the one who is accountable here; they will never be as accountable as me!"

- *Managed care and everyone else:* Like a steamroller running over all of us, managed care has had a tremendous impact on health care providers. Physicians feel their opportunities for independent practice are restricted, patients feel their choices are being limited, and nurses are in the middle advocating for patient care and resisting the limits imposed by managed care plans. Medicare restrictions on home visits cause nurses to chafe at the regulations, as they wonder what type of care will be cut next.

Review statements 1–5 in Checkpoint 9–1. Think about how the norm for handling conflict in your family has affected the way you deal with, or avoid, conflict at work. Those of us who learned that any kind of disagreement was very painful may find it more difficult to respond to conflict in a positive, open manner. If significant others in our past modeled ineffective communication skills, which culminated in rearrangement or destruction of our family unit (whatever our definition may have been), we may be baffled and confused by those who enjoy a good argument and don't feel threatened when confronted by conflict. People who learned to keep quiet and passive, then fly into a rage, may find it more difficult to bring out issues that may trigger conflict until the situation becomes unbearable.

COST OF CONFLICT

We've discussed the potential benefits of a willingness to recognize and resolve conflict, and we have identified the sources. What about the cost? When team-

---

CHECKPOINT 9-1

Consider the conflicts you've encountered in the past two weeks in your work setting. Which source of conflict was responsible for each situation? In what ways could positive resolution of those conflicts be constructive for your team and your clients?

Let's take a look at how your past may be influencing your attitude toward conflict. Answer the following as true or false.

___ 1. I am afraid of conflict. In my family, conflict meant people yelling and fighting, which always translated into heartache for someone.

___ 2. In our family, we argued for fun. The neighbors often thought we were really fighting, but it was our way of showing we cared about each other.

___ 3. My parents never raised their voices to each other. I never knew things weren't going well until they were ready to get a divorce.

___ 4. The people in our family didn't ever disagree until someone was really very angry. Then one little thing would put Dad (or Mom) into a screaming rage.

___ 5. I grew up in the only nondysfunctional family in our town. We all discussed any issues that bothered us openly and freely, and calm, insightful, respectful discussion was the norm.

---

work fails, when people are unhappy with each other or themselves, when staff feel overburdened or taken advantage of or, worse yet, powerless, a price is paid. We all know nurses who think of the work setting as an adversarial, "us against them" environment. These people usually have a negative outlook, feel powerless and victimized by the system ("I have no choice"), and will either withdraw or leave the organization. If they stay around, it is with detachment and a sense of "just putting in my time." The impact on others is significant, as this attitude is contagious. Morale drops and staff are less likely to work actively for the improvement and advancement of their agency. (Managers then consider themselves lucky if the staff are just getting the work done!)

The organizational cost of conflict may be financial, as reflected in lengthening of patient treatment due to missed treatments or care; lack of collaboration among the team members, leading to disputes over approaches to care; or staff calling in when they do not want to face a continuing negative environment.

> The impact on others is significant, as this attitude is contagious. Morale drops and staff are less likely to work actively for the improvement and advancement of their agency.

The impact can be felt on a personal level as well. By misusing avoidance, the unhappy staff member may internalize the conflict between her and another staff member, a poor resolution that affects her physically (stress ulcers, high blood pressure, maladaptive coping through substance abuse). Yet the fear of confrontation or the feeling of helplessness can be so powerful that the personal price is paid: the situation is endured, not resolved.

We have seen many efforts to incorporate assistive personnel or a more interdisciplinary approach to care fail due to the inability of staff to resolve the conflicts satisfactorily that arise when developing a team. Differences in personal values, role confusion, unclear goals, and a need for control (usually on the part of the nurse) contribute to team dysfunction. Conversely, we have witnessed many success stories where staff were willing to take the personal risk, were supported, and were able to resolve the inevitable disagreements that result when people work together. "Unchecked, conflict has the potential to divide alliances and departments. Conversely, providing an ongoing forum for differences of opinion to be voiced and understood creates an environment where expectations can be shared and ideas are more likely to be expressed openly than 'behind another person's back'" (Forte, 1997, p. 121).

CHECKPOINT 9-2

Evaluate your attitude toward conflict and your strategic response repertoire by answering the questionnaire in Exhibit 9-1. Most people use different coping mechanisms in conflict situations depending on the setting and the future implications, but use your first reaction for the questionnaire.

Exhibit 9–1 Conflict Questionnaire

	Very Unlikely	Unlikely	Likely	Very Likely
1. I am usually firm in pursuing my goals.				
2. I try to win my position.				
3. I give up some points in exchange for others.				
4. I feel that differences are not always worth worrying about.				
5. I try to find a position that is between hers and mine.				
6. In approaching negotiation, I try to consider the other person's wishes.				
7. I try to show the logic and benefits of my position.				
8. I always lean toward a direct discussion of a problem.				
9. I try to find a fair combination of gains and losses for both of us.				
10. I attempt to work through our differences immediately.				
11. I try to avoid creating unpleasantness for myself.				
12. I might try to soothe the other's feelings and preserve our relationship.				
13. I attempt to get all concerns and issues immediately out.				
14. I sometimes avoid taking positions that create controversy.				
15. I try not to hurt the other's feelings.				

SCORING: Very unlikely = 1, Unlikely = 2, Likely = 3, Very Likely = 4.

	ITEM	ITEM	ITEM	
COMPETING	1	2	7	TOTAL
COLLABORATING	8	10	13	TOTAL
COMPROMISING	3	5	9	TOTAL
AVOIDING	4	11	14	TOTAL
ACCOMMODATING	6	12	15	TOTAL

Source: Reprinted with permission of Academy of Management, PO Box 3020, Briar Cliff Manor, NY 10510-0820. *Toward Multidimensional Values in Teaching: The Example of Conflict Behaviors* (Exhibit), K.W. Thomas, Academy of Management Review 1977, Vol. 2. Reproduced by permission of the publisher via Copyright Clearance Center, Inc.

STRATEGIES FOR CONFLICT RESOLUTION

Now that you have some idea of how you react to conflict, let's review how effective your preferred coping mechanism becomes in different situations. This section's adaptations of the Thomas-Kilmann Conflict Resolution grid show how attitudes toward conflict reflect our intensity toward our own interest and the self-interest of the other viewpoints. Exhibit 9–2 also summarizes the cost and benefit of each of the choices.

Exhibit 9–2 Five Choices for Resolving Conflict among the Team

---

#1 Avoidance: "There's no problem"
Used as a short-term solution to calm down and to buy time.
Cost: It does not solve the problem.
Benefit: It allows time for cooling off and thinking.

#2 Accommodation: "You win, I lose"
Sacrificing own interests to please the other member of the team. Okay if the issue is not important to you or the resolution is short term and will be problem solved later.
Cost: It does not achieve your own interests.
Benefit: It allows for immediate solution.

#3 Competition: "I win, you lose"
For quick, decisive action on vital matters.
Cost: Other party might not be satisfied and may be resistive.
Benefit: Your goals are achieved.

#4 Compromise: "I win and lose some, you win and lose some too"
Temporary solutions to complex problems, with resolution by mutual consent.
Cost: It takes time; you may have to give up optimum goal.
Benefit: Both parties feel successful and part of solution.

#5 Collaboration: "I win, you win"
Process that evolves over time, working through feelings that have interfered with the relationship, and finding an integrative solution.
Cost: It takes strong commitment of both parties.
Benefit: It is a long-lasting solution with mutual satisfaction.

Source: Reprinted from R. Hansten and M. Washburn, How Can I Get My Coworkers to Work with Me As a Team? *Clinical Delegation Skills*, p. 258, © 1998, Aspen Publishers, Inc.

Avoidance

The first common strategy for resolving conflict is avoidance. Those who answered "Agree" on Question 1 in Checkpoint 9–1 may find avoidance to be an overused tool. It may be evidenced by the statements "I don't want to talk about it," "Let well enough alone," and "Don't rock the boat." Although avoidance works well in situations when you need more time to reflect, calm down, or get more information or input, it won't work for those situations that require your action and involvement.

A study of nurses' conflict resolution styles at three hospitals (Fowler et al., 1993) noted that nurses use withdrawal, or avoidance, as their most common coping mechanism when confronted with conflict. The authors stated that this indicated a willingness to remove themselves from relationships and possibly a lack of interest in the outcomes of the conflicts as well.

How do we decide whether to get involved? Certainly in health care it is easy for us to either brush conflict situations under the rug, leave them for the day or the next nurse, pass them off to a manager to take care of, or run in and save the day. It's certainly easy for us to put ourselves in a rescuer role when we don't need to be.

When making a decision about whether to get involved, focus on the intended outcomes. For example, what will happen if I do something about this issue? What will happen if I don't? Examine the potential costs and potential benefits, then make your decision. Further, think about whether this situation affects your own safety, security, or goals. Does it affect the safety or welfare of those committed to your care? Does this conflict get in the way of achieving your group goals? If the answer to any of these questions is yes, then your strategy of avoidance had better remain an interim tactic only. You'll need to deal with this conflict.

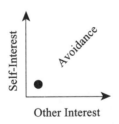

Source: Adapted from the Thomas-Kilmann Conflict Mode Instrument. Copyright © 1974, by Xicom, Inc., Tuxedo, New York. Reproduced with permission by Aspen Publishers, Inc.

Competition

Competition as a method of solving conflicts shows a great amount of self-interest and low interest in whether the other party's viewpoints are considered. We see competition as an integral part of our society, of our business world, and of the games we play in the Western Hemisphere. In the past, boys were taught how to compete through the games and sports they played. Girls were encouraged to cooperate and be "nice" to everyone, and therefore women may not feel as comfortable with win-lose situations. As we enter into health care reform, we have

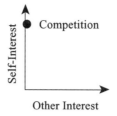

Source: Adapted from the Thomas-Kilmann Conflict Mode Instrument. Copyright © 1974, by Xicom, Inc., Tuxedo, New York. Reproduced with permission by Aspen Publishers, Inc.

discussed the idea of "managed competition" as compatible with the American way of business. The win-lose mentality works very well in some situations but is not satisfactory for making certain everyone's position is considered and for promoting a long-term supervisory relationship.

For example, if a school nurse and a school secretary have had repeated discussions about the necessity of instructing the asthmatic children how to use their metered dose inhaler properly, but the secretary refuses to do it, and the nurse observes a child in real distress being merely handed the inhaler by the secretary as she glares at the RN, an "I win, you lose" or autocratic approach to resolving the conflict may be necessary for the short term. The nurse will want to intervene immediately to be certain the child's health is not at risk and will have to overrule the secretary's actions with her own, discussing the problem later with the secretary in private. Certainly when a client's health is at risk, time is not wasted to ascertain the other party's position on the matter.

Due in part to the serious nature of health care and nursing, rules or policies are considered important guides for practice. Some rules are based on reason and excellent rationales. But, when conflicts occur in some organizations, the culture (or "the way things are done here") may encourage forced compliance. This becomes a kind of "corporate competition": rules are enforced without reasoning why they were written in the first place. The agency itself is the "we win, you lose" competitor. For example, it's necessary for everyone's safety that an agency enforces a rule that no one (except security or police) will be allowed to carry concealed weapons when coming in for care. When a client brandishes an AK-47 assault rifle and is carried bodily from the public health infection disease clinic, the "we win, you lose" method of solving a conflict may be best. But when the rule against accepting gratuities means that a nurse and rehabilitation aide are told they cannot accept a set of crocheted oven mitts from a patient who wants to thank them for all they've done for her, following the rules in "the agency rules win, you lose" approach doesn't seem to be the best choice for anyone concerned. Just as we discussed the necessity of using your nursing judgment when delegating care, choosing the correct method of solving problems rests on your assessment of the situation and choice of the most effective tactics.

Accommodation

This style of resolving conflict develops when a person is much more interested in the other person's needs or desires than in maintaining his or her own point of view. Those whose answers scored high in accommodation may use this as a comfortable method of relating to others when there is some disagreement. Accommodation is effective in a situation that doesn't matter much to you. For example, if a delegate (a home health aide, for example) states in a challenging manner that she is planning to rearrange her schedule of home visits, and this does not present a problem to you or to your clients, it's fine to be accommodating. (The nurse in charge may want to explore the situation more extensively and find out why the home health aide seems angry and challenging today.) If, however, a technician in your family planning clinic states that she doesn't think she'll provide the correct size of gloves for the nurses today, it's not time to accommodate her wishes.

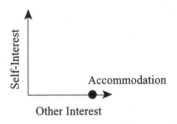

Source: Adapted from the Thomas-Kilmann Conflict Mode Instrument. Copyright © 1974, by Xicom, Inc., Tuxedo, New York. Reproduced with permission by Aspen Publishers, Inc.

The message of accommodation is this: accommodate when it's truly okay with you. Use another method of conflict resolution if you feel uncomfortable or unhappy with the situation. (For those with codependent tendencies who tend to accommodate others, we recommend Question 71 in *The Nurse Manager's Answer Book* [Hansten and Washburn, 1993] or *I'm Dying To Take Care of You* [Snow and Willard, 1989].)

Compromise

"I win some and lose some; you win some and lose some" is commonly used for conflict resolution in our society. The political process often uses compromise to

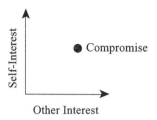

Self-Interest

● Compromise

Other Interest

Source: Adapted from the Thomas-Kilmann Conflict Mode Instrument. Copyright © 1974, by Xicom, Inc., Tuxedo, New York. Reproduced with permission by Aspen Publishers, Inc.

reach a reasonable middle ground when terribly complex issues are discussed by highly polarized groups. Each of these groups has principles or values that are ingrained to the core of each individual's personality and are at complete odds with each other. What is right and good and ethical will be very different for different individuals; therefore, it is sometimes difficult to find a conflict resolution that completely satisfies everyone. If you discovered in your conflict questionnaire that you compromise frequently, you may be aware of the very common human tendency to avoid flexibility and understanding the opposite viewpoint when your opponent is so obviously wrong and you are so obviously on the side of "good and all that is right."

Compromise allows us to move ahead in situations that are terribly complex or polarized. When changes must be made in the admissions and billing for a home health agency, conflicting ideas and positions will occur because many different publics and people will be affected. Even if all those potentially affected are involved in creating the changes in procedure, not all of the personnel may agree wholeheartedly with the end-product and may need to "give" a bit on their original positions. Mutual consent that the decision is made, and that all will implement it for the good of the whole, will allow the home care agency to continue to function as smoothly as possible during the admission and billing process and stay open!

You may experience compromise frequently in your work setting. For example, if a new admission is coming to your area but all staff are overloaded, perhaps other routine visits could be done by several nurses from another area so that the lengthier process of admission could be completed by the primary nurse who would be following the case. If a home dialysis tech asked for Christmas Eve off but ended up having to take call, perhaps another dialysis tech would share call and get the work done more quickly.

> Collaboration requires trust, a clear understanding and appreciation of each other's position, and a willingness to reframe the goal to one of mutual concern.

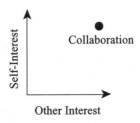

Source: Adapted from the Thomas-Kilmann Conflict Mode Instrument. Copyright © 1974, by Xicom, Inc., Tuxedo, New York. Reproduced with permission by Aspen Publishers, Inc.

Collaboration

The "win-win" approach to conflict resolution, or collaboration, is founded on the ability of each party to focus on what each wants or needs, as well as their mutual goals. In collaboration, each party contributes to the problem-solving process so that views can be integrated. All relevant issues are discussed in an open and honest manner, with mutual respect for each individual's thoughts, feelings, and ideas. Both parties "win" because they have been heard and their ideas and needs have been considered. The final resolution should be acceptable, if not preferable, to all involved. This "win-win" approach will be discussed in more detail in the Hansten and Washburn Collaborative Resolution Method later in this chapter.

As you reviewed your organization's mission, we suspect you found some statements about treating those you serve with dignity and respect. These same precepts or values are necessary to work within a situation of conflict. Although all the methods can be used effectively within an appropriate problem situation, compromise and collaboration reflect a thorough consideration of each party's needs, emotions, and issues.

Collaboration is a time-consuming approach and should be used for those problems that require participative involvement for the success of a program, those where emotions are deep, and those where there is significant need for the relationship between the parties to grow and mature. Changing care providers, adding new personnel, and redefining roles require a true collaborative effort.

Let's look at a few issues and determine what method would be best to use.

1Q: There is a conflict between the RN who supervises the oncology program in this large metropolitan visiting nurse service and the pain management protocols recommended by the physician advisor to the service.
Conflict resolution method of choice _____
Why?_____

1A: Collaboration should be attempted first because there are significant reasons to invest in this relationship: its quality will affect individuals, the team, and the patients. Both individuals are driven by the mutual goal of the most appropriate and effective patient treatment. It's possible that other personal needs are involved, and compromise may be necessary.

2Q: The rehabilitation team has worked extensively with a family regarding the home care plan for a paraplegic patient, Fred. However, one of the family members strongly believes, from a religious standpoint, that Fred should not be completing his self-catheterization. Although this viewpoint is difficult for the health care team, the caregiver has shown no change of attitude, despite many reasoned discussions.
Conflict resolution method of choice _____
Why?_____
2A: Compromise may be necessary in this situation. Reality dictates that if a procedure will not be completed due to pressure of a family member, another method may be needed. Perhaps the religious standpoint could be further explored and the exact nature or rationale of the prohibition could be discussed to find a creative solution. Perhaps the family member will not have to be involved in this procedure. When deep values, such as religious teachings, are involved, it's difficult for everyone to be totally satisfied with solutions.

3Q: Sally was brought up by an abusive, alcoholic mother. When she visits the home of an alcoholic diabetic patient, she finds herself unable to listen carefully to the concerns of this patient. When she allows herself to be honest, she figures that he's killing himself anyway and that her time is wasted when she tells him to eat right and to take his insulin and medications as ordered. It's a constant argument, with Sally telling him what to do and the patient ignoring her.
Conflict resolution method of choice _____
Why?_____
3A: Unless Sally has already embarked on an effective personal counseling journey, it may be best for her to use avoidance and ask someone else to take over his care. Awareness of her inability to deal with the inevitable conflict successfully shows respect for herself and for her patient.

4Q: Pablo, a case manager for total hip patients throughout the health care continuum in a large health care conglomerate, notices that one of the acute care facilities frequently sends total hip patients home without adequate preparation and referrals on the weekends and holidays. When he attempts to discuss this with the director of that department, she begins to shout about the level of staffing that is available during those periods.

Conflict resolution method of choice _____

Why? _____

4A: This situation calls for collaboration on the part of Pablo, who has legitimate concerns, and the department director, who seems frustrated at her staffing situation. A win-win solution will creatively address both individuals' concerns. Their mutual ground at this point is their need to assure patients' welfare.

5Q: Pat, an AIDS patient in a residential care facility, has been very angry about the facility visiting rules. She wishes to be married to her significant other, Kim, and wants to invite at least 50 friends. Her condition is declining. She is angry and shouts at you, the nurse in charge, about the "antihumane corporate policies."

Conflict resolution method of choice _____

Why? _____

5A: The nurse has every reason to accommodate Pat's need to go around the rules. The nurse may need to ask Pat to compromise on the number of guests but, if possible, can accommodate Pat's wishes. The charge nurse has very little invested in the corporate rules in this situation and will be even more satisfied if Pat "wins."

6Q: You receive a call from a home health aide who wonders whether it's OK to allow Mr. Allen to smoke with his oxygen on. She says he's agreed to be wheeled to the other side of the bedroom to smoke, and will keep the window open.

Conflict resolution method of choice _____

Why? _____

6A: "I win, you lose" is the method of choice in this situation. The patient also wins if he and his apartment complex don't go up in flames. It's an issue you may wish to discuss again with the home health aide to resolve any educational needs about the use of oxygen and flammable materials.

7Q: As a public health nurse, you are concerned about the number of teen pregnancies and HIV and other STD (sexually transmitted disease) cases in your community. You have been teaching classes, which include use of condoms as well as the choice of abstinence. The principal of a local high school describes the outrage that has been shared by a group of parents. Your obvious concern is safety and the public health. Parents are concerned that discussion of contraception and use of condoms will increase sexual activity or encourage students to engage in intercourse at an early age.

Conflict resolution method of choice _____

Why?_____

7A: This situation calls for a collaborative approach in the long run. In the short run, the nurse could attempt competition ("I will continue to teach this no matter what they say because the teens need to hear it for their own safety"), or accommodation and passive-aggressive behavior ("I won't discuss it this week, to let things cool down, and just go back to the same concepts after parents forget about it.")

Before we move on to the Hansten and Washburn Collaborative Resolution Method, let's review the sources of conflict, the beneficial and destructive consequences, and the advantages to dealing with conflict appropriately to the given situation. Please review the flowchart in Figure 9–1.

INNOVATIVE ISSUE RESOLUTION PROCESS: A COLLABORATIVE METHOD

Exhibit 9–3 outlines the collaborative resolution method. Quickly review the process steps in the figure and then proceed to the discussion. We'll be asking you to apply the process in some clinical situation that you may have encountered.

The first step in resolving issues or conflicts is to be aware of your state of mind. If you are angry and upset, your mind will be closed to creativity. If you feel threatened, your "fight or flight" response will be operant, and things will not proceed as effectively. In health care, we don't have the luxury of wasting time and money on uncontrolled, unexamined emotions.

1. Shift Your Focus. Instead of thinking about how you're being wronged, or the negative characteristics of the Neanderthal person you're dealing with, blow out the flame of anger instead of adding fuel to it. Several methods can help you remain calm and logical as you attempt to resolve an issue.

Stimulate your right brain and creativity by thinking about what is good about the problem. (We encourage you to read *Awaken the Giant Within* (Robbins, 1992) for more on positive problem solving.) For example, in the above problem (#7) of teen sex education, consider what could be positive about this issue arising.

Perhaps you are glad that this has happened now because the school year

> Identifying what's good about the problem allows you to stop the negative downward spiral of "ain't it awful" and begin to think of creative and positive options.

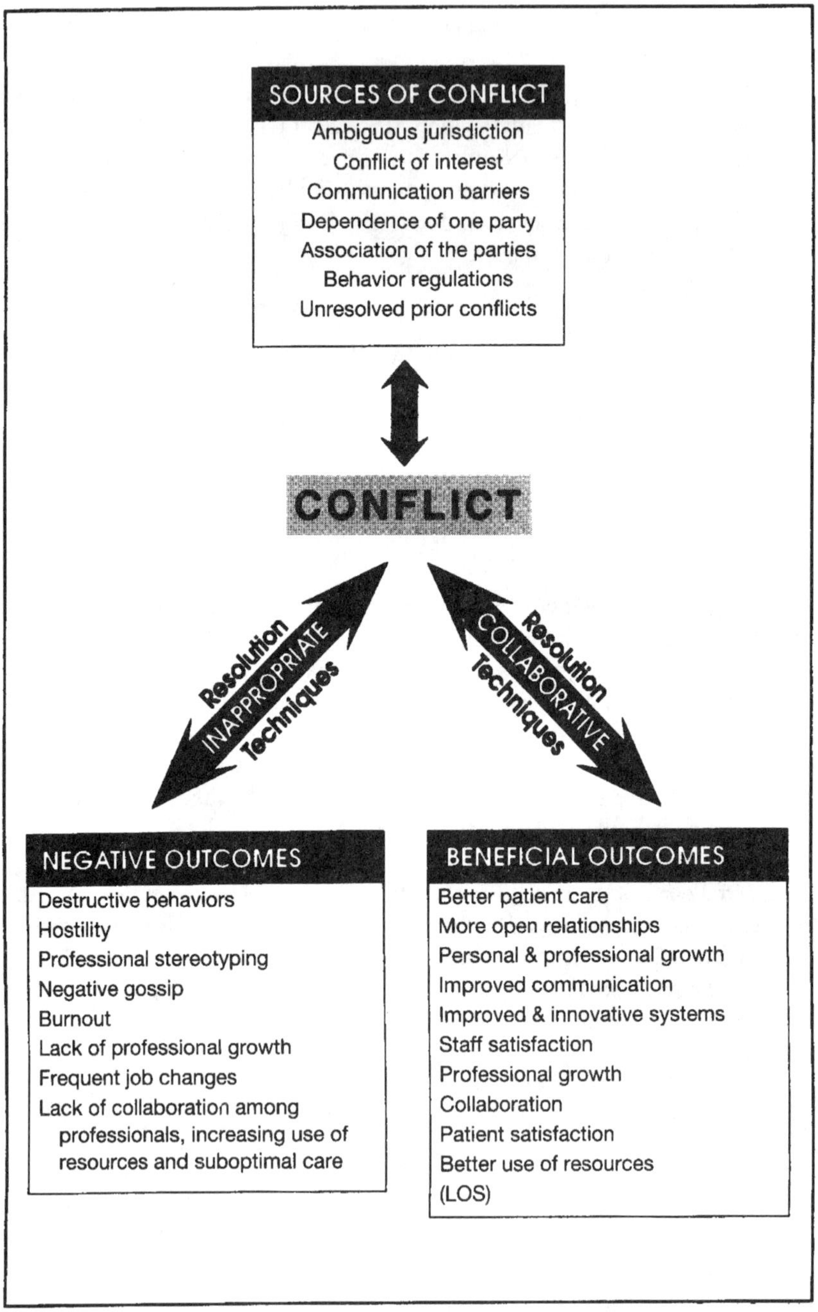

SOURCES OF CONFLICT
Ambiguous jurisdiction
Conflict of interest
Communication barriers
Dependence of one party
Association of the parties
Behavior regulations
Unresolved prior conflicts

CONFLICT

Resolution INAPPROPRIATE Techniques

Resolution COLLABORATIVE Techniques

NEGATIVE OUTCOMES
Destructive behaviors
Hostility
Professional stereotyping
Negative gossip
Burnout
Lack of professional growth
Frequent job changes
Lack of collaboration among
    professionals, increasing use of
    resources and suboptimal care

BENEFICIAL OUTCOMES
Better patient care
More open relationships
Personal & professional growth
Improved communication
Improved & innovative systems
Staff satisfaction
Professional growth
Collaboration
Patient satisfaction
Better use of resources
(LOS)

Figure 9–1 Conflict Flowchart. Courtesy of Dennis Burnside, 1998, Omaha, Nebraska.

Exhibit 9–3 Hansten and Washburn's Collaborative Resolution Method

Shift Your Focus.

What is good about this issue?
Separate the person from the problem.
Determine exactly what you want.

Create a Positive Open Attitude.

Listen and restate what the other party wants.
Be certain he or she feels heard.
Reflect and respect feelings expressed.

State Your Perception.

Use assertive language.
Express what it is you want from a factual viewpoint.
Determine what you are willing to do, or give up, to get what you want.

Establish Mutual Goals.

Determine what the other party is willing to do, or give up, to get what he or she wants.
Propose a solution that reflects your understanding of both parties' needs/desires.
Summarize each party's agreed-on actions.

Source: Reprinted from R. Hansten and M. Washburn, How Can I Get My Coworkers to Work with Me As a Team? *Clinical Delegation Skills*, p. 267, © 1998, Aspen Publishers, Inc.

is just beginning and you feel so strongly about these issues, affording a whole year of improved communication between school, nurses, students, and parents. Resolving the conflict will perhaps teach the parents about the current case data and allow them to be more active in home education. Perhaps this will allow you to get to know the community better and educate them about the role of the public

> Determine exactly what you want. Most people fail to resolve a conflict successfully because they are reacting on an emotional level and have not clearly identified their desired outcome.

health nurses and department in their community. This may sound like a Pollyanna part to collaboration, but it is essential to shift to a positive way of thinking so you can use the creativity necessary for problem solving.

Separate the person from the problem. This time-honored phrase has been used as fundamental to conflict resolution since people began to think about the process. Remember that the person who is telling you about this issue (the principal) is caught in the middle. The parents are his constituents, as are the students who need protection and education. The parents are reacting out of a misunderstanding of what is being taught. This allows you to view individuals involved dispassionately, more as a pawn to circumstance than as someone who is personally plotting against your (or the students') happiness.

Determine exactly what you want. By this time, you must be calm enough to take the energy produced by those emotions and harness it to think logically about what you'd like to reap from the time you'll spend on this issue. What is the bottom-line result you'd like to see? In this case, you probably want the teens to understand how to protect themselves from pregnancy and disease and how to deal responsibly with their sexual feelings. In the best of all worlds, the parents would reinforce and support the students' sex education.

If you are still not calm enough to think about this problem logically, then take some time to relax and calm down. Deep breaths, counting to 10, prayer, and taking a short bathroom or coffee break are useful to some. Nurses have also told us that they use such techniques as creative visualization and directive self-talk. These are not auditory or visual hallucinations. In creative visualization, you think of yourself in a safe, calm place, whether it is by a rushing stream in the mountains, fly fishing, or on your couch at home in front of a crackling fire with a cup of herbal tea. Others visualize themselves or someone they admire dealing with the issue in an effective manner. Some visualize the opposing person(s) in his or her pajamas, wearing a clown nose, or in other less threatening attire. Many people direct their self-talk, that continuous running commentary in your brain, to be positive: "I know I can handle this, I will be calm, and besides, no one will remember this day 100 years from now!"

2. Create a Positive Open Attitude. Listen closely to what the other party is saying. By continuing to keep your focus shifted from your anger to the other party's needs, and trying to understand his or her position fully, you are influencing the potential for a positive outcome to the discussion.

Listen carefully to what is being said. The principal is telling you about angry parents. How many parents are concerned, and why? As you restate what you've heard, you're clarifying and asking for more information. "So some parents have called and voiced concerns? Tell me more about what has happened."

Be certain that the other party feels he or she has been fully heard and that his or her position has been understood. "If I hear you correctly, you are feeling quite a bit of community pressure on this issue? How do you think this might affect you in your job?"

Reflect the feelings that have been expressed. In our example discussion, perhaps the principal will express concerns about being in trouble with the school board if these parents approach them with unsubstantiated stories about the sex education class. In many cases, people will not express their feelings clearly, and you may need to put yourself in their place, empathize, and then ask for confirmation. "You seem pretty nervous about this. I can certainly see where this would be of concern to you, especially with what happened recently with the football coach and the drinking on the bus. Am I on target with how I think you are feeling about this?" Naming their emotions, fears, or concerns often allows people to be less guarded, discuss the issues without hidden agendas, and solve problems more effectively. If the other party is very angry or upset, stating that you've received that message will help take the wind out of their sails. When talking with the parents, you may say "I can see this is upsetting for you and you seem to be feeling quite concerned. I would also be very concerned if I thought someone was encouraging my young teen to experiment with intercourse. I understand that your reaction is based on that perception. Let's talk about what we can do together to clarify the situation and put the students' health and safety as a priority."

Respect all feelings that are expressed. Nurses are great empathizers; we may know how we would feel in the same circumstance. However, the range of human emotions and thoughts is varied, and whatever feelings are expressed must be respected as such. Judging whether a feeling is right, wrong, or justified is not helpful and only serves to further isolate the two parties. (Behaviors, however, are subject to feedback and comment. Discussion of methods of giving feedback will be discussed in Chapter 10.)

3. State Your Perception. In this step, you are again sharing your viewpoint and what you'd like to accomplish by your discussion. Think back to our last chapter on assertiveness and use your "when you, I feel, I want" recipe as needed. For example, you may state, "I noticed that you wanted to stop the sex education pro-

> Respect all feelings that are expressed. Judging whether a feeling is right, wrong, or justified is not helpful and only serves to isolate the two parties.

gram at the high school in reaction to these parents' concerns. I felt uncomfortable about not being approached to discuss this first. Let's work on these issues together before decisions are made in the future." This statement focuses on the long-term results and the reason you are feeling distressed. "For now, let's continue with the education as it is, and set up a meeting with the concerned parents for early next week. Let's also plan for an evening meeting so that all parents can attend and hear the information that I share with the students so that there is no misunderstanding about what is being said."

In the above discussion, the nurse has looked at the problem in two ways: one is a short-term resolution (don't stop the sex education program); the other, long-term (how can we find a better system to educate the parents and avoid these problems in the future, thus keeping the teen pregnancy and STD case rate at the minimum?). The nurse has used assertive language to express feelings and stated what he or she wanted from a factual viewpoint. The nurse has also determined that he or she is willing to do at least one thing to resolve the problem: call parents and set up meetings to discuss these concerns.

What else may the RN do to start on resolving the long-term issue? She may use the meeting time to accomplish the overall goal of decreasing teen pregnancy and STD rates by educating parents and students, thus noting that this conflict may be beneficial to the community in the long run.

4. Establish Mutual Goals. In any area of health care, the patient or client's service or care must be the mutual, bottom-line objective of all parties involved. When people are reminded of their shared goals, it is much less difficult to obtain participation. "Because all of us are here to promote safe, healthy teens who do not engage in early or unprotected sexual intercourse, we can certainly agree to a method to teach them the necessary information."

Determine what the other party is willing to do, or give up, to be a part of the solution. "Will you be willing to come to hear the information I share with the students?"

Propose a solution that reflects your understanding of the needs and desires of the other party as well as your own, and then review what each party has agreed to do.

"So as principal you'll help set up the meetings for next week and the week after, and you'll let me know if any concerns come up that may affect my work with the students here. We may have to begin researching other schools and find out what they do when some parents refuse to have their children taught sex education." "As parents, you'll agree to come to a meeting, hear the content of the classes, and give me feedback regarding the classes."

This step allows us to clarify whether each party has remained clear and whether the parties agree on a course of action. Each party has "won" and will be invested in the solutions.

Although the process of collaborative resolution seems intricate and involved, there are really four main issues:

1. Shift your focus to what's possible and away from the negative feelings.
2. Create a positive open attitude by listening and respecting the other party's position.
3. State your perception and position assertively, clearly, and factually.
4. Establish mutual goals and actions based on input and participation from both parties. Use the imagery of the arrows to help you remember.

CASE STUDY ANALYSIS OF COLLABORATIVE RESOLUTION

Jamal is a community health nurse who visits a men's work release center. He has had some concerns about some nagging coughs that he's heard, particularly when he visits during early morning hours. Although most of his clients have been smokers, some also have had positive PPDs (TB skin tests) without preventive drug therapy. He's read about the growing prevalence of a multidrug-resistant tuberculosis in his geographical area and wonders whether all of the prisoners would be infected through the current ventilation system. He's brought the concerns and a plan for follow-up PPDs, chest films, and sputum samples to the physician advisor, Dr. Richards. Dr. Richards, who is also responsible for the budget of the facility, reacts angrily: "Jamal, you are just like a mother hen! I am tired of hearing about all the real or imagined ills of 'your patients!' These people are heavy smokers, have been drug abusers, and are in horrible health all around. They are going to cough in the morning, for heaven's sake! Don't you have enough to do? We can't afford to do all those tests on these people!"

Follow the process to help Jamal respond to Dr. Richards. Write down your thoughts as well as your dialogue in this situation.

1. Shift your focus. _____
   _____
   _____
   _____

2. Create a positive open attitude. _____
   _____
   _____
   _____

3. State your perception. _____
   _____
   _____
   _____

4. Establish mutual goals. _____
   _____
   _____
   _____

1. In shifting your focus, you wonder what is good about this problem. Perhaps this gives Jamal a chance to prove his clinical expertise and judgment, or an opportunity to clarify his role expectations with Dr. Richards, as they seem to be in conflict. It's certainly good that Dr. Richards is reacting at all, because he rarely seems to have an opinion on anything. Besides, it's necessary to get him involved in this potentially serious situation. In separating the person from the problem, you've identified the real problem as the health of these coughing patients. What you want is an opportunity to further assess the etiology of these coughs and rule out TB or other infectious disease agent.

2. What is Dr. Richards saying here? Is he afraid that he can't really affect the wellness of the inmates without it costing too much? Does he feel out of control of their health due to the myriad of other risk factors? He's obviously irritated. Jamal might respond, "Dr. Richards, I can see this is a frustration for you as it is for me. These people have just about destroyed their bodies before they get to us, and certainly we don't have enough money to give them all bionic parts! It's hard for us, me especially, to determine where I can best be of help to them all. Do you ever feel that way?"

3. Dr. Richards has verified this feeling of helplessness; now it's time for Jamal to share his position. "As frustrating as it may be, I am even more concerned when I hear the increasingly loud racket of productive coughs when I visit during the early morning hours. Some of the inmates are also complaining of night sweats and were never followed up on their positive skin tests. When I am confronted with all of these symptoms, I feel increasingly frightened for their safety as well as ours, and I want your help in deciding what kind of follow-up should be done with respect to efficacy as well as cost. The cost would be astronomical, both in terms of treatment and in terms of public outrage, if we had a TB problem and did nothing about it. I am willing to do overtime or whatever it takes, including getting the advice of the state TB epidemiologist."

4. Because Dr. Richards seems to be responding well to the facts now that Jamal has outlined them effectively, as well as being cognizant of the risks involved with not acting, it's time to remind him of the mutual goals. "After all, our

jobs here, as I see it, are to ensure the optimal health of these clients, given the cost constraints and the material we are given to work with! We are certainly working together for the same goals, right?"

After Jamal asks Dr. Richards for suggestions, Richards determines he'll call an old friend at the health department for some input. He'd like Jamal to call the state TB nurse specialist and find out how the state could help. As the conversation continues, Jamal wants to restate the plan. "So I will call the TB nurse specialist for assistance, and you'll talk with your friend who's been involved in the program, and we'll get together to discuss this on Friday at noon? Great! I feel better checking this out. There are just too many indications to avoid exploring the cough problem!" Jamal also knows a long-term problem is left to solve. How can he determine whether he is fulfilling Dr. Richards's expectations, or if there is a problem? Is he really a "mother hen," or was that response a result of Dr. Richards's frustration? "You know, Dick, I am wondering if we could also discuss how you feel I am doing in my responsibilities with the work release center. This is a relatively new method of providing health maintenance to these men, and I'm not sure how to interpret the comments you made earlier in the conversation. Could you think about this and we'll discuss it on Friday? I want to be able to present my concerns to you and to do my job overall, in the most effective manner, and I'd like some feedback." The physician may or may not respond now, but potentially Jamal will find out how he can better get Dr. Richards's attention without having to resolve a conflict.

CONCLUSION

Conflict, and our response to it, will always determine whether we move ahead as a profession or become paralyzed victims of circumstance, unwilling to take the risk that conflict demands. We have seen countless nurses literally stopped in their tracks, victims of everyone else's control, as they perceive the potential for conflict too great to take the chance. We have also observed many nurses who see conflict as a process of life and who have developed their skills in dealing with disagreement, just as you have mastered numerous clinical skills. Nursing is in the people business. And people don't always agree. Appreciating the benefits of that disagreement and being confident in your ability to resolve conflict will posi-

> Conflict, and our response to it, will always determine whether we move ahead as a profession or become paralyzed victims of circumstance, unwilling to take the risk that conflict demands.

tion you for the most satisfying career you can imagine. Secure in your under-standing of the basic four-step process of conflict resolution as outlined in this chapter, you will find yourself taking control of both your personal and professional growth. Isn't that the best outcome of all?

CHECKPOINT 9-3

To feel competent in dealing with the Collaborative Resolution Process, it's necessary to practice it continually. As often as we've taught these communication skills, it is still difficult for us to use them in every situation. We recommend that you think about a recent issue or conflict and role play resolving it with a friend. If you feel uncomfortable doing that, make yourself a "skill card" with the process, and keep it in your backpack, purse, or pocket to use as you plan to solve an interpersonal problem. After a conflict situation, use the process to evaluate how well you have done and where you may have needed to concentrate. Many nurses have found it effective to teach the process to their children or spouses and learn it better from teaching it.

Here are a few situations you can use to test your understanding. For further practice, look over the conflict issues listed earlier in the chapter.

1. It's near the end of a busy week, and you've asked a home health aide to make an unplanned Friday afternoon visit to a new patient who desperately needs some personal care. She responds that no, she is too tired from the week's work, and you don't ever appreciate all she does anyway.
2. At the group home for psychiatric patients, you've returned from a break and you notice from the sound of screaming and the presence of other staff members at the door of his room that one of the patients is having a serious problem. One of the attendants is on the phone, chatting about a date she is planning for the evening. You motion for her to get off the phone and help with the other patients, who are beginning to look anxious, pacing around the TV room. The attendant glares and turns her back, continuing her conversation.

3. You and your supervisor have had a disagreement about your caseload and the home health aides and rehabilitation aides working with your patients. You feel overwhelmed and unable to take on more work, and you aren't happy with the performance of your assistants. Your supervisor is adamant, and the entire agency is under terrible financial stress.

4. The director of your agency is an amiable physician who is near retirement. Recently, she has been displaying erratic behavior that may indicate she is being affected by chemical dependency or another personal problem. Yesterday before a noon meeting with the board, you encountered her on the elevator and smelled alcohol on her breath. You decide to discuss this with her assistant, who reacts angrily that you should keep quiet about it, and that she is sure the director has "everything under control."

See the end of the chapter for the answers.

ANSWERS TO CHECKPOINTS

9–3. Scenarios: suggested dialogue:

1. In shifting your focus, you realize that the real problem is not this nursing assistant but the fact that a task needs to be done and no one is agreeing to do it. You consider what is good about this problem: Perhaps you are glad to have the chance to interact with this aide, who has expressed her concerns about overwork before. Perhaps you are rested today and feel energetic about using your new conflict resolution method! You want to find someone to take over the task assignment (if not this home health aide) and to find out what's wrong with this coworker. To create a positive open attitude, you'll respond, "Wow, Mei, I can see that you are really overwhelmed! And I regret that you haven't felt appreciated, because I do appreciate your hard work and I guess I don't express it enough. We've all had a pretty rough week." In stating your perception, you may say, "But Mei, when I ask you for help, and you react by saying no right away, I feel hurt. I'd like us to look at the assignments together and see if you have other ideas about who else can be assigned to see this new patient. Some one has to complete it, and I know three of us will be overtime already." Mei may tell you that she needs

foot surgery and that she isn't feeling well. (You should certainly respond with a few caring comments.) You may also express that you've looked at the assignments and are unable to find anyone who will reach the office before 6 PM, and that you can't take on any more work yourself after opening three new cases. In establishing mutual goals, you may also state, "Mei, I know we all want the patients to get quality care and we also all want to get home and put up our feet. Would you be willing to assist with this new patient if you can call in your comments from the home and finish the charting on Monday? You could go home directly from the patient's visit, and I'll make comments for Marion to use over the weekend." Mei agrees. The next week, when time allows, discuss the long-term problem of Mei's feet, and how you and she could interact more positively regarding her assignments and the additional positive feedback she seems to require. Clarification of expectations, another concept covered earlier, will be helpful.

2. In shifting your focus, you take a few deep breaths. (If you have a split second, you may consider what is good about the problem: You finally have some objective evidence that this coworker is not performing. Usually she just disappears!) You know the real problem at hand is getting adequate assistance with the patient who is decompensating and with the other patients, who will be very upset. This is a time for using "competition" as a mode of resolution until you can work out a long-term solution. You may lightly touch your coworker and state, "Sue, I am going to help with Mr. Peters. You must check on the other patients. Now." Or, after you ascertain that the emergency is under control, you may return to Sue. You may use your assertive language and say, "I understand that it's important for you to have some time on the phone with your friends, but when I notice you are on the phone talking about a date while an emergency is going on, and you ignore me, I feel disappointed and angry, and frightened about the safety of the patients. In the future I would expect you to terminate your phone conversation and assist our patients when necessary, and schedule your personal phone time at break times." You've determined what you really want is for Sue to participate in the emergencies and supportive client care. You've determined that you are willing to make a point of resolving the issue and discussing it with Sue. Your mutual goals in this situation are safe care. Sue may have the additional goal of getting break time or free time to resolve personal issues. If that is the case, you can discuss how she can take care of those needs during breaks. A solution will certainly include all individuals being involved in caring for the patients during emergencies.

3. You begin by shifting your focus. What is good about this problem is that it has finally come to a head and that you'll be dealing with it for the good of all involved. You determine that you want to be able to do the work as

required but to have some impact on the way you supervise and evaluate the assistive personnel. You begin by discussing with the supervisor, "I know it's very tough financially here and we all want to do our best and keep the agency open, and keep our jobs. You have your hands full helping us to maintain productivity. But when I'm asked to do more than I'm sure I can do well, without having adequately trained assistants, I feel absolutely overwhelmed, and frankly, I am afraid. I'm not sure my patients are getting the care they need unless I have more time to supervise and teach these new assistants. I'm willing to take any suggestions you may have." As your supervisor understands that you are trying to work things out, she'll be able to interact with you more positively. "What I'd really like from you are some ideas on how to make certain I can supervise, train, and evaluate them and still do the necessary caseload." As the discussion continues, your supervisor may give you many worthwhile ideas, may assist in training or supervising your assistive personnel, or may modify your assignment. Remember to summarize each other's agreed-upon actions.

4. What's good about this problem? You've used your excellent powers of observation. The problem here is the potential for poor leadership and ill-advised decisions being made due to the agency director's behavior. You want someone to find out what is going on with her and to take action to help her and to protect the agency. You have another meeting with the assistant director, Maria Menendez. You begin by saying, "Maria, I know you are good friends with our director, Pam Putz, and it's tough to think there could be a problem. It's scary for all of us. But we all want to protect our agency, and indirectly our patients, if my concerns are valid. When you seemed to dismiss my objective examples of her erratic behavior yesterday, I felt even more concerned. I've lost sleep over this situation. I noted what I thought was alcohol on her breath yesterday before the board meeting, and although I could be mistaken, this could be a problem for all of us. As health care professionals, we can hardly sit by and not give some feedback to Pam. I am willing to be involved in the discussion with her, if you'd like, or be of support to you when you talk with her. Are you willing to discuss it with her? Good. Will you let me know when you've talked with her, then?" Although we haven't added the responses of Maria Menendez, she is aware that she must deal with the situation and determine what needs to be done. She also knows you aren't going to let the problem simmer when the health of a leader and the viability of the agency are involved. Good job!

REFERENCES

Forte, P. 1997. The high cost of conflict. *Nursing Economics* 15, no. 3: 119–123.

Fowler, A.R. Jr., et al. 1993. *Health Progress* 74, no. 5: 25–29.

Hansten, R., and M. Washburn. 1993. *The nurse manager's answer book.* Gaithersburg, MD: Aspen Publishers, Inc.

Robbins, A. 1992. *Awaken the giant within.* New York: Simon & Schuster.

Snow, C., and D. Willard. 1989. *I'm dying to take care of you: Nurses and codependence and breaking the cycles.* Redmond, WA: Professional Counselor Books.

RECOMMENDED READING

Anderson, K. 1993. *Getting what you want: How to reach agreement and resolve conflict every time.* New York: Penguin Books.

Fisher, R., et al. 1991. *Getting to yes.* 2nd ed. Boston: Houghton Mifflin Co.

Hargrove, R. 1998. *Mastering the art of creative collaboration.* Chicago: McGraw-Hill.

Marcus, L. 1995. *Renegotiating health care: Resolving conflict to build collaboration.* San Francisco: Jossey-Bass.

Rusk, T., with D.P. Miller. 1993. *The power of ethical persuasion.* New York: Viking Penguin.

Weeks, D. 1992. *The eight essential steps to conflict resolution.* New York: Jeremy T. Tarcher, Inc.

CHAPTER 10

Know How To Give Feedback: What Do Delegates Really Want?

Ruth I. Hansten and Marilynn J. Washburn

In Chapter 7 we discussed the need to know your delegates in terms of their strengths, weaknesses, motivation, cultural differences, and preferences. Communication is an essential skill in assessing your delegates in these areas, and the specific process of feedback will allow you to maintain a continuous cycle of effective communication that will not only assess the progress of the delegate but motivate performance as well.

Feedback is the final note in the circular process of delegation. Foregoing feedback is similar to singing the notes of the scale: do, re, mi, fa, sol, la, ti. . . . Everyone is waiting to hear "do," the last note, your words that will complete the cycle and will set the tone for the next time you work together. If they are left unspoken, you have failed to close the loop and to provide a solid foundation for the working relationship with your delegate. Lacking your feedback, the delegate may be making assumptions, filling in his or her own note.

The next time you work together, the delegate will be functioning with an unknown evaluation, and performance will be adversely affected by his or her unanswered questions. "Did I do OK? Does she think I'm a good worker? Does she even notice what I do?" Or the delegate will have formed an opinion of *you*: "She never notices, doesn't even say thank you after I've worked like a demon for her." "He never seems that busy, always sitting at the desk at the office, talking to docs while I'm running around like crazy. I hate to work with him." Or, worse yet, "I hope I don't do anything wrong, but who knows? I never get any feedback, so what does

> Feedback is the final note in the circular process of delegation.

CHECKPOINT 10-1

Think about the benefits you will realize from learning a process for giving effective feedback to your delegates. Jot down a few thoughts.

_____

_____

If delegates felt comfortable giving you constructive feedback on your communication skills, leadership, or performance, how would that benefit you and your performance?

_____

_____

_____

---

it matter? I only see the nurse once a month or so and she never says anything really when she comes out to the home."

Giving and receiving feedback takes courage. It's difficult to tell people what's going wrong, easier to talk about what is going well. It may be harder still to ask your delegate for an appraisal of your performance, and you may feel that this is unnecessary in your role. When it seems that giving and receiving feedback is the absolute last thing you want to do, it's helpful to think about the possible benefits to you and the delegate.

BENEFITS OF GIVING AND RECEIVING FEEDBACK

Some of the following responses are most commonly given to us by nurses. We hope that you identified similar benefits, as well as some that are particular to you:

- You learn how to lead the team better.
- Personal growth for both the RN and the delegate improves job opportunities for the future.
- The delegate learns and grows and is thus motivated to a more energetic effort.
- Positive performance is reinforced.
- Individual and team performance improves.

- Open communication helps overall teamwork.
- Patients receive better care.

Besides, haven't you always wondered what your delegates and coworkers thought about your performance?

THE POWER OF FEEDBACK

The value and benefit of feedback as a motivator cannot be stressed enough. Research studies repeatedly show that recognition, feedback, and constructive criticism are high-ranking factors in enhancing productivity and performance. When asked to rank work factors in terms of importance, the majority will list "appreciation of work" and "a feeling of being in on things" above the amount of pay, the loyalty from the supervisor, or the physical conditions of the job (Jenks and Kelly, 1985).

Feedback in the form of recognition is a significant factor to most of us. In a survey of nurses in the Midwest, 92 percent ranked recognition as important to job satisfaction, but 28 percent perceived this recognition to be given seldom or never. Verbal feedback was described as the most significant form of recognition, and many looked to their head nurse, nurse executive, patient, coworker, physician, and hospital department heads for this feedback (Goode et al., 1993). What an opportunity you have as a fellow colleague, knowing that a simple "thank-you" or "good job" can take so little time to say and yet can have such a tremendous impact!

A study of how both goals and feedback affect performance levels and motivation was published in 1983 by Bandura and Cervone, and its message has not changed. They found that when an individual has a challenging goal and detailed feedback (both positive and negative) is given, performance effort improves nearly 60 percent (Kouzes and Posner, 1993, p. 173). This underlines the need to discuss the preferred patient outcomes with team members when assignments are given and to evaluate progress along the way.

THE PROCESS

Many nurses would like to leave the process of feedback to the manager, believing perhaps that it is out of their realm of responsibilities and that

> When an individual has a challenging goal and detailed feedback (both positive and negative) is given, performance effort improves nearly 60 percent.

the manager has more time to devote to evaluating and supervising employees. However, regarding the process of delegation, the National Council of State Boards of Nursing (NCSBN) states,

> The delegating nurse is accountable for assessing the situation and is responsible for the decision to delegate. Monitoring, outcome evaluation and follow-up are necessary supervisory activities that follow delegation.... The delegator would be expected to provide supervisory follow-up such as intervention on the behalf of the client and corrective action (NCSBN, 1990, p. 3).

CHECKPOINT 10–2

Recall the last time someone recognized your efforts on the job or at home. How did you feel?

The feedback that you are required to give as a delegator involves some preparation in terms of assessment and analysis. *The following basic questions will be helpful in preparing you to follow up with your delegate:*

- What do I see? Is the delegate having difficulty with the task? Is the information not where I expected it to be (weekly weight not on the graphic sheet)?
- How does it affect me? Is it making my job easier or more difficult?
- What can I do about it? Can I offer additional training for the task he seems to be unable to do? Can I encourage him to share this skill with other members of the team?

When you are providing feedback to your delegates, the information shared will usually be one of the following four types (Hersey and Duldt, 1989):

1. *Clarifying:* This will involve restating your instructions, making certain that any confusion regarding the assignment is cleared up so that you both are in agreement regarding parameters for reporting and the expectations of per-

formance that you both have. "Please do Mrs. Johnson's first visit and check her blood pressure before 10 AM today, and call me with the results."

2. *Interpretive:* This particular type of feedback involves making an observation of the delegates' behavior and making assumptions about the meaning. "When Mr. Henley's daughter called and said you had not been there yet, I assumed you were taking a lunch break early." Be careful about this type of feedback—check your assumptions first!

3. *Judgmental:* Similar to interpretive feedback, this form also involves drawing conclusions, this time in the form of a value judgment regarding behavior. "You're such a slob! How can we get any work done when you leave such a mess in the conference room?"

4. *Personal reaction:* When you provide the delegate with information about your personal feelings, you are giving a strong message about how he or she is coming across. "I feel relieved when you are working with me because you do such a good job and I can count on you."

CHECKPOINT 10-3

Can you recall times when you have given feedback to coworkers that was (1) clarifying? (2) interpreting? (3) judgmental? (4) a personal reaction? How did you feel on each of these occasions? Which type was most effective for you?

GIVING FEEDBACK TO THE DELEGATE

It is easy to see by reviewing the types of feedback that potentially one can do more harm than good. You can increase the defensiveness of the delegate and further alienate the members of the team if a few simple criteria are not followed. *In further preparing your feedback message, consider the following criteria (LaMonica, 1983):*

- It is specific rather than general.
- It is directed toward behavior the receiver can do something about.
- It considers the needs of both the receiver and the giver of the feedback.
- It is solicited, rather than imposed.
- It is well timed.

> • It is checked to ensure clear communication by asking the receiver to rephrase the message to make certain he or she understands.

Keeping these criteria in mind, let's look at a method for giving feedback. Our proposed recipe can be used for both positive and negative feedback. For our example, let's use the situation of a new student nurse who has been working with you. You've noticed that Brenda does an excellent job in working with patients who have been diagnosed with cancer and are in the beginning stages of the grief process. You'd like to comment on how wonderful it has been to work with Brenda.

Who needs to be told this information? Brenda, certainly, needs to know how you feel. It would be helpful for Brenda if your evaluation of her expertise were shared with her instructor as well. When you have positive feedback to share, feel free to shout it from the rooftops and tell everyone. Letting others know about Brenda's performance is certainly positive to the general atmosphere of the work setting. Just be certain to let the person most involved hear it first! However, if the feedback is negative, then only Brenda should hear the news. It may, of course, be necessary for the manager and the instructor to hear about problems. (Be sure to tell any person that you'll be sharing the information with the manager or supervisory person prior to doing so.) Resist telling stories to others about the errors individuals have made. Adlai Stevenson said, "If you throw mud, you get dirty." Confidentiality in performance feedback of a negative nature is essential, and betraying confidences will cause the speaker to look bad as well.

When the feedback discussion takes place is also essential. As soon as you are aware that feedback needs to be shared, time should be planned to make certain it occurs. If emergency circumstances dictate that feedback will need to wait, then tell the person as soon as possible that you'll need to talk with him or her and set up a time. It is human nature to avoid the unpleasant, but in health care we do not have the luxury of avoiding giving performance feedback of a negative nature because human lives are at stake. (Think of late feedback you've been given about a circumstance that took place several months earlier. It isn't effective for either learning or motivational purposes.)

Where the feedback session occurs is also important for the success of the discussion. Obviously, negative feedback is never given in public, whereas praise is wonderful to hear in any setting. Negative feedback given without discretion to the time and place will belittle the importance of the message and be ineffective because the receiver will generally react defensively due

> Adlai Stevenson said, "If you throw mud, you get dirty."

to the shame of being reprimanded in public. Instead of being useful, this is destructive to the results intended.

THE SUPERVISORY VISIT

As reviewed in Chapters 3 and 7, the Health Care Financing Administration (HCFA) has a few regulations regarding the frequency of supervision of personal attendants and home health aides. Our discussion of the law also included the recognition that the definition of supervision includes not only initial guidance, but periodic inspection as well. This regulated form of feedback assures that the work of the delegate will be monitored and evaluated for effectiveness, competency, and safety. When your presence is required at a supervisory visit in the client's home, what better time to use the following feedback model to maximize the visit.

THE FEEDBACK MODEL

1. Get the delegate's input before proceeding.
2. Give credit for the delegate's efforts.
3. Share your perception of what you have observed, read, assessed.
4. Explore the situation more fully with the delegate: discuss gaps in perceptions, causes of the problem.
5. Get the delegate's solution to the problem.
6. Agree on an action plan.
7. Set a time to check on progress.

APPLICATION TO THE DELEGATION PROCESS

As Georgia, an RN, plans to give feedback to Natalie, she reviews the plan of care for Mr. Logan, the 66-year-old dialysis patient whom Natalie has been caring for. The supervisory visit is scheduled for 10 AM, during Natalie's scheduled time to be caring for Mr. Logan. Earlier this week, the client's daughter-in-law called Georgia to praise Natalie and to say how delighted they were that she was so reliable, and well-liked by her dad.

1. Getting the delegate's input is essential and is the step that people often miss. In this case, Georgia knows that Natalie has asked for a week off, and would like to have her assignment changed when she gets back. Georgia will need

CHECKPOINT 10-4

Give proposed responses to the situation that follows between Georgia, Natalie, Mr. Logan, and his daughter. Use the feedback model below.

1. Get the delegate's input before proceeding. "Natalie, how do you feel things have been going?"
2. Give credit for the delegate's efforts.
3. Share your perception of what you have observed, read, assessed.
4. Explore the situation more fully with the delegate: discuss gaps in perceptions, causes of the problem.
5. Get the delegate's solution to the problem.
6. Agree on an action plan.
7. Set a time to check on progress.

to have a private discussion with Natalie during the early part of the visit to find out Natalie's views on how things are going.
2. There is no substitute for giving credit for others' efforts. Once Georgia determines what Natalie thinks of how the case has been going, she needs to recognize Natalie's hard work and the efforts she has been making. This is essential! No one likes to be criticized all the time, and we all appreciate the recognition that we have been working hard (even if this is not the case, almost all of us believe we have been extending the hardest effort!)
3. It's now time to share the perceptions Georgia has about Natalie's work. She needs to share the comments of the daughter-in-law, and to review the case from her perspective. Mr. Logan will be needing continued assistance for the next two months, until he moves to Florida to be with his niece. He and his family would like to have Natalie continue, and so would Georgia.

Maintain and preserve the self-respect of delegates by being respectful in your manner and speech. Asking yourself what you want delegates to remember from the conversation will help you to set the correct tone. Do you want them to remember how angry and upset you were? If so, be prepared for the situation to repeat itself, as a display of anger will allow delegates to focus on your behavior, not theirs. It's a fact of human behavior that we tend to remember process, how something was said, much more readily than what was said. A calm, objective manner will overcome that tendency and keep the focus on the message, not your emotions. Insisting that Natalie stay with the case, that she has no opportunity to take a vacation and to change assignments, will only alienate the relationship. Giving in to frustration, and reminding Natalie that Mr. Logan has had three home health aides in the past three weeks, will not serve any benefit.

4. As the situation is explored, Georgia shares her assessment of Natalie's performance, noting how reliable she has been, coming on time, and working hard to please Mr. Logan's very specific demands.

5. Getting input and discussion from the delegate, Natalie responds that she has been taking twice as long with this visit, and it puts her behind for the rest of the day. Mr. Logan is lonely and likes to talk, and always seems to have one more request before she leaves. As input is received from the delegate, remember that performance problems are generally due to a combination of several factors: Delegates may not understand their role or your expectations. They may not know that the way they are performing their role does not correlate with what you desire, or that it doesn't measure up. Barriers may be present in the environment (those systems problems), or they may not understand how to do their job or why it is supposed to be done the way you want it to be. They may need further education or closer supervision. Or they may lack the necessary motivation to do the job right. Natalie's solution in this case is simply to transfer to another assignment, and not have to worry about ol' Mr. Logan's demands. She does, however, like Mr. Logan and his family and feels bad that he will have to have another aide.

6. Georgia reviews some options for setting limits, and suggests that together she and Natalie talk with Mr. Logan and his daughter-in-law about realistic requests, and what is included in what Natalie is to provide as supportive and personal care. The length of the visit will also be reviewed. Natalie is agreeable to this action plan, and willing to continue with the case—if they can work things out so she can stay on time with her daily schedule.

7. The discussion during the remainder of this visit goes smoothly, with all parties agreeing to the scope of Natalie's care, and to the time frame of the visit. Nancy, the daughter-in-law, agrees to check in with Mr. Logan and Natalie, and to call Georgia if there are any concerns. Natalie agrees to do so as well.

Now, let's use the feedback model process to give negative feedback.

Mike, the PT aide, has been doing range of motion exercises on Martha, a 42-year-old MS client. She called you today in tears, saying that Mike was very rude and hurt her during his visit today. You know you need to give feedback to Mike before his next visit to Martha, so you page him and ask him to call you this afternoon at the office.

You: How have your visits been going with Martha? I had a phone call from her today, and I was wondering if you were doing OK with her exercise routine. Did she seem upset during your visit?

Mike: That old bag! I feel sorry for her, lying around all day and just waiting for me to come and move her a little so she isn't bored! No, she didn't seem upset, just stiff. Her muscles are getting more atrophied, and she doesn't do anything to help herself.

You: I'm sorry you feel that way, Mike. I know many of your patients have told me you do an excellent job, and I appreciate your willingness to take on extra patients. In Martha's case, she was rather upset and stated that you were rude and hurt her during her therapy today.

Mike: Wow! I'm sorry! I didn't mean to hurt her, but maybe I upset her when I said I thought she was getting a little stiffer and should be getting out more.

You: Sometimes it's hard to hear that things are not getting better, and we do not know that they aren't in Martha's case. What do you think you should do now to get things back on track? Martha was pretty upset.

Mike: How about if I give her a quick call and tell her I didn't mean to be rude, and that I'll work with her more gently tomorrow?

You: Great idea, Mike. I'm sure she'd appreciate hearing from you. Let me know how tomorrow goes, okay?

Now give feedback to your office staffer, Joe. Lately, he has been giving you referrals that are incomplete in one way or another, missing the age of the client, or having the wrong street address.

Follow the process or role play a feedback session. Describe the setting. Then follow the steps of the feedback process.

A possible conversation would proceed as follows:

Marion: Joe, how have things been going for you here with respect to your role and work?

Joe: Pretty well, Marion, but I feel a bit like my skills are being underused. You know I want to become a mental health professional instead of an intake coordinator. Otherwise, I think the job is okay.

Marion: I think it's great that you want to advance your career and if I can help in any way, let me know. One thing that will be very important as you learn a new role is accuracy. I'd like to talk to you about the referral forms you have been giving me in the past two days. The referrals for Mr. Jesup and Mr. Kile had the wrong addresses, and Mrs. Brady's did not list her age. I know it's tough to get the information from the client or hospital sometimes, but it delays our care of the clients if I have to

CHECKPOINT 10-5

Review the conversation between Mike and you and match the steps of the performance feedback process on the following chart:

1. Get the delegate's input before proceeding.
2. Give credit for the delegate's efforts.
3. Share your perception of what you have observed, read, assessed.
4. Explore the situation more fully with the delegate: discuss gaps in perceptions, causes of the problem.
5. Get the delegate's solution to the problem.
6. Agree on an action plan.
7. Set a time to check on progress.

go back and correct these forms. How do you think this should be resolved?

Joe: Marion, as much as I hate the detail work, I guess I have been slipping. I can see how it would be frustrating for you all. I'll pay more attention and make sure I have all the blanks filled correctly.

Marion: Great! I'll let you know if I find any more missing information, and I appreciate the effort. Thanks!

Practice Feedback Scenarios

1. In your family planning clinic, an assistant who also performs secretarial work has decided to telephone the patients with their human immunodeficiency virus test results before consulting with you, the RN who generally counsels patients about these issues.
2. You have heard about a new colleague drawing blood without using gloves during her home visit. Someone needs to talk with her.
3. A personal attendant has been discussing confidential information about clients while in the office getting supplies.
4. In a joint visit, the social worker talked with a client's family to plan nursing home placement. After the social worker left, the family complained about the "condescending attitude" that was displayed.

5. A physician who is the consultant for the school nurses' immunization clinic met with some of the community leaders at an evening holiday open house. He had evidently had something alcoholic to drink because his breath smelled quite strong, although his behavior didn't seem altered. One of the community leaders asked, "Is this clinic run by someone with a drinking problem? I think that drinking alcohol is a bad example for the people of this community, where substance abuse is very high. You need to tell the doctor we don't want to smell alcohol on his breath again!" Margaret, one of the school nurses, has to decide whether to give this feedback to the physician, but is afraid of the impact on the clinic if she doesn't.
6. Maria, the home health aide on the weekend call list, routinely complains about having to care for clients who are "just going to die anyway."
7. Greta has come in to work late several times in the past week.

REQUESTING AND RECEIVING FEEDBACK

As you can see from our model, feedback requires an exchange of information to be most effective. You can give recognition (and we certainly recommend it!) in a one-way communication format and still have a positive impact. However, allowing the delegate to offer input too will set up a two-way communication process that is much more meaningful and can lead to longer lasting results.

> When the delegate feels that his or her input is valued, you are building trust and a positive working relationship. The input you receive can help you to further improve your performance as well and make working together easier and more beneficial for the patient.

Great supervisors ask for feedback from their staff not only in terms of clinical data or reports on how the systems are working in their area but on their own performance. RNs who ask for input on their personal performance from their delegates will soon capture the respect and admiration of their teammates. Receiving feedback graciously allows the RN to hear the other person's point of view without being defensive or angry. The RN can further explore the points being made and decide whether the feedback is something that he or she can use to improve his or her performance or behavior in the job setting.

It is important to understand that some delegates may have difficulty in participating in a two-way communication process. Others may welcome the chance and overwhelm you with their opinions! To make certain the process stays on track, you may want to review what is expected (clarifying expectations again) so that you foster an environment in which you are all working together to improve delivery of care.

On a periodic basis, it's important to ask such questions as:

- How did these assignments work for you?
- Is there anything I could have done that would have made the day/shift/case better for you?
- How am I doing, in your perception?
- What am I doing that works well?
- What should I be working on, in your opinion?
- What ideas do you have that I could use to make things work better here?
- Did the instructions I gave you help, or was there a better way for me to communicate with you?

Being open to such feedback allows your delegates to know you think you are human too, and fallible. They will feel less defensive themselves when you must give them negative feedback or criticism if they know you are willing to receive it yourself. And certainly everyone will feel more free to give the positive feedback needed to keep everyone's self-esteem and motivation at the highest level.

UPWARD FEEDBACK

Most of our discussion so far has been on providing information to the delegates in terms of their performance, to ensure their competency in performing delegated tasks. When soliciting feedback from delegates, you are, in effect, asking them to provide "upward feedback," or evaluative information to a superior. This can be difficult for many, because the fear of reprisal may hinder their desire to be honest. Consider your own situation—are you comfortable in providing feedback to your supervisor?

Unfortunately, we have worked with some organizations where the "chain of command" was strictly enforced and communication flowed only in one direction. This top-down approach has a significant negative impact on teamwork, morale, and productivity. It is sad to see such outdated management practices in any organization, but there are ways around the limitations imposed by such a command/control environment.

If you find yourself in a situation where providing feedback to a superior is forbidden and you must continue to work in that setting, you can speak to these

CHECKPOINT 10–6

Consider the following situations:

1. Why is it so important, as an RN, to ask for feedback from others on the team?
2. Think about a situation in which you've been delegating to others. What questions could you ask to determine how you are doing?
3. Arlene, a school nurse, has given many instructions to the parents who help out in the high school when she's at another school in her area. The school secretary tells Arlene that a parent was assisting when a girl came in with some concerns, and then the girl left the office sobbing. The secretary overheard the assisting parent telling the girl loudly that "you should have just said no! Well, you'd better call your parents about this pregnancy or I will!" How would you give feedback and further instructions to the assisting parent?
4. Frank, a nurse working in a poison control center, has trained a new assistant. This nurse is relatively inexperienced, and Frank is quite concerned about the first few times that she'll be on alone. How can Frank receive some feedback from his new assistant about the training process and his supervision style while giving feedback to the new nurse?

See the end of the chapter for the answers.

individuals using the assertive strategy of "I messages." Rather than focusing on "you are never around when I need you," consider rephrasing the message as "I need to know where I can reach you if we get another referral for involved diabetic care." If you are not getting any feedback from this supervisor and would like to find out how you are doing, don't criticize him or her for lack of performance ("You never give me any feedback—how am I supposed to know how I'm doing?"). Instead, use the I-message technique and state, "I need to have some information from you about how I am doing. I have been here at the agency for three months now, and I'd like to know if I am performing OK."

Recall what we discussed in the chapter on communication: Before sitting down to give feedback to a superior, be clear on the outcome you would like from

CHECKPOINT 10–7

Using I messages, give upward feedback in the following situations.

1. The agency supervisor frequently places you on weekend call more often than any other member of the staff.
2. The client care coordinator was yelling at you in the office in front of your coworkers. She does this frequently.

the conversation. In the previous example, the person giving the I message was clear that she wanted some feedback right away. That nurse may also have had additional outcomes in mind, ranging from "I'd like to meet with you every two months during the orientation period so I am clear on how I am doing" to "Let me know only if I make a mistake; otherwise we'll talk again in a year." The outcomes you wish will vary, and being certain of what you really want will go a long way in making your points clear and in gaining the ear, and the respect, of your boss.

Often nurses allow position and chain of command to foster a helpless, "victim" mentality. As professional nurses, you are accountable for the safety of your patients, and working conditions such as those above may hamper your ability to provide that care. It is essential to be able to provide feedback to those persons who are in a position to affect your ability to provide safe care.

In Situation 1 of Checkpoint 10–7, if you are feeling overloaded and you question your ability to provide adequate care to the patients in this assignment, you must give this feedback to the area supervisor. Consider using an I message such as "I am concerned about this assignment. I will need some assistance with Mr. Smith when I speak to the family about their abuse of his care. Will you be available?" Without being directly confrontational, or offering judgmental feedback on the director's ability to make fair assignments, you have let her know your specific concerns and that you will need assistance throughout the shift.

Situation 2 involves a situation that makes the work setting less than pleasant when allowed to continue. Taking control of the situation, you may consider using an I message to redirect the supervisor to another location: "I appreciate your comments and would like to have further feedback, but I need to step into the supply room to get a suture removal kit." Once removed from the public arena, you may continue your discussion with additional assertive techniques (see Chapter 8). As time and the situation dictate, using the entire feedback model to give upward feedback is also effective.

CONCLUSION

Giving and receiving feedback can be risky business, but the potential for building more positive working relationships outweighs these risks. Remembering the step-by-step process and preparing your message before you speak will help you to make this a more meaningful part of your role as a professional nurse. From the impact of a simple "thank-you" to the detailed exchange of the evaluation of the performance of a new task, feedback closes the loop of the delegation process. As a result, you are fulfilling your legal obligation to monitor, evaluate, and follow up, and the patients are reaping the benefits. Good job!

ANSWERS TO CHECKPOINT

10–6.

1. The RN, as leader of the team, must set the stage for listening to others' perceptions, being open to growth, and being nondefensive. You will engender the respect of your coworkers as you teach them how to give and receive feedback. Your nurse practice act states that you must supervise your delegates, and this means giving feedback on their performance. They'll accept feedback from you much more happily if you are able to accept it yourself. You can grow and learn from constructive information sharing. Giving feedback and discussing goals can improve performance effort up to 60 percent.
2. Use the questions preceding this checkpoint or others that fit your situation exactly.
3. Follow the feedback model, being certain that you get input from the parent first. You may have to explain the school district's policy on confidentiality.
4. Follow the feedback model. Be prepared with a few questions for the new assistant that would, when answered correctly, help him feel more comfortable with her knowledge. Be certain to listen to how well he has been orienting her.

REFERENCES

Goode, C., et al. 1993. What kind of recognition do staff nurses want? *American Journal of Nursing* 93: 64–68.
Hersey, P., and B.W. Duldt. 1989. *Situational leadership in nursing.* Norwalk, CT: Appleton & Lange.
Jenks, J.M., and J.M. Kelly. 1985. *Don't do—delegate!* New York: Franklin Watts.

Kouzes, J., and B. Posner. 1993. *Credibility*. San Francisco: Jossey-Bass. The original study cited was from A. Bandura and D. Cervone, "Self-Evaluation and Self-Efficacy Mechanisms Governing the Motivational Effects of Goal Systems," *Journal of Personality and Social Psychology* 45 (1983).

LaMonica, E. 1983. *Nursing leadership and management, an experiential approach.* Monterey, CA: Wadsworth Health Sciences Division, 139.

National Council of State Boards of Nursing. 1990. *Concept paper on delegation.* Chicago: NCSBN.

CHAPTER 11

Know How To Evaluate and Solve Problems: How Well Has the Delegation Process Produced the Outcomes I Wanted To Achieve?

Ruth I. Hansten and Marilynn J. Washburn

It's 8 AM and your interdisciplinary team meeting is beginning. As an aside, a home health aide (HHA) mentions to you, the supervising registered nurse (RN), "By the way, on Saturday, Mr. Peterson, your patient on Oak Street, complained of chest pain and was diaphoretic when I was doing his bath. I decided it was because he'd been coughing too much after I fed him, so I asked the daughter to give him a sleeping pill after I left. I left a message on Joan's answering machine when I remembered it because she is the case manager for Mr. Peterson." Wondering if the issue was discussed when the aide reported off to the on-duty weekend RN, you immediately call Mr. Peterson's home, and the daughter reports that he's been having periods of syncope and times when he "feels like his heart is pounding out of his chest." You take immediate action to correct the clinical problem, notify the physician's office of the presenting symptoms, and send him to the ER according to the physician's request. You also discuss the situation with others, and do some short-term and long-term problem solving.

As in any situation involving people and judgment, there are several possible problems as well as several times when the error could have been caught before it was too late for the patient. As a good problem solver and expert critical thinker, your concerns have surfaced like this: In this case, one would expect the nursing assistant to have known that all complaints of chest pain in a patient like Mr. Peterson who requests complete resuscitation must be reported immediately to the nurse in charge for the weekend, not the case manager. She was definitely overstepping her job description by diagnosing the origin of the pain and taking her own interventions. Besides, a patient having pain of any kind that was causing diaphoresis and much discomfort would require intervention. What happened with the discussion when the HHA reported off to the weekend supervising nurse? You remember that Joan, the case manager, was not scheduled to work the weekend and has been on vacation. Was anyone supervising the HHA this weekend or was this a communication failure? What happened to the notification process regarding who is on duty? Yet a few more questions remain: What has the HHA been taught regarding reporting of symptoms? What has the daughter been taught about reporting syncope and other episodes to the agency? What was happening during the feeding if the patient was coughing so much? Is there a learning problem or a clinical problem as well?

CHECKPOINT 11-1

Keeping in mind what you have learned about the delegation process, what went wrong in this situation?

_____

_____

_____

_____

EVALUATION: CONTINUOUS, PROBLEM RELATED, AND PERIODIC

Evaluation is a familiar word and process to all RNs. Evaluation, as a part of the nursing process, is continuous, as we consider whether our interventions are achieving the projected outcomes for each nursing diagnosis. In this chapter, we'll discuss evaluation of the delegation process itself. How well the process is working will yield important information on the performance of the systems we have created and the people to whom we delegate. Evaluation will allow us to give useful feedback, both positive and negative, and to learn from the feedback that is given to us by our coworkers. In this chapter we'll cover some of the issues that we have discovered commonly interfere with successful completion of the process.

One of the most productive stages of the delegation process includes the portion covered in this chapter: evaluation of the results of the process, with a careful analysis of each step of the process to ensure that the cycle of delegation has been complete and effective. In the situation above, evaluation of a problem situation yields important information for the growth of the personnel involved and for improving the quality of the care delivered. Often, when evaluating, we discover that we've missed some essential points from preceding parts of the process. There were many potential errors in the "chest pain" incident:

- Before we question the people involved and find out more, we can at least assume that the delegate did not report appropriately or in a timely manner.
- We can also question whether the weekend nurse on duty was informed of the problem, and if so, what she did about it.
- Checkpoints between the supervising RN and the delegate were missing or the communication was incomplete when the report process occurred.
- A long-term view of the situation will certainly reveal that the nursing assistant's performance must be evaluated and feedback given in relation to her past performance.
- The communication systems to alert personnel about what to report and to whom may need some attention, as well as the on-call or weekend assignment structure.
- There is a question about what happened when the HHA was feeding the patient. At this point, one may question why the patient was coughing? Was there any relationship to feeding technique?

Within any organizational setting, there is the need for continuous (ongoing), incident-related, and periodic evaluation. Whether it is broken down on a shift-by-shift, daily, case, product line, program, or delegate basis, evaluation is integral. Just as the nursing process of assessment, planning, intervention, and evaluation is a circular, never-ending continuum, evaluation is a continuous part of the delegation process; the delegating nurse constantly checks reality with what was projected in terms of job descriptions, expected behaviors, and outcomes. The feedback related to the process of evaluation is received in two forms:

1. Data reporting and the RN's personal assessment of the client situation and the actual process by which care is delivered will yield some of the information necessary to evaluate both the process and the people performing it.
2. Performance feedback (see Chapter 10) is a two-way, reciprocal action in which the RN coaches and guides the delegates and receives feedback from them related to the RN's performance as well.

Evaluation of specific problems or situations, whether they have to do with personal performance or systems performance, will consistently be a part of the RN's job in his or her appraisal during the delegation process. Feedback must be given, and problem solving, both short-term and long-term, is necessary.

Periodic evaluation considers the effects of systems and people performance on the overall goal achievement of the team. What outcomes have been expected, and what outcomes have been evidenced? The RN looks for what is working well, what problems or trends need attention to improve the quality of care, and takes steps to resolve recurring issues. Periodic evaluation of the performance of the team members is also a part of this type of evaluation.

The evaluation phase of the delegation process is represented graphically in Figure 11–1.

CONTINUOUS EVALUATION

Checkpoints, Timelines, and Parameters for Reporting

Depending on the community setting in which you work, you have integrated a method by which you can receive and give feedback or share information and clinical data on a regular, ongoing basis in your clinical work. The communication is two-way: to and from you as the RN and to and from the delegates. This data sharing makes it possible for you to evaluate the clinical situation and to make decisions about further assessment and interventions that may be necessary for a specific patient or case. In a psychiatric group home setting, for example, the supervising RN may receive data from assistive personnel several times throughout the day about a client who is experiencing an acute depressive episode. He or she may also spend one-on-one time with that patient to make decisions about further treatment modalities. Getting the necessary data in a timely manner from the assistive personnel depends on having checkpoints, timelines, and parameters for reporting.

As we have discussed previously in this book, it's essential for you to know what you want. Knowing what kinds of things you need to find out from assistive personnel is fundamental to your ability to clearly express your requirements to the delegates. We again review the journalist's list of questions necessary for evaluation: who, what, when, where, how, and why.

> Be clear with the delegate about:
> - *Who* should be doing which tasks, and to *whom*
> - *What* kinds of data are necessary
> - *When, where,* and *how* it will be reported to you

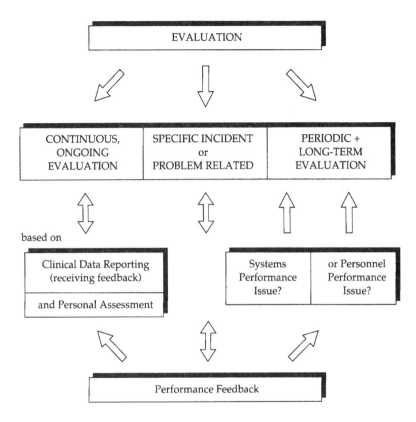

Figure 11–1 The Evaluation Process. *Source:* Reprinted from R. Hansten and M. Washburn, Know How To Evaluate, *Clinical Delegation Skills*, p. 301, © 1998, Aspen Publishers, Inc.

This is basic information that is often assumed to be understood, and the expectation is not shared by all delegates and supervisors. (Is it okay to chart only essential information? What kinds of data are important?) *Why* shows delegates what kinds of things you are concerned about and helps them grow while they become another set of eyes and ears. For example, if a delegate is assigned a group of tasks, including data collection such as glucose testing, he or she needs to know when to report to you results that are abnormal and what constitutes "abnormal." Parameters for reporting are essential and are often forgotten, especially when you delegate to another RN who is new to your area. Keep in mind that when you became a new RN, you weren't sure what to expect, and assistive personnel won't know either. Guidelines for reporting help avoid unpleasant surprises. Wherever you work, take time to think about how you implement the following and whether the communication is in a written and/or oral format.

- **Checkpoints:** How often do you get together to share data? (This is a two-way street, as shown by the double arrows in Figure 11–1.) What are your agency policies about how often you must perform supervising visits? Where and how can delegates find you if needed?

- **Timelines:** Are all personnel certain of when to report which data? Which are okay merely to chart and which need immediate attention? How often should the delegate expect that you'd report changes or update them on the client's situation? Are you clear about this expectation when delegating?

- **Parameters for Reporting:** Are you worried about the drainage on the Mrs. Smith's dressing? If so, how much would it be expected to decrease as the wound heals? Are you wondering whether Mr. Potter's daughter has been in the home with him to discuss transport to the rehabilitation center for physical therapy (PT)? How soon do you need to know about the travel arrangements that have been made? Just as you appreciate (and need!) specific parameters for reporting patient condition changes to the physician, your delegates need specific parameters as well. Do you provide them?

If you found the answers to the questions above were difficult to come by or if the questions raised some concerns about whether information is being shared appropriately and in a timely manner, now is the time to determine what can be done about interruptions in the continuous flow of important information among the members of the health care team. As we discuss the problems that may become evident as a part of your evaluation process, you can use some of the suggestions to help you solve the communication flow issue.

Learning and Communication Styles

As you thought about how you are giving and receiving clinical information and feedback continuously with members of your health care team to evaluate whether outcomes have been achieved, you may have overlooked the importance of understanding how people best learn. This one issue commonly creates problems in the delegation process that become evident as you gather data and evaluate, and it is closely related to how well you assessed your delegate and acted on those assessment data.

Considering global versus linear learning styles, as well as visual, auditory, and kinesthetic learning styles, will help you communicate more effectively throughout the delegation process.

People have preferred modes of learning that may affect their ability to retain and implement your instructions to them. Let's take a closer look at how learning and communication styles may influence the manner in which you discuss the work to be done with the delegates and the achievement of outcomes.

Global versus Linear Learning

Some of the delegates need to know the total, overall goals and the global picture before they are able to begin working most effectively; others want more detailed instructions about the steps to be accomplished, with less regard for the total view. When discussing the work at hand, it's best to give the overall outcomes to be achieved for the motivational value and for those who need that type of information to get started, while giving more detailed information to those who need it. For example, if you are discussing hospice care, you will want to tell the team about the outcomes you wish to achieve with Mrs. Ventelli: "The multidisciplinary team group, along with the patient and family, determined that we'd all work for the goal of keeping her home for Christmas with a home health aide coming in twice daily for chores and personal care for the three days she wants to stay there [overall picture for the global learners]. This means we'll be gradually increasing her PT and trying some other pain medications. This graph will give the aides a full picture of the goals and outcomes the team and patient are anticipating, and consequently their roles as members of the home care team. Let me know before the next time I visit how well the plans for Christmas at home have progressed" [more detail for the linear learners]. In this way, each person on the team is clearer about the work he or she needs to do and what kind of information you are expecting in return.

Visual, Auditory, and Kinesthetic Learning

Those of you who were very glad that we've included graphic representations and models to aid in your assimilation and integration of the material are probably visual learners. Very observant, these people may have difficulty understanding or remembering oral directions. (Have you ever been given directions verbally at the convenience store or gas station when what you really wanted was a map of the area?) It is very frustrating for visual learners to hear directions only. These people will be able to do their jobs more effectively if given written directions, and even better when the care map or plan is visually represented by symbols or in a graph-like format. Visual delegates may want to make up their own assignment sheets or write up personal notes (often called "brains" in many settings) to make certain they are organized and will give appropriate feedback to the RN in a timely manner. It's best when written information on assignments and reporting timelines is available, for clarity and legal reasons as well as to facilitate the accomplishment of the process. We'll discuss the topic of documentation more fully later in this chapter.

Many organizations have specific (written) policies for reporting times and checkpoints, for example. Certainly all health care organizations across the continuum expect some kind of formal charting of patients' responses and other clinical data. Computerized patient clinical data may be available in a real-time manner; however, it is not a substitute for the RN's interpretation and discussion of the implications with the delegates.

Auditory learners need to hear from you. They won't be satisfied with a written assignment, but will want to discuss it with you. This is their preferred method of communication, and despite the time it takes to talk about what needs to be done and how, it's essential to save time later by being clear in asking for and receiving feedback or clinical data reporting. We have observed negative consequences in systems where delegates were given only written instructions to be followed, without discussion, before beginning their work. Because health care in any setting is a dynamic process, what is written as an instruction one minute may be inaccurate at best, dangerous at worst, in the next minute. Relying on "routine" in any setting has created many problems. Be aware that some of the problems may be related to the necessity of auditory learners to hear from you personally. This can especially challenge the "lone" workers in home health care who may require more conversation and may find themselves telephoning for more input.

> Visual learners want to "see" what you're telling them in a written or graphic format; auditory learners want to hear from you; kinesthetic learners want "hands on" practice or assistance.

With so many delegates speaking English as a second language, it's important to understand the necessity of clarity in both written and oral communication. When determining delegates' ability to understand, get immediate feedback from them by asking them what their plan for the day/shift/case is. Although it is uncomfortable to determine these issues, it's even more uncomfortable when unclear communication causes a patient problem. Many organizations use written universal symbols to help multilingual patients, staff, and families understand each other.

Kinesthetic learners are those who need to "do" rather than hear about it. Some delegates may feel comfortable with trying to complete a task with verbal instruction, but kinesthetic learners will need to experience an active learning process of watching and helping with the task or procedure, then doing it with a supervising nurse. When giving instructions such as parameters for reporting, it may not suffice for this delegate to be told that "wrapping the patient's amputation stump will be just like in your skills lab." For these delegates, you may need to go with them to the patient's home and describe and show them what you mean, allowing them to practice. When asking a delegate to complete a patient's clothing checklist, paying special attention to suicide prevention articles, it won't suffice for them to read the procedure and discuss it with you. They'll have to work through it in a patient situation with a supervising nurse to feel comfortable with the process.

Because all of us have a combination of preferences of learning modes, it's best to use as many of them as possible when communicating and asking for feedback in the form of data reporting. Keep in mind that just because a delegate may have a combination of styles that is different from yours doesn't mean it will detract from his or her ability to do the job. It does mean, however, that you will need to adjust your methods of communication as you learn what works best with that staff member. (For additional information on learning styles and the principles of learning, we recommend Anderson's (1990) *Patient Teaching and Communicating in an Information Age*.) Before you proceed, turn to Checkpoint 11–2 and complete it.

Importance of Personal Assessment

Although we have mentioned this previously, whether you are evaluating achievement of outcomes on a patient-by-patient basis, doing ongoing evaluation as the case progresses, evaluating a specific unusual occurrence, or completing a more global evaluation of the processes and systems you are using for delivery of care, nothing can substitute for your own personal assessment and evaluation. Using assistive personnel has allowed RNs to gather data with the additional eyes and ears of others, leaving time for the RNs to perform professional nursing tasks and processes more thoroughly. However, keep in mind that the RN is the supervising authority. You are being paid to use the nursing process, solve problems, and think about maintaining and improving the quality of the care or service provided to your clients on a short-term and long-term basis. Nothing can substitute for the time you spend evaluating the situations you are faced with each day.

CHECKPOINT 11-2

1. Thinking about your communication links in the system in your workplace, how do you make certain you respond to the preferred learning and communication styles of those with whom you work?

   _____

   _____

2. Have you ever been frustrated with those with different learning styles? For example, what would the following example lead you to believe? (Use information you have learned in all the preceding chapters.)

   "I have *told* the billing clerk several times today to complete the insurance forms and to send them as soon as possible, and it hasn't been done yet." Is Delegate A

   a) lazy?
   b) hard of hearing?
   c) new to the English language, so that she may not have understood?
   d) a visual or kinesthetic learner who needs written instructions or actual demonstration?
   e) of a culture that differs from yours, so that she may not interpret your instructions as a priority due to your method of communication?
   f) lacking motivation and being resentful and subordinate?
   g) misunderstanding what you expect?

   Looking at this example, it would seem that further assessment and evaluation is necessary to determine what is really going on here. Does the RN have the extra time and energy to spend in frustration and anger, or would time be better spent finding out what the real issue is behind this? (You have learned many skills for working with these issues: the assertiveness formula, the collaborative resolution model, and the feedback process. You have also learned how to assess the delegate to determine how to delegate effectively based on your appraisal.)

Besides evaluating the results achieved by your interventions according to your treatment plan as in the nursing process, you must evaluate the efficacy of the delegation process and the performance of the delegates. If you are a public health nurse who has been examining the data of the growing rate of tuberculosis and AIDS in your community and has reviewed reports of specific cases from many assistive personnel, nothing can substitute for on-site assessment and evaluation of selected patient cases. If a medical assistant or LPN often gives the injections in your well-baby clinics, supervising the process and observing and evaluating his or her ability to perform the functions of the job description are essential to your ability to evaluate the systems you are using as well as the performance of the delegates. When you've made a home assessment visit, you know that no other professional or assistant can better synthesize the medical, psychological, social, and practical aspects of the patient and family's life to determine the plan of care and how best to capitalize on the patient's strengths.

When you work in the community and in homes, you are able, in a moment's time, to "eyeball" a patient and observe any changes in condition. In a few seconds, you have taken in the patient's respiratory rate, depth, and comfort; skin color and moisture; body habitus and expression—all the visual and auditory cues. Asking a short question will allow you to make a preliminary assessment of cognitive functioning as well. Combining your observations with the clinical data and your experience with your scientific knowledge is a part of the art of nursing. Sometimes all of this assessment occurs over the telephone as you ask the right questions to each family member's response. You use this special art to evaluate, decide what additional data are needed, and conclude what else needs to be done. The patient assessment and/or evaluation data that you complete by your clinical assessment also yield valuable information about the delegation process and how well it is going. Are the delegates completing care? Are changes in condition being reported appropriately? How does the environment appear? Where have other care providers concentrated their efforts? How are we proceeding as a team in achieving the planned outcomes?

Evaluation is another part of the delegation process that encourages you to make decisions about what data can be gathered by others and what data must be generated by your own senses. Again, nursing judgment must be used in each specific situation to determine how much of the evalua-

> When you've made a home assessment visit, you know that no other professional or assistant can better synthesize the medical, psychological, social, and practical aspects of the patient and family's life to determine the plan of care and how best to capitalize on the patient's strengths.

CHECKPOINT 11-3

Consider your own work environment. What kinds of information about the effectiveness of the delegation process and the performance of the delegates can be obtained from your own personal assessment? What kinds of information do you retrieve from your evaluation of the patient, the chart, or other written materials?

_____

_____

_____

---

tion can be based on reports and data collected by others, just as which tasks to delegate and the amount and type of supervision needed were determined in each situation in the beginning of the delegation process. A pulmonary nurse specialist at a receiving agency is the very best person to determine which questions to ask nurses at the hospital before transport of a ventilator patient to a community setting, rather than chatting with the ward clerk prior to discharge. Nothing can substitute for the "eyeball" assessment and evaluation of the situation by a nurse. Even though this book is dedicated to helping nurses make the very best use of assistive personnel, we wish to caution all nurses to maintain patient contact so that the delegation process, and assistive personnel, can best be evaluated.

Give yourselves credit for that art of nursing, the judgment based on your experience and scientific knowledge. Think about how often we use it in our daily lives: when you and a friend are at the mall and you see someone walking past, you might comment, "Boy, that person has COPD: looks like he left the oxygen at home!" or "My goodness, that pregnant woman has 4+ pitting edema up to her calf, and with that flushed face I wonder if she's had her pressure taken recently?" Or, in conversation with a friend at church or the grocery store, you might say, "With the sleep and appetite disturbances, I wonder if he's tried drugs or psychotherapy for that depression. Has he ever said anything about feeling like he'd like to never wake up? Any other suicidal ideation?" It's impossible to take the nursing process or the "art" out of a nurse at any age or in any setting. Because your nursing abilities are second nature, don't assume

> Nothing can substitute for the "eyeball" assessment and evaluation of the situation by a nurse.

that all humans are endowed with these special abilities, but instead, give yourselves credit for your expertise and use it for evaluating and improving the care we provide!

SPECIFIC INCIDENT OR PROBLEM RELATED EVALUATION: CRITICAL THINKING

Because you are the supervising nurse, incidents or problems will definitely occur, if not daily, then at least frequently enough that these "unusual occurrences" will consume a fair amount of your time. Evaluating the situation is essential for resolving the problem or situation. In the first situation we discussed (the case of the chest pain), there were many possible errors, and several times when the problem could have been resolved. For example, ongoing checkpoints and two-way feedback were missing, as the HHA did not report appropriately to the correct RN. If the on-duty RN had been notified, she or he may have been able to step in. If the case manager RN had received her message, there would have been immediate clinical action.

The RN who was notified (albeit a day late!) stepped in immediately when the information was shared to solve the short-term problem: finding out whether the patient had a myocardial infarction (MI), and what kind of treatment was necessary to provide immediately. After the emergency issues were resolved, another concern remained. Why did this problem occur, and how could it be prevented from happening again? In this case, evaluation of the problem uncovered the need for more information from the other RNs involved (to determine what steps would be necessary) and for performance feedback for the nursing assistant. (In Chapter 10 we discussed the process of performance feedback. As Figure 11–1 illustrates, performance feedback supports the entire evaluation process.) Now let's take a closer look at the RN's responsibility for evaluating incidents and resolving problems.

Many nurses have reported to us that they wish their managers were better at resolving problems and incidents. They often share their frustration with the slow progress they've seen in improving and repairing systems and personnel's performance. These RNs have clearly evaluated specific incidents or have determined trends or recurring problems. They have begun the evaluation and problem-solving process by analyzing situations and coming up with ideas of what is wrong and what should be done. Most of the work in resolving the problem is already complete! Ideas like these should be shared and used with the managers of the departments to improve the quality of care and outcomes achieved, instead of being kept bottled up in individual and collective frustration! The managers cannot possibly "fix" everything (including people's performance) alone. Each RN has the accountability to be involved in the short-term and long-term improvement of care.

Critical thinking skills are essential as professional nursing moves increasingly into cognitive work rather than task-oriented psychomotor practice, that is, brain-work: coordination, leadership of the interdisciplinary team, focusing on outcomes rather than merely tasks.

Defining Critical Thinking

As discussed in Question 52 of *The Nurse Manager's Answer Book* (Hansten and Washburn, 1993), and again in our *Toolbook for Health Care Redesign* (Hansten and Washburn, 1997), there is a step-by-step process to use when evaluating an incident or problem. We have used this model with countless health care professionals and have incorporated research related to critical thinking skill development.

As nurse executives and managers call for improved critical thinking on the part of their staff, educational groups have responded by concentrating on these skills. The National League for Nursing requires schools of nursing to teach, measure, and evaluate improved critical thinking of nursing students. Many studies from various perspectives have evaluated this topic, leading to improved methods of teaching critical thinking. Although varying definitions are seen in the literature, this skill set is basically creative problem solving as a continual process. *A sample of definitions follows.*

"Critical thinking is a certain mindset or way of thinking, rather than a method or a set of steps to follow. Critical thinking is clear thinking that is active, focused, persistent, and purposeful. It is a process of choosing, weighing alternatives, and considering what to do. Critical thinking involves looking at reasons for believing one thing rather than another in an open, flexible, attentive way"(Kyzer, 1996, p. 66).

"Critical thinking is a complex form of thinking and can be defined as the rational examination of ideas, inferences, assumptions, principles, arguments, conclusions, issues, statements, beliefs, and actions. It is reasoning in a way that generates and examines questions and problems. During this type of thinking, the individual weighs, clarifies, and evaluates evidence, conclusions and arguments"

(Bandman, 1988, as quoted in Stark, 1996, p. 168). "The process of critical thinking may actually be part of and integrated into an individual's inner self, incorporating intuition and feelings in the problem-solving process" (Gross, 1991, as quoted in Stark, 1996, p. 168).

Critical thinking is "purposeful, self-regulatory judgment which results in interpretation, analysis, evaluation, and inference, as well as explanation of the evidential, conceptual, methodological, criteriological, or contextual considerations upon which that judgment was based" (Facione and Facione, 1996, p. 129).

Despite some variance in definitions, it is clear that critical thinking, ongoing problem solving from an organizational and clinical perspective, and clinical nursing judgment are closely aligned. Intuition has also been discussed as a part of critical thinking. A recent study, based on qualitative research showing that the use of intuition in clinical judgment making is an important part of the critical thinking process, gives evidence that as the level of nursing proficiency increases from beginner to expert, and as the amount of clinical experience increases, the use of intuition to make clinical nursing judgments increases significantly (Polge, 1995).

How does one recognize expert critical thinkers, besides the fact that patient problems are resolved effectively and potential errors are avoided? Instead of stating, "This is the way we've always done it," they move beyond the norm or daily routine to being open to possibilities and asking "why?" They look for patterns and trends in individual patient situations as well as patients in a category, such as a disease process. They see the big picture, use intuition, and get input from others when solving problems (Stark, 1996, p. 169). In what almost seems like an updated Scout Creed, educational research indicates that the ideal critical thinker is

- habitually inquisitive,
- well-informed,
- trustful of reason,
- open-minded,
- flexible,
- fair minded in evaluation,

- honest in facing personal biases,
- prudent in making judgment,
- willing to reconsider,
- clear about issues,
- orderly in complex matters,
- diligent in seeking relevant information,
- reasonable in the selection of criteria,
- focused in inquiry, and
- persistent in seeking results that are as precise as the subject and the circumstances may permit (Facione and Facione, 1996, p. 130).

Further research with hundreds of graduates nationwide has shown that critical thinking skills and the disposition toward critical thinking are vitally important in the exercise of workplace decision making, leadership, clinical judgment, professional success, and effective participation in a democratic society (Jones, 1994). Certainly this is not a new thought to nurses and nurse managers and the patients who reap the results of noncritical thinkers in various situations; for example: a nurse notes that there are two HIV+ girls in a high school but doesn't think to follow up with further case finding or preventive education; a nurse observes from the chart that all previous children in this family were failure-to-thrive infants but doesn't think the new baby requires a visit or suspect family or parenting problems; a nurse pages the same physician again and again with no response as the patient's condition deteriorates, but the nurse does not problem solve beyond that same paging number until the patient arrests.

Several principles seem to emerge related to research results:

- Certain individual characteristics assist the individual to gain critical thinking skills, including
  - foundations of knowledge and experience
  - attitudes of openness and attentiveness
  - thinking strategies (thinking from all perspectives, seeing patterns, gathering all facts and ideas)
  - skills (problem solving, prioritization, technical, time management, assertiveness, negotiation, communication) (Kyzer, 1996, p. 4).
- Critical thinking can be learned.
- Once an individual obtains concepts, theories, and knowledge, personal experiences

combine with that memory to become "productive memory" or the basis for critical thinking (Whiteside, 1997, p. 154).

- Use of a model can assist nurses in clinical areas to improve their ability to think critically (Whiteside, pp. 159–160).
- The organization shares some responsibility in providing barriers or supports to critical thinking.

Organizational Barriers and Supports for Critical Thinking

The barriers and supports of an organization for problem solving and critical thinking deserve additional commentary. The organization that has characteristics similar to those of individuals who are effective critical thinkers will help improve those skills in the nurses it employs. For example, if the characteristics in

---

Exhibit 11–1 Organizational Evaluation for Critical Thinking Facilitation

❑ Organizational culture or rules that would cause an individual employee to avoid creative problem solving and risk taking have been changed, and the new culture encourages empowerment and rapid action on problems.

❑ Critical thinking is modeled by managerial levels, with on-site mentoring focused on coaching rather than blaming.

❑ Education focuses on improving these abilities with use of case studies, experiential learning, and guided problem solving with expert mentors and preceptors.

❑ Education evaluates its effectiveness and does not attempt to do too much in too little time.

❑ Preceptors and mentors are also used for orientation, cross-training, or focused development activities.

❑ Multidisciplinary teams share their experiences and work together with open communication so that learning can take place across disciplines.

❑ Participative management is present, with supportive employee-managerial relationships.

❑ Mistakes are seen as a chance to learn and grow, and the punitive aspects are deemphasized.

❑ Questions, new ideas, and risk taking are supported.

Source: Data from Sharpening Your Critical Thinking Skills, *Orthopaedic Nursing*, Vol. 15, No. 6, pp. 66–76, © 1996.

Exhibit 11–1 are true of your organization, your road to expertise in this pivotal skill will be swift! Use Exhibit 11–1 to evaluate your organization for support of the process.

Strategies for improving critical thinking in an organization stem from improving the organizational climate by practicing critical thinking in all areas and rectifying those areas in the list above that need improvement. Loosening up to develop new ideas and risk-taking behaviors may mean using games, exercises, role playing, puzzles, or any number of strategies that open up the creative, right side of the brain. Use of case studies or other simulated experiences will help produce the episodic memory necessary for building up experience and the potential for using that invaluable intuition. Most effective is the on-site mentoring of a clinically astute manager, supervisor, or clinical nurse specialist who is able to ask the right questions and help staff in real-time coaching as incidents occur. (See our discussions of managerial rounds, easily adaptable to home visits and supervisory visits, in *Toolbook for Health Care Redesign*, Hansten and Washburn, 1997, pp. 20–22, 236.)

Potential benefits of focusing on critical thinking skill development for all health care workers in an organization are numerous. Although it is difficult to draw a direct cause-effect relationship with the improvement of thinking and the improvement of patient care, nursing leaders across the country tell us they expect to see the following improvements related to enhanced critical thinking:

- improved patient care as measured by fewer accidents or errors (falls, medication errors, omissions), decreased length of stay or length of treatment in each care area, fewer return visits to the hospital, emergency department, or intensive care unit
- better patient satisfaction related to appropriate discharge instructions, attention to patient priorities while under care of an RN, smooth transitions from one point of care to another
- increased resolution of problems, care issues, system glitches
- less blaming, more "How can I fix this problem?"
- improved staff morale and less turnover in all disciplines as interdisciplinary teamwork improves and as all workers feel more empowered to effect change both within the patient care realm and with organizational systems

Personal Accountability for Developing Critical Thinking Skills

Your job as a critical thinker is exciting and rewarding: Developing these skills will assist you in your goal of delivering excellent patient care and will allow you to solve some of the problems that have frustrated you and have been an impediment to your practice! See Exhibit 11–2.

We have developed the checkpoints and case studies in this book to assist in development of critical thinking skills. Although we cannot provide actual mentorship or experiences in this written format, we have attempted to begin the process that can be used by clinical instructors to develop preceptorships, real-time case studies, and peer consultation. Based on our work with thousands of nurses across the nation, we recognize that the use of a model or a guide will provide an essential link for those who are learning creative problem solving and are developing their critical thinking skills.

Falkof and Moss's classification scheme (Girvan, 1989) uses four levels of questioning for improving critical thinking: When the nurse in charge of an agency discovers two staff have called in sick today, the following questions will help him critically think through this situation:

Exhibit 11–2 Personal Accountability for Developing Critical Thinking Skills

> ❑ As you identify your current point in the journey from novice to expert, consider how you can continue to grow through additional education, consultation with those more experienced when questions occur, working enough to immerse yourself in your specialties. Consider obtaining certification in your current specialty.
>
> ❑ Reflect on the way you think, and review those steps you miss most often.
>
> ❑ Learn from your mistakes and the mistakes of others. "What steps in the process did I (or my unfortunate colleague) miss this time?"
>
> ❑ Recognize your personal indicators that alert you to when you aren't able to think as well, such as illness, short staffing, or stress at home that reduces focus on work issues. Redouble efforts at that time to resist jumping to conclusions, not challenging your assumptions, or being close-minded due to time constraints. This may include stress-reduction techniques or asking a coworker to hear your thinking out loud.
>
> ❑ Participate in or lead discussions of clinical scenarios.
>
> ❑ Participate in a mentorship or preceptor program, either as a participant or as a mentor. You will learn as you teach others.
>
> ❑ Trust your intuition, your gut feelings. If something (a lab value, a physical assessment parameter, an organizational problem) seems odd or out of the ordinary, ask why.
>
> ❑ Use the four types of questions and/or the positive problem-solving process (see below) as a model for intermittent measurements of your critical thinking processes.
>
> *Source:* Data from Sharpening Your Critical Thinking Skills, *Orthopaedic Nursing*, Vol. 15, No. 6, pp. 66–76, © 1996.

1. *Factual questions*—test knowledge and comprehension—develop the thinking skill of cognition and memory. "How have we staffed when this has occurred in the past? Who is present and what are their abilities? Which patients are scheduled for visits today? What skill levels are needed to care for these patients today?"

2. *Interpretive questions*—test application and analysis—develop convergent thinking. "What principles can be used to assign based on acuity and patient needs, and how can we apply them today? How can we apply past knowledge to the current patient population?"

3. *Creative questions*—test ability to synthesize information—develop divergent thinking. "What can I do to meet our staffing needs for today? What other ways can I think of to do safe patient care, given the people we have today, if no help is possible? What care tasks can be done differently, or what can be left for later, or done by someone else? What other methods can we use to obtain help? Which patient's visit can be delayed?"

4. *Evaluative questions*—test ability to evaluate—develop affective thinking skills (Girvan, 1989). "How will I evaluate the outcomes we achieve by trying to solve this staffing problem from a present and long-term perspective? What is good about this problem? How will I know if we have been successful at the end of this day?"

Positive Problem-Solving Process

Think back to the clinical problem we discussed at the beginning of the chapter. We will use this example to discuss the process of positive problem solving, then use the additional examples of the case studies for practice. If you become frustrated during this process, consult with a peer or a mentor to assist you. Remember that the critical thinking process is continuous and doesn't stop after one or two potential solutions have been tried and found wanting. Results are measured, and if the right solutions haven't been found, the process returns to the beginning.

1. *What signs cause you to think there is a problem?* Think about the frame of reference, reasons that this problem may exist, attitude, and assumptions. Be very specific about the exact nature of the problem, incident, or error. (Patients who complain of chest pain need assistance. A patient didn't get appropriate care because the RN didn't know about his symptoms. The symptoms weren't reported.) Use the following questions to define the problem further:

- How is my frame of reference affecting my interpretation of this situation? (Because I did not work the weekend, I don't know what happened. I may have oriented the HHA and thought better of her abilities; therefore, I may suspect the RN was told and didn't act on it.)

- What are the reasons that this problem may exist? (Is this a performance problem? Is there shared accountability with the RN and the assistive person who did not report the symptoms? Is this an educational need, i.e., does the nursing assistant not understand what to report or to whom? In what ways did the weekend on-call system fail, or was it clear to everyone but the HHA what needed to be done?)

- How does my attitude affect this problem-solving process? (Do I dislike that nursing assistant and hope she gets fired? Do I have a bias that the weekend RNs do not supervise the HHAs adequately? Do I think that this patient should not opt for further treatment?)

- What are my assumptions? (I need to verify what happened. I need to talk to all involved to find out each person's perceptions of the truth. As yet, we don't know what really happened from patient being fed to the chest pain to the reporting to either RN.)

2. What is good about this situation? To challenge your brain, identify three positive aspects of the situation. (Remember collaborative resolution? This step allows the creative juices to flow. When we ask this question, we begin to change our mind-set. Instead of "Oh no, not another problem!" we can open up the creative right brain to begin to see other possible solutions. Try it in your personal life; it really works! We encourage all readers to apply this question to all situations that they encounter when the same old problems keep reappearing. The statement "Oh, No! We are out of suction catheter sets for the 30th time this month!" should be a trigger to use the full positive problem-solving process and, especially, to ask what is good about the problem. (The good things about the patient situation in the example are numerous: The patient didn't die; this incident allows us to teach the assistant and the other nurses, to look more closely at our methods of communicating on the weekend, to look at how nursing assistants have been taught what things to report, and to evaluate whether that program is working effectively.)

3. What should have been happening instead of what did happen? Discuss specific and measurable criteria. These will be your criteria for knowing when the problem has been effectively resolved. (The HHA would have reported the pain to the correct RN; the RN would have intervened to resolve the pain issue; the HHA would have known whom to call when; and most important, the patient would have had relief of pain and appropriate treatment for his discomfort and arrhythmias.) In the long term, this type of miscommunication of relevant and critical patient data will not occur. From an organizational perspective, one of the most glaring problems in this example is that an assistive person did not report serious data in a timely manner. She made a decision about the implications of the patient's complaint and decided to make an intervention on her own. We would be able to tell that the problem was resolved if this staff member reported appropriately at all times (in a timely manner and to the correct person). Another problem may be a lack of information sharing throughout the weekend and unclear knowledge about weekend call. If a system were set up by which weekend information sharing could be as effective as during the week, then positive outcomes for all patients would result. The outcomes for the patients would ultimately be avoidance of untreated pain and complications, and smooth and effective clinical results, including shorter courses of treatment and fewer returns to acute care. In this situation, absence of lawsuits based on poor quality of care could be another outcome.

4. Do I need to do something about this? Ask yourself this question to determine accountability and ownership. The following questions will help determine when you should get involved. Some of us like to be involved in everything, but we become overly taxed and ineffective from spreading ourselves too thin and assuming others' responsibilities. Other individuals seem to take accountability more lightly and would not consider this to be their problem to solve. To determine that, ask these questions:

- *Does it affect me, my patients, or our team goals? (Yes!)* Also ask yourself this related question: Is this a real problem or is it something I can let go? (No, patients' lives could be threatened if I let this go.)
- *What will happen if I don't do anything about this?* (Patient care would suffer. This is a good reason to deal with the incident. It's also true that someone else may do something about it, but I am not willing to allow this kind of incident to continue. Even if I were not the supervising nurse, I must act in the best interests of the patient in an emergent situation.)
- *What will happen if I try to resolve this problem?* (Be aware that addressing a problem can cause conflict, but don't let concerns about conflict get in your way. You know how to deal with that. Keep your mind on what may happen that will be better: If these communication problems are solved, perhaps lives will be saved and care will be more effective as reporting will be enhanced. Also be aware of organizational politics. If this nursing assistant is the branch director's best friend, you'll have to weigh that into the equation. However, we hope that you will respond ethically, and put the client or those you serve in the priority position.)
- *Am I the person who can solve this problem (or prevent this type of incident from occurring in the future), or should this problem be dealt with by another person or department?* Consider who else may be affected. (In the chest pain incident, the short-term situation definitely required the action of the nurse

caring for Mr. Peterson. The long-term solution for this problem will rest with that RN as well as the manager. The errors are too serious to leave for quick, undocumented verbal feedback.) Consideration of who else may be affected by your action or inaction will help you determine other stakeholders. For example, have other nurses had problems with weekend reporting? Is there a call notification problem that all staff need to be involved in solving?

5. What can we do about these problems? Consider three possible solutions in terms of the following:

- immediate corrections of the short-term problem
- long-term resolution so the situation does not occur again
- people/departments/resources that need to be involved
- the solutions' potential side effects for other individuals and departments
- a timeline for evaluation

Without judging the feasibility of each idea, list some possible plans for resolving the problem. (After resolving his clinical needs, Mr. Peterson's nurse may list a variety of ideas: (1) fire the nursing assistant, a solution that would require the manager's help; (2) educate the nursing assistant about what to report and to whom; (3) plan for better communication throughout the day on the weekends; (4) ask other nurses for ideas; (5) research the situation more fully and get feedback from all of the people involved; (6) determine if other HHAs have educational needs, learning what and when to report; (7) talk to the manager about this and give him or her a list of possible alternatives.)

Consider what should be done first. (In this case, the nurse decides to get more information from the others and then talk to the nurse manager. The manager will need to know about this very soon because of the risks inherent in the situation, and will want to be involved. The nurse will also think of how to improve supervision on the weekends and discuss potential plans with the manager at the same time.)

Be certain you have considered the solutions' potential side effects for other departments or individuals. (What will happen to staffing if this individual is fired? What could happen if she improves? What if we need to increase weekend RN coverage and that means we all have to work more weekends?)

Plan the steps for implementation of the solutions or follow-up, keeping in mind the positive results you will enjoy because of your efforts. Remember the need to involve all individuals who will be affected when changes are made. (Depending on the amount of responsibility given to Mr. Peterson's nurse in the job description, she will be working with the manager to give performance feedback to the assistant and the other nurses who may have been involved. The manager, or perhaps the other RNs if they have a "hiring/firing" supervisory role, will probably be engaged in the progressive discipline process for the assistive person and in evaluating the HHA education program!)

Evaluate your results by the objective criteria you designed. Is the situation/ problem vanishing? (Is the nursing assistant reporting all information? How is your system of weekend communication working? Are you getting the information you need from the assistive personnel? When will you judge that the nursing assistant is competent?)

If related incidents continue to occur, the solutions aren't working and a new plan needs to be developed. (Perhaps this nursing assistant will never report appropriately and it's time for her to progress to a different job.) It's possible that the real problem hasn't been defined or that the symptoms you saw were caused by something else. Perhaps the facts weren't fully disclosed or you did not fully research the incident. Maybe communication with all those who needed to be involved hasn't occurred or the solutions haven't been given enough time to do their magic! Again, remember the process is ongoing—continuous, just as is the nursing process—and includes evaluation to be certain that the applied solutions are still working.

We encourage each professional nurse to complete as much of the problem-solving process as is authorized in his or her work setting. As we have noted, managers must be notified of problems and should be involved in developing and carrying out the solutions. But as reforms in our national system continue and health care adopts the business trend of flattened hierarchies, increased accountability and responsibility will be granted to each employee. Each RN will become more empowered to act in the best interests of the patients for whom he or she cares and will be more involved in activities that once were considered the province of managers.

The five-step process of evaluation and follow-up for specific incidents or problem situations can be applied to any clinical setting. To review the steps just outlined, see Exhibit 11–3.

The process of evaluation of a specific situation or incident includes many of the principles of the conflict management process as well as the nursing process. Evaluation must focus on the short-term situation as well as on how the problem could be avoided in the future.

PERIODIC EVALUATION

Whether you are a staff nurse working with assistive personnel, or are involved in upper management, you will need to take time for periodic evaluation of the work and how the delegation process has been proceeding. Remember that the same process applies to the evaluation you may do when families or other care

Exhibit 11–3 A Positive Approach to Problem Solving

The following worksheet can be used as a teaching tool for positive problem solving.

1. What signs tell you that something is wrong here? What is the exact nature of the problem, incident, or error? Be specific. Consider your
   - frame of reference (shift, position, etc.)
   - reasons that this problem may exist
   - attitude (do you have a personal investment or bias?)
   - assumptions (have you verified the evidence?)

2. What is good about this situation? Identify *three* aspects of this situation that are *positive*.

   _____

   _____

   _____

3. What should be happening instead of what did happen? These are your criteria for success. Be specific and measurable so that you know when you have solved the problem.

4. To determine accountability and ownership, ask yourself: Do I need to do something about it?
   - Does it affect me, my patients, or our team goals?
   - What will happen if I don't do something about this?
   - What could happen if I do?
   - Should I be solving this problem, or do I need someone else (who is affected)?

5. What can be done about it? Consider *three possible solutions* in terms of:
   - immediate corrections of the *short-term* problem
   - *long-term* remedies so the situation does not occur again
   - people/departments/systems/resources that need to be involved
   - the solutions' potential side effects to others
   - a timeline for evaluation

   _____

   _____

   _____

Source: Adapted from R. Hansten and M. Washburn, *Toolbook for Health Care Redesign*, p. 193, © 1997, Aspen Publishers, Inc.

> As an RN, you'll need to use your nursing judgment, in addition to policies and insurance requirements, to determine when your periodic evaluation should occur.

providers, hired by the patient or family, deliver care. Depending on the site in which you work, this may be on a shift-by-shift basis, as each case is finished, or every several months.

We have worked with more than one organization that had recently changed the skill mix for the professional nurses and the assistive personnel. When their work was completed, assistants went home without reporting what had happened during those hours. It's obvious that this created some difficult situations as the RNs attempted to find out what had been done, how the patients responded, and what was left to be completed. The RNs spent a lot of time looking for charted information and asking the patients or family members. Although their observations and phone calls to the patients' homes afforded them valuable information about the performance of their delegates, some of the information could have been handled much more efficiently by verbal or written communication. It's obvious that evaluation needs to be done on a basis that is adequate not only to ensure communication of relevant clinical data for optimal patient care quality and outcomes but also to allow the RNs to fulfill the requirements of state law. As nurses use their professional judgment, they have the prerogative to determine whether the state law requirements for evaluation visits are frequent enough to ensure patient care quality in each given situation. (That's clinical judgment and critical thinking!)

One community care agency developed a policy that required RNs to meet with the HHAs and rehabilitation aides twice a month to discuss progress on the long-term cases. Nurses who complained at first about the amount of time this would take discovered that it actually saved them time when they reflected on whether the plan of care was working, gave and received feedback from their delegates, and decided whether the system and the personnel were performing as required.

CHECKPOINT 11-4

Think of a problem incident or situation that has occurred in your facility or work setting in the past month. Was it related to the delegation process? Was it related to problems within the system or with the performance of personnel, or both? How did you go about helping to solve it, immediately and long-term?

The team members were able to celebrate the outcomes they achieved with their patients as well!

A parish-based respiratory facility for rehabilitation of asthmatic and COPD (chronic obstructive pulmonary disease) patients employed respiratory therapists, physical therapy/occupational therapy aides, a secretary/receptionist, and an LPN (LVN), all supervised by an RN parish nurse. In this situation, the team met at the beginning and end of each case not only to plan the care and evaluate outcomes, but also to evaluate their process of delegation. Often personnel performance issues were discussed and feedback was given. Each time, the RN asked for feedback about how the system was working for the delegates, and ultimately for the patients and their families.

When the clinic expanded its services to include general respiratory patients who were receiving ongoing outpatient care from the pulmonologists, some of whom were being referred to the rehabilitation clinic, the periodic evaluation of the system and personnel performance changed. The managing RN evaluated personnel on a quarterly basis, and systems' functioning was discussed in the staff meetings every month. The case-by-case evaluation of outcomes for the rehabilitation clinic patients continued. The staff handled personnel performance issues as they came up by using the feedback process, as we discussed in the previous chapter.

Overall evaluation includes asking some questions related to the delegation process. At the end of the week, for example, an RN may ask the questions listed in Exhibit 11–4. When you have reviewed these questions, proceed to Checkpoint 11–5.

Exhibit 11–4 Questions for Overall Evaluation

1. Did we accomplish our goals? What patient outcomes have been achieved?
2. If so, did the outcomes have anything to do with the manner in which work was delegated and assigned? If so, what worked well so that I can use it again the next time?
3. What didn't work? Why?
4. If there was a problem, did it have anything to do with how I delegated?
   a. Did I know my own job description, roles, and responsibilities?
   b. Did I allow any personal barriers to get in the way?
   c. Did I know the roles, job descriptions, and characteristics of my delegates?
   d. Did I match the jobs to the delegates appropriately? Were jobs prioritized?
   e. Did I communicate clearly and assertively?
   f. Was conflict handled?
   g. Did I use checkpoints, timelines, and parameters for reporting?
   h. Have I given feedback as needed, both negative and positive?

Source: Reprinted from R. Hansten and M. Washburn, Know How to Evaluate, *Clinical Delegation Skills*, p. 323, © 1998, Aspen Publishers, Inc.

CHECKPOINT 11-5

Susan and Joe, HHAs, returned from their home visits on Friday afternoon about 2 PM and sat in the break room having a cup of coffee. The secretary thought it was odd that they were back from their visits so early. When Audrey, their team RN, called in to the office prior to one of her last visits, the coordinator mentioned this to Audrey for follow-up. What could have gone wrong with the delegation process in this situation? Use the questions in the preceding checkpoint to assist you.

See the end of the chapter for the answers.

CASE STUDY ANALYSIS OF EVALUATION

In this case study, we will review the three types of evaluation (continuous, periodic, and specific problem related) and setting up timelines, checkpoints, and parameters for reporting in a community health setting.

Continuous Evaluation: Bob, a visiting nurse in a large metropolitan area, is supervising a challenging child abuse case. The mother has had two previous children who were mentally disabled from what has been surmised to have been head trauma. Previous charges against her were unproved, so the judge awarded custody of her new twins to this natural mother, despite the concerns of the social worker, child welfare worker, mental health professional, and mental health worker. Until the case can be appealed, Bob is attempting to coordinate the team's activities as well as supervise a chore worker who has been placed in the home to help purchase and prepare the food and provide some assistance with feeding the babies. How will Bob best evaluate and give necessary instructions to Evelyn, the chore worker?

_____

_____

_____

Discussion: Bob will discuss the case with the chore worker and plan to visit at least twice weekly himself. The chore worker, Evelyn, will understand the global picture in terms of the desired outcomes (the twins to be healthy and safe, the mother to be able to handle the situation) and will be given details, both written and oral, about what to look for: signs that would indicate Mom is not coping well, problems with the infants, and how to recognize if Mom has been using drugs again. Evelyn and Bob will make the first visit together to be certain the step-by-step process of care and reporting is followed. In this way, the mother will know what to expect from both Evelyn and Bob in the ensuing weeks. Evelyn will be able to tell Bob how quickly he or the caseworker (or 911) should be notified if problems occur and will report to Bob after each visit for at least the first month. On each visit, Bob will evaluate the babies, the mother, and the care that Evelyn is doing.

In this case we've reviewed some of the basic principles of evaluation on a continuous basis—discussing the parameters, timelines, and checkpoints for reporting. Bob will have given and received feedback (clinical data reporting) from a clinical situation based on Evelyn's data gathering and his own personal assessment.

Periodic Evaluation: Beginning on a daily basis, then moving to a weekly, biweekly, and monthly basis, Bob completed a more long-term, periodic evaluation of the plan of care and outcomes and how the team's process was proceeding. At the end of one month, which proceeded rather smoothly, Bob and the rest of the interdisciplinary team discussed the case. Bob evaluated the plan against the goals and projected outcomes: Is the mother able to cope with the twins, based on the support she has been given? This is being measured by whether the twins are gaining weight and thriving, a lack of evidence of abuse or neglect, and the mother's self-report of being in control. The assessment of all the support professionals agrees with the mother's statement that she has been able to care for the babies and herself without incident. Despite all the concerns of the staff, periodic evaluation yields positive results. Based on our evaluation model, what two questions does Bob need to ask himself at this point?

_____
_____
_____

Discussion:

1. How is the system working? (So far, so good. We'll need to keep up the continuous evaluation and communication, however. We seem to have matched the right person with the right work, and our communication in the delegation process has been effective.)
2. How is the personnel performance affecting the results of this case? (The people involved have been doing an excellent job! It's time for positive feedback for all the professionals who have been so deeply concerned and involved in this case!)

Specific Incident Evaluation: The twins seemed to be consuming formula at a faster rate, and this meant Evelyn had to pick up groceries more often. One day, on returning home from the market, she noted that their mother was fast asleep on the couch, a cigarette burning in the ashtray, while the twins were howling from hunger. It was difficult to arouse Mom, so Evelyn fed and changed the twins. The mother stated she had been up late the night before trying to get them settled and was exhausted. Evelyn, having been an exhausted new mother herself, decided not to report this incident as a possible problem unless it occurred again. Several days later, the twins were again screaming as Evelyn arrived, but this time Mom had left the used syringe on the kitchen table. How would you, as a supervising RN, evaluate this incident? Use the questions in the table in Checkpoint 11–6 to guide your evaluation.

DOCUMENTATION AND THE DELEGATION PROCESS

As we travel the country talking to nurses during and after seminars and consulting projects, we are often asked, "How do I document the delegation process?" We have several recommendations, based on the particular situation and the degree of seriousness of the problem. Many nurses voice concerns about creating visible "proof," in the form of documentation, to demonstrate that they have indeed completed their responsibility as a supervisor of a delegated act.

To record the process of evaluation and feedback, many facilities have developed policies, procedures, or forms to be completed. For example, if a specific problem or error has occurred, you may be asked to fill out an "Unusual Occurrence Report" or "Incident Report." In these cases, follow the guidelines you've been given at your workplace. Generally, the actual observable problem is recorded in the chart objectively, but any interpersonal performance feedback is not documented on the patient record. (For example, if a fall occurred, record that it occurred and what you did to care for the patient. The facility incident report is generally a form that is used for communication to the health care agency's insurance company and often asks who was responsible for the incident and what form of follow-up was done.) Personnel feedback and evaluation are documented on such forms as interim performance progress notes, performance appraisal forms, or other anecdotal notes that are often kept by managers. As a delegating nurse, you may be asked to give written information to your manager about what you've discussed with your delegate when performance has been exceptional in either direction.

Documentation of the matching of the jobs to the delegate is often completed through assignment sheets or daily task lists. We recommend that you check to find out whether these are saved, and for what time period, in your department. We also recommend that you keep notes on your daily activities. Whatever method you currently use to keep track of your work for the case, or the shift, is an acceptable way to make that notation that you talked to Pam about the difficulty

CHECKPOINT 11-6

Answer each question.

1. What signs tell you something is wrong here?
   The potential problem could have been reported earlier.
2. What's good about this incident?
   The twins are okay. The drug abuse evidence will help get the children ultimately to a safe foster home. This is a great teaching example to use for the future.
3. What should be happening?
4. Do I need to do something about it?
5. What is the exact nature? Objective criteria to know if solved?
6. What can be done?
7. Positives and negatives for each solution.
8. Plan steps and implement short- and long-term solutions.
9. Evaluate short-term results by objective criteria.
10. Evaluate long-term. Solved?

(Are new/additional strategies needed?)

See the end of the chapter for the answers.

she was having in performing a task, but if the problem continues or becomes more serious, you will want to use a more formal method of documentation and alert the appropriate management person.

When you've done the delegation process well, following all the steps, and a delegate makes an error, how can you support your decision to delegate that task? Your decision is endorsed by delegating according to state statutes, your facility job description, and validated competencies or skill checklists. You will save your notes from the day that record you did instruct and verify competency. (This information is not charted in the patient record, however.) Many organizations have established guidelines and policies about delegating that may also support your decision. Your manager will document your follow-up and feedback given to the delegate in some way, and an "Unusual Occurrence Report" will be completed according to specific agency rules.

An excellent example of documentation of delegation by RNs to unlicensed care providers in specific settings (such as residential programs for the developmentally disabled, licensed adult family homes, and licensed boarding homes for assistive living) has been used by the state of Washington's Department of Social and Health Services. As Harris points out,

> "Specific policy and procedures must be written by a facility to delineate the scope of responsibilities to be delegated. . . . The successful completion of training and/or competency evaluation as required under (Medicare regulations of 1989) would be the minimum requirement for delegation of additional responsibilities to a home health care aide. Additional criteria include demonstration of ability to perform instructions from professional nurse; demonstrated successful interaction with home care team; interest and initiative for this responsibility; and additional training and supervision for a delegated responsibility" (Harris, 1993, p. 55).

The following forms have been developed by the state of Washington in collaboration with Aging and Adult Services to provide a backup to the nurse delegation provisions in the nurse practice regulations. The first form (Exhibit 11–5) is a checklist to assist the nurse in determining whether the delegation is appropriate and the assistant has had adequate training. The second form, Delegation of Nursing Care Task (Appendix 11–A), specifies the setting, the specific tasks to be delegated, and includes important information such as the telephone numbers of the assistive personnel who are authorized to perform those tasks. Patient/client consent is an essential element, and this form features a space for documentation of the procedures and steps, predictable outcomes and how to deal with them, and potential side effects and complications and appropriate actions. When a new nurse assumes care of a patient in a group home or other authorized care setting, another form has been developed that ascertains that the RN knows the client, the plan of care, the skills of the nursing assistant, and the delegated task. There can be no question that the RN must follow the delegation process carefully! If the nurse determines that the delegation must be rescinded due to the assistant's performance, another form will support tracking of the supervision process. If a change of physician orders for delegated medications occurs, the RN must verify the change with the physician, and must decide whether a site visit is necessary, whether delegation must be rescinded, or whether the new task can be added to the instruction list.

As delegation to unlicensed health care personnel becomes even more widespread in the future, documentation such as this will be adopted across the health

Exhibit 11–5 Checklist for the Delegation of Specific Nursing Tasks

Delegated Task	Client/Patient

YES NO

❑ ❑ Does the nurse hold a current license to practice as a registered nurse in Washington?

❑ ❑ Is the setting in a certified community residential program for the developmentally disabled, a licensed adult family home, or a licensed boarding home contracted to provide assisted living services?

❑ ❑ Is the task within the nurse's areas of responsibility (scope of practice)?

❑ ❑ Has the specific care task been approved for delegation?

❑ ❑ Has the nurse assessed the patient's clinical and behavioral status and determined the patient to be in a stable and predictable condition that does not require the nurse's frequent presence and evaluation?

❑ ❑ Has the nurse considered the potential risk of harm for the individual patient and determined that the task can be properly and safely performed by the nursing assistant?

❑ ❑ Has the nurse analyzed the complexity of the nursing task and determined the knowledge, psychomotor skills, and training needed by the nursing assistant to competently perform the task?

❑ ❑ Has the nurse assessed the level of interaction required, considering language or cultural diversity that may affect communication or the ability to accomplish the task to be delegated, as well as methods to facilitate the interaction? Has the nurse verified that the nursing assistant:

❑ ❑ is currently registered or certified as a nursing assistant in Washington State in good standing without restriction?

❑ ❑ has a certificate of completion issued by the Department of Social and Health Services (DSHS) indicating completion of Core Delegation Training for Nursing Assistants?

❑ ❑ is willing to perform the task in the absence of direct or immediate nurse supervision and accept responsibility for his or her actions?

❑ ❑ Has the nurse assessed the ability of the nursing assistant to competently perform the delegated nursing task in the absence of direct or immediate supervision?

❑ ❑ Has the nurse informed the patient, or authorized representative, of the delegation and the nursing assistant's training and obtained written, informed consent from the patient, or authorized representative?

❑ ❑ Has the nurse taught the nursing assistant how to perform the task, including return demonstration under observation to verify competency to perform the task safely and accurately, and documented the

continues

Exhibit 11–5 continued

YES	NO	
		training? Has the nurse provided specific and written delegation instructions to the nursing assistant that the nursing assistant understands, including the following:
❏	❏	the rationale for delegating the nursing task
❏	❏	that task is patient specific and not transferable
❏	❏	that task is not transferable to another nursing assistant
❏	❏	the nature of the condition and purpose of the delegated nursing task
❏	❏	the procedure to follow to perform the task
❏	❏	the predictable outcomes and how to deal effectively with them
❏	❏	the risks of the treatment
❏	❏	the interactions of prescribed medications
❏	❏	how to observe and report side effects, complications, or unexpected outcomes and appropriate actions to deal with them, including specific parameters for notifying the registered nurse, the physician, or emergency services
❏	❏	the action to take in situations where medications are altered by physician orders
❏	❏	how to document the task in the patient's record
❏	❏	how task was taught, including content and that a return demonstration was correctly done
❏	❏	If delegating administration of PRN medications, has the nurse provided written parameters specific to an individual patient that provide guidelines for the nursing assistant to follow when deciding to administer the PRN medication and the procedure to follow for administration?
❏	❏	Is there a plan of nursing supervision describing how frequently the nurse will supervise and evaluate the performance of the delegated nursing task by the nursing assistant and reevaluate the patient to ensure continued appropriateness of delegation, which must occur at least every 60 days?
❏	❏	Has the nurse completed any records required by the Secretary of Health for evaluation?

NURSING ASSISTANT'S NAME	NURSE'S SIGNATURE

Source: Reprinted from State of Washington Department of Social and Health Services.

care continuum. If you are concerned about the absence of adequate job descriptions or competency checklists, or you feel you need a form such as those in Exhibit 11–5 and Appendix 11–A, begin now to identify how you can be involved in planning documents to record your professional practice.

CONCLUSION

Evaluation is an integral part of our daily nursing practice. Unfortunately, we rarely take enough time to carefully appraise our ability to use this part of the nursing (and delegation) process. In this chapter, you've found this topic explored in its various facets, emphasizing the need for continuous evaluation throughout the shift, visit, or case so that clinical and performance feedback can be offered effectively to correct any problems that may be occurring. The use of checkpoints, timelines, and parameters will assist you in that process. Nothing can substitute for your own personal assessment and evaluation of a situation, because you are uniquely prepared by your scientific education, your experience, and your intuition. When a specific incident occurs, you use critical thinking skills, then move forward using the positive problem-solving process to challenge assumptions creatively and implement logical, planned solutions, continuously measuring for success along the way. When you function in a leadership or supervisory role (and nearly 100 percent of nurses do!), you implement periodic evaluations of how the delegation process is working and how assistive personnel are functioning, so that planned client outcomes can be achieved most effectively. Evaluation allows us to make the system work better and to applaud what's working well in our team efforts.

CELEBRATE THE SUCCESS OF THE TEAM!

Whether you work in a school, a parish, community agencies, a public health department, or any other health care arena, health care is a serious business. Supervising other people and delegating work to them is a complex and often anxiety-laden proposition. But when you learn to delegate properly, using the skills we have presented in this handbook, you'll gain the confidence needed to grow professionally, and safe, effective, high-quality patient, family, and community care can be delivered.

Due to the stressful nature of working with others, nurses may focus only on the potential for error and the actual problems that occur. It sometimes seems they have little time to do anything else. However, as an RN and as a leader of your health care team, you are in the very best position to help your coworkers focus also on the most wondrous work you are doing! The outcomes of your efforts are evidence of the existence of that which is good and full of light in this harried, violent, and often frightening world.

CHECKPOINT 11-7

1. Think of all the people who help you when you are involved in a particularly challenging case. List them and what they do.

    Example: Maintaining at home a quadriplegic who is depressed, chemically dependent, angry, has large decubitus ulcers, and is a diabetic.

    a) parish nurse: found the case by tracking a prayer chain list and hearing of a recent 911 call for assistance for hypoglycemic episode

    b) agency billing clerk and/or secretary: researched method to obtain financial assistance from various sources and ordered supplies

    c) respiratory therapist: taught the patient and care providers to use a new, more compact portable ventilator

    d) agency LPN: developed a positive relationship with the patient while changing the many dressings

    e) HHA: reports progress and symptoms carefully, and performs excellent personal care, training the attendant to do so

    f) student nurse: talked with the occupational therapist about a plan for therapy that would include the patient writing novels by using a voice recognition computer

    g) pastoral care: helped the patient attend Narcotics Anonymous meetings and encouraged him in the 12-step program

    h) social worker: connected patient to agencies that will assist

    i) physical therapist: taught the attendant and patient how to avoid additional skin breakdown

    j) nutritionist: planned specific meals to keep blood glucose levels within reasonable limits

    k) neighborhood pharmacist: planned entrance into the methadone program and monitors progress

l) case manager RN: assessed the situation and the patient, planned the care with other disciplines, and coordinates all the disciplines

m) physicians: ordered necessary tests, treatments, and participated in the planning

n) hospital emergency department RNs: communicated the pattern of admissions to ER and collaborated in a patient care planning meeting to present coordinated efforts

o) the patient and his significant others (should the patient be the last one on the list or the first?)

p) insurers or managed care organization: involved in planning the care and providing reimbursement to avoid further costs and improve outcomes for this patient

q) psychologist: visits the patient and works through anger and chemical dependency issues

Who else can you think of?

This exercise helps us recognize the necessity of effective team functioning for positive patient outcomes, and the complex and rewarding role of the RN in coordinating that care.

2. Discuss with your coworkers the successes you have enjoyed in the past week.

3. How can you and your team plan to celebrate your successes more often?

You have helped create a new family, a haven for love and nurturing, because you and your team provided family planning information or infertility therapy and prenatal care; you taught the mother about nutrition and sexually transmitted diseases and made sure she received financial assistance. Or you may have been the nursing care team who helped train the mother's labor coach and helped with baby's first baths, or supervised and supported the new family as they attempted a sleepy adjustment at home.

Perhaps you were a part of the nursing care team that helped keep another disabled child in school, teaching the teachers to suction, providing therapy in the rehabilitation setting, or identifying the child's need for preventive care to avoid a trip to the pediatric ICU. Maybe you are one of the groups of health care

> Victories are continual, each day, in all settings of the health care continuum, whether you saved a life today or gently cared and supported as a peaceful, sheltered death ensued. Nurses are there, in the most challenging, difficult, joyful, or tragic episodes of human life. And you are not alone.

professionals intent on finding the answer to preventing this child's disability through research or public health measures. Maybe it was your team that helped someone's grandmother come to terms with Grandfather's inability to recognize her or his past. Or you may have been the ones who treated Grandfather when his suicide attempt followed the first diagnosis of his disease. Across the span of life, you have been there for them, working together as a team.

So recognize your unique contribution to this world, and recognize all the people who help make it happen. And celebrate the success of the team!

ANSWERS TO CHECKPOINTS

11–5. Using the questions preceding the checkpoint, consider possible alternatives. Evaluation of this day may show that the following could have occurred: Personal barriers of the nurses could have been in the way; perhaps they did not assign all the work they could have to the aides, consistent with their job descriptions. Perhaps the RNs did not know the extent of responsibilities that could be assigned or did not trust Susan or Joe, or perhaps Susan and Joe did not complete their work. Supervisory visits or checkpoints may not have occurred recently for these patients and may need to be completed to be certain that care is being completed well. Susan and Joe may have thought they completed all their work because they did not complete the plan of care for each client, or perhaps visits were canceled. Did all RNs communicate clearly and completely the extent of the work that needed to be completed by the two assistive personnel? Perhaps a system needs to be set up for people to assist others when their work is completed, such as reporting in to the coordinator or an RN leader for further assignments. Other issues could be part of the problem: disorganization, people unfamiliar with the agency, inaccurate assessment of the workload, performance of the RNs in their supervisory capacity, and/or the competence of the delegates.

11–6. (Refer to steps as given in Exhibit 11–3.) 1. What signs tell you something is wrong? Evelyn could have reported the first problem so that Bob could have visited to determine whether drug abuse was a problem. 2. What is good? Evelyn reported it now and was very observant. The twins are still intact. 3. What should be happening? If all had gone well, she might have reported this earlier, or one of the other professionals could have seen other signs. The objective criteria we'd use to determine whether the problem was solved are that any and all possible symptoms of drug abuse or child abuse or neglect in the home would be reported for further follow-up. 4. Should we do something? Yes, this may be a good chance to give more instruction to Evelyn. It will help other patients in the future. 5. What should Bob do? Bob should talk with the manager about his plan but will probably give feedback to Evelyn and determine if this is a learning need or if Bob should have communicated his expectations more clearly, or if there is a system glitch. Is it to be expected that a new mother would be difficult to rouse? This is certainly difficult to tell, and Bob should be careful to be positive about all that Evelyn did well in this situation. Also, he should determine whether she left him a message about this that was not given to him. First Bob must secure emergency care for the mother and the twins; then he must look at how the incident occurred and how to avoid it in the future, using his feedback model to let Evelyn know about his concerns.

REFERENCES

Anderson, C. 1990. *Patient teaching and communicating in an information age.* Albany, NY: Delmar.

Bandman, E. 1988. *Critical thinking in nursing.* Norwalk, CT: Appleton & Lange, 5–6.

Facione, N.C., and P. Facione. 1996. The disposition toward critical thinking. *Journal of General Education* 44 (May/June): 129–136.

Girvan, J. 1989. Enhancing student decision-making through use of critical thinking/ questioning techniques. *Health Education* 20, no. 7: 48–50.

Hansten, R., and M. Washburn. 1993. *The nurse manager's answer book.* Gaithersburg, MD: Aspen Publishers, Inc.

Hansten, R., and M. Washburn. 1997. *Toolbook for health care redesign.* Gaithersburg, MD: Aspen Publishers, Inc.

Harris, M.D. 1993. Competent, supervised, unlicensed personnel will contribute to high-quality, in-home health care. *Home Healthcare Nurse* 11, no. 6: 55.

Jones, E.A. 1994. Defining important CT skills for college graduates to achieve. Paper presented at the Sixth International Conference on Thinking. Boston, MA.

Kyzer, S.P. 1996. Sharpening your critical thinking skills. *Orthopaedic Nursing* 15, no. 6: 66–76.

Polge, J. 1995. Critical thinking: The use of intuition in making clinical nursing judgments. *Journal of the New York State Nurses Association* 26, no. 2: 4–9.

Stark, J. 1996. Critical thinking for outcomes-based practice. *Seminars for Nurse Managers* 4, no. 3: 161–171.

Whiteside, C. 1997. A model for teaching critical thinking in the clinical setting. *Dimensions of Critical Care Nursing* 16, no. 3: 152–162.

APPENDIX 11–A

Delegation of Nursing Care Task

<table>
<tr>
<td colspan="2"></td>
<td>Date</td>
</tr>
<tr>
<td>Client/Patient's Name</td>
<td>Social Security Number</td>
<td>Birth Date</td>
</tr>
<tr>
<td>Facility's Name

Owner's Name</td>
<td colspan="2">Facility Address

Telephone Number</td>
</tr>
<tr>
<td>Setting
❏ Certified Community
   Residential Program for
   Developmentally Disabled

❏ Licensed Adult Family Home

❏ Licensed Boarding Home
   Contracting To Provide
   Assisted Living Services</td>
<td colspan="2">Diagnosis</td>
</tr>
<tr>
<td colspan="3">Specific Nursing Care Task(s) To Be Delegated

   ❏ Medication Administration (if checked, list medications below):

      ❏ Oral _____

      ❏ Gastrostomy tube _____

      ❏ Topical (skin/nose/ear/eye) _____

      ❏ Vaginal suppository _____

      ❏ Rectal suppository _____
      Known allergies: _____</td>
</tr>
</table>

Source: Reprinted from State of Washington Department of Social and Health Services.

- ❑ Dressing change using clean technique
- ❑ Urinary catheterization using clean technique
- ❑ Enema
- ❑ Ostomy care in established and healed condition
- ❑ Blood glucose monitoring
- ❑ Gastrostomy feeding in established and healed condition

Nature of client/patient's condition and purpose of task (Include rationale for delegating the nursing task and evidence of patient's stable and predictable condition.)

RN's Signature	Telephone Number	Date

NURSING ASSISTANT

Nursing Assistant Name(s)	Telephone Number(s)	Date(s)

CLIENT/PATIENT'S CONSENT

I have been informed of the delegated nursing care task, the expected results, the possible risks, and the nursing assistant's level of training. I consent to having the above nursing assistant(s) perform the nursing task as directed by the registered nurse.

Client/Patient's (or Authorized Representative) Signature	Telephone Number	Date

If you have any complaints or concerns, call 1-800-562-6078 (toll free).

Procedures/Steps To Follow To Perform the Task (Include procedure for contacting RN for additional help.)	Predictable Outcomes and How To Deal with Them	Potential Risks/Side Effects/Medication Interactions/Complications, and Appropriate Actions To Deal with Them (Include what to observe for and report, what to do, and who to contact.)

PRN MEDICATIONS: TO BE COMPLETED ONLY IF PRN MEDICATIONS ARE DELEGATED

Medication	What Is Medication For?		
Medication Dose (i.e., four (4) mg)	Amount To Be Given (i.e., one tablet, one teaspoon)	Schedule (i.e., every six (6) hours)	Route (i.e., by mouth, under tongue, transdermal)
Not To Exceed (Number of doses in a specified amount of time, i.e., six tablets in 24 hours)			
To Be Discontinued If (Specify adverse reactions, side effects, or when medication should no longer be given.)			
Medication May Be Given If (Specify reason medication is needed, i.e., specific complaint or behavior.)			

NURSING CARE TASK CONTINUATION		
Complete only one task per page.		
Client/Patient's Name	Date	Page ___ of ___
Procedures/Steps To Follow To Perform the Task (Include procedure for contacting RN for additional help.)	Predictable Outcomes and How To Deal with Them	Potential Risks/Side Effects/Medication Interactions/Complications, and Appropriate Actions To Deal with Them (Include what to observe for and report, what to do, and who to contact.)

NURSING CARE TASK: ASSUMPTION OF DELEGATION		
		Date
Client/Patient's Name	Social Security Number	Birth Date
Facility's Name	Facility Address	
Owner's Name	Telephone Number	

1. Reason for another RN to assume delegating responsibility:

    _____

    _____

2. I agree that I know the client/patient, the plan of care, the skills of the nursing assistant, and the delegated task. I agree to assume responsibility and accountability for this delegated task and to perform the nursing supervision.

3. The nursing assistant and client/patient have been informed of this change.

RN's SIGNATURE	DATE

If you have any complaints or concerns, please call 1-800-562-6078 (toll free).

NURSING CARE TASK FOLLOW-UP EVALUATION: RESULTS OF SUPERVISION OR RESCINDING ORDER				

NURSING CARE TASK FOLLOW-UP EVALUATION:
RESULTS OF SUPERVISION OR RESCINDING ORDER

Client/Patient's Name   Nursing Assistant's Name

Include Date, Client/Patient Care Outcomes, Observations of Nursing Assistant's Performance, and if redemonstration or remedial training was necessary. Explain any negative outcomes and action taken.

RN's Signature | Date | Nursing Assistant's Signature | Date

Rescinding Delegation (Describe reason for rescinding delegation, date, time, and plan for providing the task or alternative plan to ensure the continuity of care.)

Task Rescinded: _____

RN's Signature | Date | Nursing Assistant's Signature | Date

If you have any complaints or concerns, please call 1-800-562-6078 (toll free).

NURSING CARE TASK:
PHYSICIAN MEDICATION CHANGE ORDERS

Client/Patient's Name	Nursing Assistant's Name

Actions Required When Physician Changes Medication Orders (Record date, time, and initial as each step is done.)

❏ 1. The delegating RN must be notified: _____

❏ 2. The RN must verify change in medication or new medication order with the physician: _____

❏ 3. The RN can continue delegation for change in medication dosage or change in type of medication for the same problem providing the client/patient remains in stable and predictable condition (include new order and instructions given to nursing assistant):

_____
_____
_____
_____

❏ 4. For new medications, the RN must review the criteria and process for delegation and decide on the following actions:

   ❏ Add the new medication to the delegated task list (list medication and instructions):

_____
_____
_____
_____

   ❏ Make a site visit prior to delegation: _____

   ❏ **Rescind delegation (complete Nursing Care Task: Rescinding Delegation, and attach).**

RN's Signature	Date	Nursing Assistant's Signature	Date

Complaints regarding delegation of specific nursing tasks may be reported to the Aging and Adult Services Administration, Department of Social and Health Services (DSHS), by calling 1-800-562-6078. All complaints specifically related to nurse delegation will be referred to the Nursing Quality Assurance Commission.

Addresses and Telephone and Fax Numbers for State Boards of Nursing

Alabama Board of Nursing
PO Box 303900
Montgomery, AL 36130
334/242-4060; Fax 334/242-4360

Alaska Board of Nursing
Dept. of Commerce and Economic
  Development
Division of Occupational Licensing
3601 C Street, Suite 722
Anchorage, AK 99503
907/269-8161; Fax 907/269-8156

American Samoa Health Services
Regulatory Board
LBJ Tropical Medical Center
Pago Pago, AS 96799
684/633-1222; Fax 684/633-1689

Arizona State Board of Nursing
1651 E. Morten, Suite 150
Phoenix, AZ 85020
602/255-5092; Fax 602/255-5130

Arkansas State Board of Nursing
University Tower Building
1123 South University Avenue,
  Suite 800
Little Rock, AR 72204
501/686-2700; Fax 501/686-2714

**California Board of Registered
  Nursing**
PO Box 944210
400 R Street, Suite 4030
Sacramento, CA 94244
916/322-3350; Fax 916/327-4402

**California Board of Vocational
  Nurse and Psychiatric
  Technician Examiners**
2535 Capitol Oaks Drive, Suite 205
Sacramento, CA 95833
916/263-7800; Fax 916/263-7859

Colorado Board of Nursing
1650 Broadway, Suite 670
Denver, CO 80202
303/894-2430; Fax 303/894-2821

Source: Reprinted from R. Hansten and M. Washburn, *Clinical Delegation Skills*, pp. 343–347, © 1998, Aspen Publishers, Inc.

Connecticut Board of Examiners for Nursing
Division of Health Systems
   Regulation
410 Capitol Avenue, MS #12HSR
#340308
Hartford, CT 06134
860/509-7624; Fax 860/509-7286

Delaware Board of Nursing
Cannon Building, Suite 203
PO Box 1401
Dover, DE 19903-1401
302/739-4522; Fax 302/739-2711

District of Columbia Board of Nursing
Dept. of Consumer and Regulatory
   Affairs
614 H Street, NW, Room 904
Washington, DC 20001
202/727-7468; Fax 202/727-7662

Florida Board of Nursing
4080 Woodcock Drive, Suite 202
Jacksonville, FL 32207
904/858-6940; Fax 904/858-6964

Georgia Board of Nursing, Registered Nurses
166 Pryor Street, SW, Suite 400
Atlanta, GA 30303
404/656-3943; Fax 404/657-7489

Georgia State Board of Licensed Practical Nurses
166 Pryor Street, SW
Atlanta, GA 30303
404/656-3921; Fax 404/651-9532

Guam Board of Nurse Examiners
PO Box 2816
Agana, GU 96910
001/671/475-0251; Fax 671/477-4733

State of Hawaii Board of Nursing
PO Box 3469
Honolulu, HI 96801
808/586-2695; Fax 808/586-2689

Idaho Board of Nursing
PO Box 83720
Boise, ID 83720
208/334-3110; Fax 208/334-3262

Illinois Department of Professional Regulation
James R. Thompson Center
100 West Randolph, Suite 9-300
Chicago, IL 60601
312/814-2715; Fax 312/814-3145

Indiana State Board of Nursing
Health Professions Bureau
402 West Washington Street,
   Room 041
Indianapolis, IN 46204
317/232-2960; Fax 317/233-4236

Iowa Board of Nursing
State Capitol Complex
1223 East Court Avenue
Des Moines, IA 50319
515/281-3255; Fax 515/281-4825

Kansas Board of Nursing
Landon State Office Building
900 SW Jackson, Room 551-S
Topeka, KS 66612-1230
913/296-4929; Fax 913/296-3929

Kentucky State Board of Nursing
312 Whittington Parkway, Suite 300
Louisville, KY 40222-5172
502/329-7006; Fax 502/329-7011

Louisiana State Board of Nursing
3510 N. Causeway Boulevard,
    Suite 501
Metairie, LA 70002
504/838-5332; Fax 504/838-5349

**Louisiana State Board of Practice
    Nurse Examiners**
3510 N. Causeway Boulevard,
    Suite 203
Metairie, LA 70002
504/838-5791; Fax 504/838-5279

Maine State Board of Nursing
158 State House Station
Augusta, ME 04333-0158
207/287-1133; Fax 207/287-1149

Maryland Board of Nursing
4140 Patterson Avenue
Baltimore, MD 21215-2299
410/764-5124; Fax 410/358-3530

**Massachusetts Board of
    Registration in Nursing**
100 Cambridge Street, Suite 1519
Boston, MA 02202
617/727-9961; Fax 617/727-2197

State of Michigan
CIS/Office of Health Service
Ottawa Towers North
611 W. Ottawa, 4th Floor
Lansing, MI 48933
517/373-9102; Fax 517/373-2179

Minnesota Board of Nursing
2829 University Avenue, SE,
    Suite 500
Minneapolis, MN 55414
612/617-2270; Fax 612/617-2190

Mississippi Board of Nursing
239 North Lamar, Suite 401
Jackson, MS 39201
601/359-6170; Fax 601/359-6185

Missouri State Board of Nursing
3605 Missouri Boulevard
PO Box 656
Jefferson City, MO 65102
573/751-0681; Fax 573/751-0075

Montana State Board of Nursing
Arcade Building, Lower Level
111 North Jackson
PO Box 200513
Helena, MT 59620-0513
406/444-2071; Fax 406/444-7759

**Dept. of Health and Human
    Services Regulation and
    Licensure**
Credentialing Division—Nursing/
    Nursing Support Section
PO Box 94986
Lincoln, NE 68509
402/471-4376; Fax 402/471-3577

Nevada State Board of Nursing
1755 East Plumb Lane, Suite 260
Reno, NV 89502
702/786-2778; Fax 702/322-6993

New Hampshire Board of Nursing
Health and Welfare Building
#6 Hazen Drive
Concord, NH 03301-2657
603/271-2323; Fax 603/271-6605

New Jersey Board of Nursing
124 Halsey Street, 6th Floor
PO Box 45010
Newark, NJ 07101
201/504-6586; Fax 201/648-3481

New Mexico Board of Nursing
4206 Louisiana Boulevard, NE
Suite A
Albuquerque, NM 87109
505/841-8340; Fax 505/841-8347

New York State Board of Nursing
State Education Department
Cultural Education Center,
   Room 3023
Albany, NY 12230
518/474-3845; Fax 518/473-0578

Commonwealth Board of Nurse
   Examiners
Public Health Center
PO Box 1458
Saipan, MP 96950
670/234-3211; Fax 670/234-8930

North Carolina State Board of
   Nursing
3724 National Drive
Raleigh, NC 27602
919/782-3211; Fax 919/781-9461

North Dakota Board of Nursing
919 South 7th Street, Suite 504
Bismarck, ND 58504-5881
701/328-9777; Fax 701/328-9785

Ohio Board of Nursing
77 South High Street, 17th Floor
Columbus, OH 43215
614/466-3947; Fax 614/466-0388

Oklahoma Board of Nursing
Registration and Nursing Education
2915 North Classen Boulevard,
   Suite 524
Oklahoma City, OK 73106
405/525-2076; Fax 405/521-6089

Oregon State Board of Nursing
800 NE Oregon Street #25, Suite 465
Portland, OR 97232
503/731-4745; Fax 503/731-4755

Pennsylvania State Board of
   Nursing
PO Box 2649
Harrisburg, PA 17105-2649
717/783-7142; Fax 717/783-0822

Commonwealth of Puerto Rico
Board of Nurse Examiners
Call Box 10200
Santurce, PR 00908-0200
787/725-8161; Fax 787/725-7903

Rhode Island Board of Nursing
Registration and Nursing Education
Cannon Health Building, Room 104
#3 Capitol Hill, Room 104
Providence, RI 02908
401/277-2827; Fax 401/277-1272

State Board of Nursing for South
   Carolina
110 Centerview Drive, Suite 202
Columbia, SC 29210
803/896-4550; Fax 803/896-4525

South Dakota Board of Nursing
3307 South Lincoln Avenue
Sioux Falls, SD 57105-5224
605/367-5940; Fax 605/367-5945

Tennessee State Board of Nursing
426 Fifth Avenue North
1st Floor—Cordell Hull Building
Nashville, TN 37427
615/532-5166; Fax 615/741-7899

**Board of Nurse Examiners,
State of Texas**
PO Box 430
Austin, TX 78767
512/305-7400; Fax 512/305-7401

**Texas Board of Vocational Nurse
Examiners**
William P. Hobby Building, Tower 3
333 Guadalupe Street, Suite 3-4000
Austin, TX 78701
512/305-8100; Fax 512/305-8101

Utah State Board of Nursing
Division of Occupational and
  Professional Licensing
Heber M. Wells Building, 4th Floor
160 East 300 Street, PO Box 45802
Salt Lake City, UT 84145-0801
801/530-6628; Fax 801/530-6511

Vermont State Board of Nursing
109 State Street
Montpelier, VT 05609-1106
802/828-2396; Fax 802/828-2484

**Virgin Islands Board of
Nurse Licensure**
Veterans Drive Station
St. Thomas, VI 00803
340/776-7397; Fax 340/777-4003

Virginia State Board of Nursing
6606 West Broad Street, 4th Floor
Richmond, VA 23230-1717
804/662-9909; Fax 804/662-9943

**Washington State Nursing Care
Quality Assurance Commission**
Department of Health
Olympia, WA 98504-7864
360/753-2686; Fax 360/586-2165

**West Virginia Board of Examiners
for Registered Nurses**
101 Dee Drive
Charleston, WV 25311-1620
304/558-3596; Fax 304/558-3666

**Wisconsin Department of
Regulation and Licensing**
1400 East Washington Avenue
Madison, WI 53708-8935
608/266-2112; Fax 608/267-0644

Wyoming State Board of Nursing
2020 Carey Avenue, Suite 110
Cheyenne, WY 82002
307/777-7601; Fax 307/777-3519

**National Council of State
Boards of Nursing**
676 North Saint Clair Street,
  Suite 550
Chicago, IL 60611-2921
312/787-6555; Fax 312/787-6898
http://www.ncsbn.org

INDEX

educational resources, 102–104
mission statement, 90–94
nonunion environment, 88–89
for practice, 84–104
quality program, 98–102
redesign impact, 97–98
service approach, 101
Health care reform, 16–19
job analysis, 150
Health maintenance organization, 22
Hierarchy of needs, 202
Home Care Aide Association of America,
  50, 181
Home Care Aide I, 182
Home Care Aide II, 182
Home Care Aide III, 182–183
Home health agency
  Health Care Financing Administration,
    scope, 76–77
  planning, 77
Home health aide
  assignment, 157
  defined, 63
  fastest growing job category, 37
  role, expansion, 176
  training, 103
Home health care
  Balanced Budget Act, 18–19
  change, 11–12
  environment, 13–14
  fraud, 101
  growth, 37–39
  hospital nursing
    adaptations, 112–113
    differences, 112–113
    transition stressor, 112
  impact of delegation, 12, 13
  move from acute care to community-based
    settings, 110–117
    adaptations, 112–113
    benefits, 115–117
    indications of success, 113–115
    stressors, 112
  multidisciplinary approach, 37
  new world of, 12–29
  nurse
    assessing strengths, 127
    personal barriers, 117–127
    preparation test, 117
    task vs. outcome orientation, 122

  value added, 122–123
  personal benefits, 115
  setting, 23
  supervision, 37
  treating whole human being, 36
Home health care agency
  categories, 23–24
  Medicaid, 23–24
  Medicare, 23–24
  restructuring, 25
  types, 23–24
Homemaker, defined, 63
Hospital, development, 84
Hospital nursing, home health care
  adaptations, 112–113
  differences, 112 113
  transition stressor, 112

I

Infusion pump, 35
Institutional policies, 185
Insurance, 17
Intentional caring, 140–141
Interprofessional Workgroup on Health
  Professions Regulation, 180
Intervention
  communication, 7
  conflict resolution, 7
  matching job to delegate, 7
  nursing process, 147–151
  prioritizing, 7

J

Job analysis, 148–151
  breaking job into parts, 148–149
  example, 150–151
  health care reform, 150
  knowledge, 149
  matching job and delegate, 149–150
  personal traits, 149
  skills, 149
Job cut, 24
Job description, 185–188
  mission statement, 190–191
    unofficial expectations, 191–193
  registered nurse, 187

drawing blood, 71
group home, 41–42
job description, 187–188, 190
long-term care, 40–41
National Council of State Boards of
    Nursing, 175–176
nonacute setting, 40
personal feelings about, 118
responsibilities, 188
skilled nursing facility, 40–41
task list, 175–176
training, 103–104
use, 40–42
Unprofessional conduct, defined, 64

V

Validated competency list
    associate degree registered nurse, 189

licensed practical nurse, 189
    nursing assistant, 189
Values, 91–94
Values statement, elements, 190
Visual learning, 291–293
Voice, communication, 233

W

Work, changing nature, 24–25
Work organization, training, 123
Working with others, organization, 134–135
Workload analysis, 162